Experience and the World's Own Language

A Critique of John McDowell's Empiricism

RICHARD GASKIN

CLARENDON PRESS · OXFORD

OXFORD
UNIVERSITY PRESS

Great Clarendon Street, Oxford OX2 6DP

Oxford University Press is a department of the University of Oxford.
It furthers the University's objective of excellence in research, scholarship,
and education by publishing worldwide in

Oxford New York

Auckland Cape Town Dar es Salaam Hong Kong Karachi
Kuala Lumpur Madrid Melbourne Mexico City Nairobi
New Delhi Shanghai Taipei Toronto

МИС   With offices in

Argentina Austria Brazil Chile Czech Republic France Greece
Guatemala Hungary Italy Japan Poland Portugal Singapore
South Korea Switzerland Thailand Turkey Ukraine Vietnam

Oxford is a registered trade mark of Oxford University Press
in the UK and in certain other countries

Published in the United States
by Oxford University Press Inc., New York

© Richard Gaskin 2006

The moral rights of the author have been asserted
Database right Oxford University Press (maker)

First published 2006

British Library Cataloguing in Publication Data
Data available

Library of Congress Cataloging in Publication Data
Data available

Typeset by SPI Publisher Services
Printed in Great Britain
on acid-free paper by
Biddles Ltd, King's Lynn, Norfolk

ISBN 0-19-928725-2   978-0-19-928725-3

1 3 5 7 9 10 8 6 4 2

Preface

John McDowell has had a significant impact on contemporary philosophy. His writings span a broad spectrum of systematic and historical topics, including the philosophy of language, the philosophy of mind, the theory of knowledge, moral philosophy and aesthetics, and the philosophies of Plato, Aristotle, and Wittgenstein. The considerable impact which his thought has had is hardly surprising. McDowell's writings have an inspirational quality which cannot be overlooked and is indeed, in a sense which is hard to make precise, uncanny. And the inspirational qualities of his pronouncements are by no means restricted to the written word: as a former undergraduate and graduate student of McDowell's, I can attest, as I am sure many others can,[1] to the almost mesmerizing quality of his lectures and tutorials. Quite apart from these stylistic features, anyone with even a modest degree of philosophical erudition will, on reading virtually any part of his output, appreciate that something philosophically profound is being investigated with an extraordinary application of intellect. It quickly becomes clear to the student of McDowell's thinking that, for all its diversity, that thinking is fed and unified by a powerful philosophical vision.

How that vision is to be characterized is not as straightforward a matter as I for one formerly imagined it to be, but there is no doubt that as one reads through McDowell's *oeuvre* one feels the gravitational pull of a strong intellectual mass; or one might say (to change the metaphor) that one detects the presence of a reservoir of energy which irrigates the outlying fields of labour. Twenty years ago I should have said unhesitatingly that that centre of gravity or reservoir of energy was, simply, realism—or, as McDowell himself might say, a sane realism: realism about the objects of experience,

---

[1] Cf. Lockwood 1989, p. 148.

including secondary qualities, about moral and aesthetic value, and about rule-following and meaning. But that characterization would probably be too positive, for over the years it has become increasingly apparent that McDowell sees himself as pursuing a more quietist agenda, and he himself has recently indicated that he regards his writings as springing from an opposition to anti-realism (taken as a positive thesis), and so as pursuing an anti-anti-realistic programme, rather than as aiming to argue directly for realism.[2]

The following study focuses on a cluster of central aspects of McDowell's thinking, namely his treatment of the nature of experience, of the relationship between mind and world, and his handling, in the philosophy of language, of the distinction between sense and reference. Much of my source material derives, inevitably, from the seminal *Mind and World*. But it follows from what has been said that we must expect to encounter matters relevant to the topics I have singled out for examination in all parts of McDowell's output, and I have not hesitated to cite evidence from texts and contexts whose ostensible subject matter was remote from the point at issue in cases where it seemed to me that there was a relevant connection to be made. But with a few exceptions, largely confined to footnotes, I have resisted the temptation to follow the many interesting paths that diverged from my chosen route. In adopting the policy of scouring McDowell's texts, quite generally, for material relevant to the investigation of my selected topics, I have perforce relied on and exploited that sense of an intellectual centre of gravity of which I spoke above, to the extent of treating McDowell's writings, which have of course been published over a period of more than thirty years, as though they issued instantaneously from a single point of view, except where we encounter an express indication of a change of mind, or where, in the absence of any such indication, charity would nevertheless demand that we register such a change. McDowell himself remarked in 1998 that he felt he had been 'single-minded' over the

---

[2] 1998*b*, p. viii; 1998*c*, p. 356; 2000*a*, pp. 112–14.

years,[3] and in fact the occasions on which we need to take note of an express or implicit change of mind are rare. Any residual historical inaccuracy incurred by my policy of treating McDowell's *oeuvre* in this unified way is, I believe, amply compensated for by the philosophical rewards of so proceeding.

My main aim in this study is not descriptive, but polemical.[4] I aim to show that McDowell's attempt to revive the doctrine of empiricism in what he calls a minimal form is crucially undermined by an error he commits in the philosophy of language. Following ancient tradition rather than Frege's radical departure from that tradition, McDowell locates concepts at the level of sense rather than at the level of reference. But this, I argue, is a mistake. Correcting it requires us to follow Frege in his location of concepts at the level of reference, but also to go beyond Frege and locate not only concepts but also propositions at that level; and doing so requires us, I suggest, to take seriously an idea which McDowell mentions only to reject, that of objects as speaking to us 'in the world's own language'. I shall further contend in the course of my discussion that, even given the correction I recommend, if empiricism is to have any chance of success it must be still more minimal in its pretensions than McDowell allows: in particular, it must abandon the individualistic and intellectualistic construction which McDowell places on what he calls the 'order of justification'— the way experiences justify empirical judgements—and it must grant conceptually structured experience not merely to mature human beings but also to infants and non-human animals. I am not, however, opposed to the very idea of a minimal empiricism, so long as it is set up in the right way—provided it is, as I put it in the course of my study, not *minimal* in McDowell's sense, but *minimalist* in a sense I will make clear—and so long as it is embedded in the context of a correct semantics for sentences and

[3] 1998*b*, p. vii.
[4] Readers looking for a more descriptive and synoptic treatment of McDowell's philosophy may be directed to recent studies by Tim Thornton (2004) and Maximilian de Gaynesford (2004).

their parts; to that extent my critique of McDowell's attempt to
establish a minimal empiricism seems to me at any rate, despite the
many points on which I criticize his manner of executing the
project, to be co-operative and constructive in overall tenor rather
than merely destructive or hostile.

In preparing this study I have tried to take account not only of
the whole gamut of McDowell's writings but also of as much of the
ever-growing secondary literature as I could locate. I am grateful to
McDowell himself for letting me see two unpublished typescripts:
'Transcendental Empiricism', and 'Sellars and the Space of Reasons'.
But in view of their unpublished status I have not cited them or
taken account of them in my characterization of McDowell's position.[5] I am much indebted to the two anonymous readers for the
Press, who made some cogent criticisms of the manuscript and
offered some useful suggestions for improvement. My colleague at
Liverpool Logi Gunnarsson also read through a draft of the entire
book and gave me detailed written comments from which I bene-
fited considerably. In 2004 I offered some graduate classes on *Mind
and World* at Liverpool and I learned much from the contributions
of the participants, especially Obie Hickmott. I began writing the
book during a period of leave jointly sponsored by the University of
Liverpool and the Arts and Humanities Research Board; I am
grateful to both institutions for the opportunity to get well into
the project before having to resume normal duties. My
colleague Michael McGhee has been of considerable assistance to
me at all stages of the project, and Peter Momtchiloff of the Press has
been a splendidly sympathetic editor throughout. Finally, my main
debt of gratitude is to my family—to my parents, to my wife
Cathrin, and to my sons Thomas and Markus—who, as ever, have
given me constant support and encouragement.

---

[5] Actually, the first of these typescripts has been published in a Greek translation
(McDowell 2003). I am grateful to my colleague Yiota Vassilopoulou for helping me
obtain a copy of this translation. But because of the relative inaccessibility of this
publication, I decided not to count it as a source for McDowell's views. (In fact that
did not impose a handicap, given the wealth of other material substantially overlapping
with this essay.)

Contents

Der Mensch spricht nicht allein—auch das Universum spricht—
alles spricht—unendliche Sprachen.

Human kind is not alone in speaking—the universe speaks
too—everything speaks—languages without end.

Novalis

I

Minimal empiricism and the 'order of justification'

I.1. MINIMAL EMPIRICISM: INTRODUCTORY

Empiricism is the doctrine that our capacity to know about the world is derived, mediately or immediately, from sense-experience. In its extreme manifestation the doctrine takes the form of asserting that there is, as the familiar scholastic tag has it, nothing in the mind which has not reached it through the senses.[1] But few philosophers who would count themselves empiricists have defended the doctrine in such a pure form: for example, the logical positivists, empiricism's most prominent twentieth-century disciples, admitted, alongside the class of synthetic truths known *a posteriori* through the medium of sense-experience, a class of analytic truths known *a priori* without any involvement of the senses, the analyticity of these truths, and the concomitant possibility of *a priori* knowledge of them, being grounded in their establishment by linguistic convention. (The positivists' dichotomy was a descendant of Hume's distinction between 'matters of fact' and 'relations of ideas'.)[2] To capture an

---

[1] The tag circulates in a number of more or less equivalent versions. Aquinas has: *nihil est in intellectu quod non sit prius in sensu* (*De Veritate* q. 2 a. 3, §19). The principle is derived from Aristotle: *De Anima* 432a7–8. See Stern 1999, p. 252 on Hegel's attitude to the principle.

[2] *Enquiry concerning Human Understanding*, IV.1.20 (1975, p. 25). Cf. *A Treatise of Human Nature*, III.1.1 (1978, p. 458).

empiricism of the positivists' (and of Hume's) stamp, one would need (at least) to amend the traditional tag so as to make it read something like 'nothing *enters the mind from the world* which has not reached it (exclusively) through the senses', a formulation which is meant to close off the possibility that the mind might acquire *a priori* knowledge of worldly matters of fact (whether necessary or contingent such facts), but which leaves it open that the mind may contain more than the *a posteriori* knowledge it has acquired by dint of sense-experience.

With the decline of logical positivism after its zenith in the inter-war period the doctrine of empiricism has fallen on hard times, but recently there has been an attempt by John McDowell to win respectability for a version of empiricism which he calls 'minimal' or 'transcendental' empiricism,[3] according to which

the very idea of thought's directedness at the empirical world is intelligible only in terms of answerability to the tribunal of experience, conceived in terms of the world impressing itself on perceiving subjects. (1996*a*, p. xvi)[4]

In so characterizing his minimal empiricism, as aiming to render intelligible the relation between thought and reality, McDowell is consciously offering us a persuasive definition. Traditionally empiricism has been understood in the way in which I explicated it in my opening paragraph, that is to say as a doctrine intended to account specifically for the possibility of *knowledge*; McDowell corrects and expands this conception, so that in his hands empiricism becomes a doctrine about the possibility of *content*. The narrower epistemological focus of the tradition is, on this approach, an inchoate expression of something deeper, namely a worry not merely about the sources and credentials of our claims to knowledge, but about how our minds can be in touch with an objective reality—and in

---

[3] The former terminology is prominent in the introduction to the paperback edition of *Mind and World* (1996*a*, pp. xi–xxiv), the latter in his Münster lecture (2000*a*, pp. 3–18). Both terminologies are employed at 2002*a*, p. 287.

[4] Cf. 1995*a*, pp. 231–2, 289; 1999*a*, pp. 95–7; 2000*a*, p. 4.

particular, as the quoted passage makes clear, how they can be in touch with the empirical world—at all.[5]

I.2. MINIMAL EMPIRICISM: SOME INITIAL DIFFICULTIES

McDowell does not (so far as I am aware) anywhere define what he means by the 'empirical world'. One might presume that he means the experienced world, that is, the world of which we can and do have sense-experience. But the empirical world cannot simply be identified with what *we* experience by means of *our* (five) senses: for McDowell is (rightly) ready to allow that there might be secondary qualities detectable by Martians but not by us,[6] hence keyed to a kind of sense-experience other than any with which we are familiar, and there can be no doubt that, for McDowell and in actual fact, any such qualities would belong to the empirical world. So the empirical world must be so defined that *any* genuine kind of sense-experience can yield access to it. But what counts as a genuine kind of sense-experience? In trying to answer this question we clearly face a threat of circularity, for there may be no independent conceptual entry-point to the relation of mutual dependence between the notions of 'empirical world' and 'experience'. The empirical world consists of what is or can be experienced, but it seems that no limits can be set in advance on what is to qualify as experience: the only requirement we can specify is the—in the context, trivial—one that objects of experience must belong to the empirical world. The difficulty which arises here, of providing some non-trivial way of characterizing the empirical world, or alternatively of supplying a non-trivial account of what is to qualify as (genuine) experience, so as to provide a way into the circle connecting these two notions, is indeed a

[5] 1994, pp. 146–7; 1995*a*, p. 232; 1996*a*, pp. xiii–xiv; 1998*e*, p. 121; 2000*a*, pp. 3–4. Cf. de Gaynesford 2004, pp. 9–10.
[6] 1994, p. 123 n. 11; 2000*a*, p. 95.

fundamental one. Of course this is a problem which confronts everyone, not just McDowell; but given the centrality to McDowell's thinking of the relationship between thought and the empirical world one might have expected him to provide more illumination than he does on the question what the empirical world is, and how its presumably constitutive connection with experience is to be conceived. A related difficulty is the following.

In the statement of his minimal empiricism which I quoted above McDowell speaks quite generally of *thought's* directedness at the empirical world, and an obvious problem in understanding this characterization lies in establishing the parameters of the 'thought' whose directedness at the empirical world is to be rendered intelligible. In other formulations of the doctrine of minimal empiricism, McDowell speaks of the way that doctrine can help us to understand how *empirical* thought can be directed at the empirical world, and I take it that we are licensed to read this restriction into formulations, such as the one I have quoted, which do not mention it explicitly.[7] But we must ask how much the restriction conveys. Is it intended to leave open the possibility that there are or could be *non-empirical* ways in which thought is directed at the world? Are there non-empirical ways in which things reach the mind from the world, to put it in the terms of the amended tag (§1)? McDowell is unclear on this point. In one passage he seems to leave open the possibility that 'answerability to how things are includes more than answerability to the empirical world';[8] but elsewhere we find him tentatively suggesting that to rephrase the question how thought is directed at the world so as to make it the question how empirical thought is directed at the empirical world 'would not be to add anything',[9] a remark which implies that answerability to the world just is answerability to the empirical world.

At all events, whether or not McDowell is prepared to allow a sense in which thinking is answerable to a non-empirical world, it

---

[7] See the characterizations of minimal empiricism given at 1996*a*, pp. xii, xv, and xvii.
[8] 1996*a*, p. xii.   [9] 1999*a*, p. 88.

seems clear that, for him, any such relation between thought and a non-empirical world would have to be essentially secondary and parasitic, dependent on a primary directedness of specifically empirical thinking towards the empirical world (whatever that is). As he puts it at one point,

thought can intelligibly be of the objective at all . . . only because we can see how there can be conceptual occurrences in which objects are manifestly there for thinkers, immediately present to their conceptually shaped *sensory* consciousness. (1998*d*, p. 465, emphasis added)

This passage does not rule out the possibility that some thinking about, and some answerability to, the objective world might be non-empirical in nature—that some world-directed thoughts might be grounded in the availability of a non-sensory route between world and mind—but it does imply that thinkers can be entitled to entertain such thoughts only if their sensory access (however this is to be defined) to the empirical world is already and anyway firmly in place. As Robert Brandom puts it, McDowell 'insists that anything that does not have perceptual experience does not have concepts either'.[10] So whatever we are to say about the objective credentials of non-empirical thinking—thinking engaged in, for instance, pure set theory—at any rate we can say that the existence of a subject conceived as an empirically uncontaminated locus of such thought is, for McDowell, not a conceptual possibility. This point is crucial both to the position which he calls 'naturalized platonism', according to which our human responsiveness to reasons is essentially dependent on our status as living, embodied beings, and to a transcendental argument which McDowell offers connecting conceptual capacities and sensory intake, and according to which each of these is required if we are to make sense of the other, and if we are to make sense of the objective bearing of thought quite generally. I shall examine naturalized platonism in Chapter II, and the transcendental argument in Chapter III: in these discussions the two issues I have

[10] 2002, p. 93.

raised so far in this section—the absence in McDowell's writings of a non-trivial characterization of the empirical world, and the question whether he takes thought to be answerable to more than the empirical world, however that is to be defined—will be in the background of my discussion.[11]

Looking at the characterization we have of minimal empiricism, according to which the very idea of empirical thought's directedness at the empirical world is intelligible only in terms of its answerability to the tribunal of experience, conceived in terms of the world's impressing itself on perceiving subjects, there is a further respect, distinct from the one I have already mentioned, in which one might wonder whether it escapes triviality. I have noted that the expression 'empirical world' is to be construed as meaning the world which is or can be accessed in sense-experience (however exactly that is to be delimited). But given that construal, one might ask: how could empirical thought's directedness at the empirical world be intelligible *other* than in terms of 'answerability to the tribunal of experience'? In fact I think this worry can be allayed: I can see three moves we might make, on McDowell's behalf, in response to any charge of triviality that might be lodged on the score of this worry. First, we might say, it is by no means trivial to claim that answerability to the experienced world must be understood in terms of answerability to *experience itself*; secondly, the appeal to answerability serves to insist on the obtaining of a *normative* connection between experience and empirical thought, and that surely travels some epistemic distance beyond the mere idea of world-directedness; and thirdly, the suggestion that the 'tribunal of experience' must be conceived in terms of the world's

---

[11] As far as empirical beliefs of a theoretical nature are concerned, McDowell's idea, following Sellars in *Empiricism and the Philosophy of Mind* (1956, §38; 1997, p. 78), is that not only do they depend for their warrant, and intelligibility, on observations, but it is also the case that observations are in turn constitutively dependent on a 'conceptual repertoire employed in articulating a world view': 1998*a*, pp. 427–8; cf. 1998*d*, pp. 434–6, 462–6; 2000*a*, pp. 13–14; 2002*a*, pp. 287–8. It is important to McDowell, *qua* empiricist, to insist that there is a good distinction to be drawn between (unmediated) observational beliefs and (mediated) theoretical beliefs: 1995*a*, pp. 291–2. But, apart from a brief reappearance in Ch. III (§8), this point will not concern me in what follows.

impressing itself on perceiving subjects serves to insist on the obtaining of a *causal* connection between the world and perceiving subjects, and that again, it is at least plausible to suppose, tells us something non-trivial about the way McDowell is thinking of experience. But adverting to these three aspects of McDowell's minimal empiricism, in order to deal with the worry I have mentioned, so far from closing the investigation, raises a host of new, and pressing, questions. Let us start by asking: how are these three features of minimal empiricism supposed to fit together?

I.3. McDOWELL'S EMPIRICISM: OVERVIEW AND PROSPECTIVE

Fundamental to McDowell's minimal empiricism is the claim that the world-directedness of empirical thought involves both rational or normative connections between world and thought on the one hand, and causal connections on the other. Putting it in general and abstract terms for the moment, we can say that the rational connections ensure that empirical thought can be *correct or incorrect*,[12] while the causal connections guarantee that empirical thought is genuinely *about* the empirical world:[13] taken together, these connections ensure that empirical thought is not empty—that it is not, as McDowell likes to put it, mere 'frictionless spinning in a void'.[14] This way of expressing McDowell's position is crude because it leaves the precise relata of the rational and causal relations unspecified. One

---

[12] See e.g. 1994, p. 26 (cited below in the text, §4); 1996*a*, pp. xi–xii; 2000*a*, p. 16.

[13] See e.g. 1994, p. 150; Afterword, Part 1; 1996*a*, pp. xvii–xviii; 2002*b*, p. 178. Thornton denies (2004, p. 204) that causation plays a role in McDowell's thinking about experience, but that seems to me clearly a misinterpretation. I shall be exploring causation's role in McDowell's picture of experience in Ch. II.

[14] See 1994, pp. 11, 18, 66, 68. A similar structure of constraints is proposed by Brandom (1994, p. 235), who criticizes McDowell's use of the image of 'friction' on the basis that it is a *causal* image clumsily employed to illustrate a point about the *rational* constraints on thought: see 1995*a*, p. 244 with n. 5. But on my reading of his strategy, the image is intended by McDowell to emphasize the need for *both* a rational *and* a causal connection between mind and world.

answer to the question I posed at the end of the previous section, involving a rather literal reading of the characterization of minimal empiricism which I have quoted (§1), would suggest the following way of setting up the rational and causal relations. There are three terms in play and two relations. In the first place, a causal relation obtains between the world and experience: that is, worldly events are the cause and experiences the effect. (The worldly events must of course act *on perceiving subjects* to produce the effect—the part of the transaction mentioned by McDowell in the quoted passage.) In the second place, a rational relation obtains between experience and (empirical) thought. But if that is the position, to label it a 'minimal' empiricism would surely be a misnomer: we would have to do rather with a substantial empiricism, one which conceived experience, in Lockean style, as an interface between subject and world, rendering the subject's contact with the world essentially indirect. Of course, anyone familiar with McDowell's writings will immediately recognize this position as one he has strenuously sought to combat, so that to read the quoted characterization in that way would certainly run counter to his intentions not only in *Mind and World*, from which the quotation is drawn, but in others of his writings.[15]

But it seems to me that, its opposition to McDowell's intentions notwithstanding, such a reading of the charaterization of minimal empiricism which I have quoted would not be merely frivolous: for there are indications in McDowell's *oeuvre* that, despite his clear intention to the contrary, he is committed by what he actually says to an empiricism of a substantial and contentious variety. There are three features of McDowell's position that at least raise a suspicion that his empiricism is more substantial and contentious than he officially allows: his handling of the causal relation constituted by the world's impressing itself on experiencing subjects; his view of the nature of experience and its relation to empirical thinking and judgement; and his approach to the question of the mentality of

---

[15] Esp. in his essay 'Criteria, Defeasibility, and Knowledge', 1998*c*, pp. 369–94. See also 1998*b*, pp. 342, 358; 1998*c*, pp. 225–6, 272–3; 2000*a*, pp. 14–17; 2002*b*, p. 191 n. 18.

human infants in the pre-linguistic phase of their development and non-human, non-linguistic animals (for convenience I shall henceforth abbreviate this cumbersome phrase to 'infants and animals'). I examine these features in turn, in Chapters II, III, and IV respectively.

To anticipate, I shall argue that the first feature, while unsatisfactory in other respects—and indeed in respects which reveal a fundamental flaw in the way McDowell tries to execute his project of integrating what (following Wilfrid Sellars) he calls the 'logical space of reasons'[16] into the natural world—does not as such commit him to a substantial empiricism; the second and third aspects, on the other hand, do commit McDowell to more substantial and controversial doctrines than the espousal of minimal empiricism purported to bring in its train. These doctrines, individualistic and intellectualistic, are deeply unsatisfactory aspects of McDowell's thinking on the relation between mind and world. I shall suggest, in Chapter V, that to provide a convincing diagnosis of the presence of these undesirable doctrines in McDowell's brand of empiricism we need to look in a surprising place and focus on what might at first sight seem a rather abstruse feature of his philosophy, and one that has (so far as I am aware) hitherto escaped notice: namely his understanding of the sense–reference distinction as that applies to concept-expressions. Offering this diagnosis will, I hope, incidentally provide a counterexample to Richard Rorty's claim that the philosophy of language as it is conducted in the post-Fregean, analytic tradition (what he calls 'pure' philosophy of language) 'has no epistemological *parti pris*, nor, indeed, any relevance to most of the traditional

---

[16] Sellars 1956, §36; 1997, p. 76: 'In characterizing an episode or state as that of *knowing*, we are not giving an empirical description of that episode or state; we are placing it in the logical space of reasons, of justifying and being able to justify what one says'. In quoting this passage McDowell likes to correct the phrase 'that of knowing' to 'one of knowing' (see e.g. 1994, p. 5 n. 4; 1998c, p. 415 n. 5) in order to 'allow that a concept of knowledge might be applied to non-rational animals too' (1998c, p. 395 n. 2). The correction is indeed desirable on stylistic grounds, though I do not see that the change connects with the reason McDowell gives for making it. (But the point that, on McDowell's view, non-rational animals are capable of knowledge will be important below: Ch. III, §10.)

concerns of modern philosophy'.[17] On the contrary, I believe—and I
hope that this study will contribute towards showing—that the
analytic philosophy of language is the context in which our deepest
metaphysical and epistemological concerns should be addressed.

It will emerge that the deep source of the unsatisfactory ways in
which his thinking goes beyond an uncontroversial minimal empiricism is McDowell's tacit commitment to an unacceptable Kantian
transcendental idealism or, more simply, to nominalism—a doctrine
which is of course intellectually distinct from empiricism, but which
has, as a consequence of what Sellars calls the 'predominantly nominalistic proclivities of the empiricist tradition',[18] been closely associated with empiricisms of a rather substantial variety. (Locke's
conceptualism is a variety of nominalistic empiricism which is
perhaps most familiar nowadays to the student of philosophy.)
Finally, in Chapter VI, I will argue that, in order to unpick ourselves
from the nominalistic entanglement into which McDowell's thinking has led us, we need to rehabilitate an idea from which McDowell
officially dissociates himself: that the world speaks its own language.
The resulting linguistic idealism, involving as it does a philosophically pregnant sense in which the world is linguistically structured,
provides, I will suggest, the only intellectually safe environment for
the cultivation of a minimal empiricism worth defending.

I.4. THE SIMPLE MODEL OF EMPIRICAL CONTENT

I have mentioned that it is important for McDowell that experience
not be conceived as an interface, something intervening between
perceiving subject and world, limiting the direct reach of the mind to
what lies on the interface (sense-data, percepts), and thus rendering
the subject's perception of the world lying beyond the interface—as
we would be forced to conceive it—essentially indirect. Instead

---

[17] 1979, p. 257.   [18] 1956, §6; 1997, p. 21.

McDowell wants us to conceive of experience, when all goes well, as a kind of openness to the world, ensuring that the mind's contact with the world is direct: for the sake of a label, we might call this the 'conduit' conception of experience.[19] It informs such passages as the following:

[T]he idea of conceptually structured operations of receptivity puts us in a position to speak of experience as openness to the layout of reality. Experience enables the layout of reality itself to exert a rational influence on what a subject thinks. (1994, p. 26)

When we are not misled by experience, we are directly confronted by a worldly state of affairs itself, not waited on by an intermediary that happens to tell the truth. (1994, p. 143)[20]

What these passages and others like them suggest is that we should read the characterization of minimal empiricism which I quoted in §1 not as positing three relata—world, experience, and empirical thought—with a causal relation running between world and experience and a rational or normative relation running between experience and empirical thought, as I suggested in §3, but rather as positing just two relata—world and empirical thought—linked by two distinct relations—a causal one and a rational or normative one—with experience conceived not as a further *relatum* in this picture but as the *relation* connecting the two posited relata.

McDowell certainly attributes a mediating role to experience, for example in a passage which comes shortly after the characterization of minimal empiricism which I quoted in §1:

we can make sense of the world-directedness of empirical thinking only by conceiving it as answerable to the empirical world for its correctness, and we can understand answerability to the empirical world only as mediated by

---

[19] McDowell frequently includes some such qualification as 'when all goes well': see e.g. 1994, p. 113, 2000*a*, p. 9, and the passage from 1994, p. 143 I go on to cite in the text. The image of openness to the world is the leitmotif of de Gaynesford's study of McDowell's philosophy (2004).

[20] Cf. 1995*a*, p. 237; 1998*c*, pp. 362, 392.

answerability to the tribunal of experience, conceived in terms of the world's direct impacts on possessors of perceptual capacities. (1996*a*, p. xvii)

Elsewhere we are told that 'experience is simply the way in which observational thinking is directly rationally responsive to facts'.[21] But the idea seems to be that experience performs this mediating role without derogating from the directness of the relation between thought and world—without functioning as an intermediary or interface which *gets in the way* of thought's direct access to the world. The directness of thought's access to the world has the two aspects we have already noted: we might say that, on McDowell's view, experience is, when all goes well, that special way in which we are connected to the world when our empirical thought is both caused by worldly events, and normatively guided by—answerable for its correctness to—the way the world is. I shall call this understanding of the way experience mediates between world and mind in the genesis of empirical thought and judgement the 'simple model of empirical content'; it is intended to encapsulate the conduit conception of experience.

I.5. THE 'ORDER OF JUSTIFICATION'

But this simple model, which surely captures what McDowell means to put forward, cannot, on the face of it, be squared with everything he says about the role of experience in securing the world-directedness of empirical thinking and, correlatively, of the empirical judgement which that thinking aims to deliver. In particular, we must take note of the following apparent antinomy.[22] In *Mind and World*

---

[21] 1998*a*, p. 406. Cf. 1994, p. 142; 1995*a*, pp. 231–2; 1996*a*, pp. xii, xx; 1998*c*, p. 393 n. 45; 1999*a*, pp. 92, 95–6.

[22] This antinomy is pointed out by Brandom: 1995*a*, pp. 253–5. Cf. his 1998, p. 372. A parallel difficulty to the one I examine here concerns McDowell's appeal to the notion of experience as a mediator between thought and reality, mentioned in the previous section: I postpone discussion of this related difficulty until I come to deal with the 'highest common factor' conception of experience in Ch. III, §7.

McDowell speaks of the normative relation of answerability as the 'order of justification',[23] and he says two apparently opposed things about this order. In some passages he tells us—what the simple model would predict—that the *world* is 'ultimate in the order of justification'.[24] In one such passage we are told that in the 'order of justification' experiences lie along a line whose end-points are the world and minds.[25] (Experience's position on this line is evidently not conceived to coincide with either of the end-points.) But in other passages we are told that *experience* is ultimate: 'when we trace the ground for an empirical judgement, the last step takes us to experience'.[26] This apparent antinomy is complicated by the presence on the scene of what might look like a third candidate for ultimacy in the 'order of justification'—'thinkable contents', about which we are told not only that they are ultimate in the 'order of justification', but also that they are 'contents of experiences'.[27] To take this third candidate first, it seems fairly clear that the contents in question are not intended to constitute a genuinely distinct candidate for ultimacy in the 'order of justification', but are instead meant to be located either in the mind or in the world: but which?

The context in which they are introduced, in the second lecture of *Mind and World*, would suggest that the thinkable contents in question are in the mind rather than in the world, for we are told that 'when we trace justifications back, the last thing we come to is still a thinkable content; not something more ultimate than that, a bare pointing to a bit of the Given'.[28] The *comparatio deterioris* surely implies that the thinkable contents in question are intended to be mental as opposed to worldly entities, for if they were intended to be

[23] 1994, pp. 29, 133–5, 146. Cf. 2000*a*, pp. 9–13.

[24] See esp. 1994, pp. 34, 39 (2nd paragraph: on the 1st paragraph see further below in this section), 42, 146, 165; 1998*a*, p. 426. The idea of our answerability in judgement to the world is prominent in McDowell's 2000*b*.

[25] 1994, p. 146: I will discuss this important passage in more detail below (Ch. II, §2).

[26] 1994, p. 10. See further 1994, pp. 49 n. 6, 67, 125; 1995*a*, pp. 234, 236; 1999*a*, p. 90.

[27] 1994, pp. 28–9 (on this passage see M. Williams 1996, pp. 105–6, 108).

[28] 1994, pp. 28–9.

the latter, one would have expected McDowell to write ' . . . not something more ultimate than that, such as a bit of the Given': in other words, the fact that the unsuccessful candidate for ultimacy is characterized as a *pointing*—and thus as a mental rather than a worldly entity—suggests that the successful candidate is, likewise, a mental entity. This argument is perhaps rather too tenuous to support a confident decision on the interpretative question before us, but comparison with a subsequent passage from the same lecture, where McDowell says that the 'conceptual contents that are passively received in experience bear on, or are about . . . the world',[29] confirms that, at least in this part of his text, McDowell is locating the thinkable contents that are ultimate in the 'order of justification' at the mental as opposed to the worldly level. For adopting the opposing position, according to which the world rather than experience is ultimate in the 'order of justification', would require him to speak of the thinkable contents that are ultimate in the 'order of justification' not as *bearing on*, or being *about*, the world, but as simply *being* (bits of) *the world*.[30] And, as we have noted, there are plenty of texts in which McDowell advances this opposing position. So it would seem that, on the face of it, McDowell does not offer us a consistent line on where the 'order of justification' terminates.[31] But I think it is possible to interpret the relevant texts in such a way as to defuse the appearance of antinomy, as I shall now explain.

---

[29] 1994, p. 39.
[30] So, rightly, Larmore 2002, p. 198; cf. Christensen 2000, p. 898. In his reply to Larmore McDowell (2002*a*, p. 295) misses the force of Larmore's criticism, by focusing on how *thinkers* relate to the world: but Larmore's point is that the passage wrongly distances experience's *contents* from the world. I take the passage to be not simply a slip, as Larmore supposes (though he is of course right that the passage is in at least *prima facie* conflict with the claim that experience reaches out and embraces the world), but an indicator of a mistaken understanding of the conceptual which dominates McDowell's thinking, and which accounts for a number of unsatisfactory aspects of his philosophy: this will be the theme of Ch. V.
[31] Cf. Brandom's accusation (1995*a*, pp. 252–5; 1998, pp. 372–3) that McDowell is guilty of an equivocation on the notion of answerability (sliding from the notion of answerability to the world to that of answerability to experience).

I.6. FROM THE COMPLEX TO THE SIMPLE MODEL OF EMPIRICAL CONTENT

The *initial* picture which McDowell intends to offer us of the role of experience in securing content for empirical thinking and judgement is indeed more complex than the simple model suggests: we are invited to contemplate, in the first instance, a structure articulated into empirical world, experience, empirical thinking, and empirical judgement, but related in more complicated ways than was envisaged in §3. (Since nothing turns on preserving the distinction between empirical thought and empirical judgement in this context, I shall simplify my discussion by in effect identifying them, treating 'judgement' as a suitable label for the resulting composite moment in the generation of empirical content.) My suggestion now is that, according to McDowell's initial model, a rational or normative relation runs not only between experience and judgement, as envisaged in the model I offered in §3, but also between world and experience; a causal relation runs not only between world and experience, but also between experience and judgement. On this last feature—the inclusion in the model of a causal relation running from experience to judgement—we may note that McDowell objects to Donald Davidson's coherentism on the basis that it is not saved from charges of idealism by 'crediting intuitions with a causal impact on thoughts', and he adds that 'we can have empirical content in our picture only if we can acknowledge that thoughts and intuitions are rationally connected';[32] but he does not say that there cannot *also* be a causal relation between intuitions [i.e., experiences] and judgements, and remarks elsewhere suggest that he would not be hostile to including that feature in what I am characterizing as his initial picture of the way experience secures empirical content for judgement.[33] So I think we may as well include it. (But this feature of the

---

[32] 1994, pp. 17–18. Cf. his criticisms of Quine at 1994, p. 134.
[33] See e.g. 1994, pp. 68, 71 n. 2; 1998*c*, p. 151; 2000*a*, p. 92; 2002*b*, p. 178.

model will not be of great importance for me: in my critique of
McDowell's handling of the role of causation in experience, in
Chapter II, I shall be focusing on the causal relation that he undeniably locates between the world and experience.) Call this conception
of the way experience mediates between world and mind in the
genesis of judgement the 'complex model of empirical content'.[34]

The idea now is that, with the complex model, as I have characterized it, in place, we are entitled to move to the simple model's
conception of the role of experience in securing empirical content for
judgement. In other words, if we start by conceiving experience as
the complex model has it, that supposedly entitles us to progress to
conceiving it as the simple model has it, namely as something that
simply mediates between subjects and world, enabling subjects to be
open to the world, enabling them to embrace the world in their
minds. Putting it in yet another way, if we start by setting up a model
of the genesis of empirical content in which experience figures as a
relatum, then provided we set the model up in the right way we will
be entitled to graduate to a different model in which experience is
conceived as a *relation*. How exactly this entitlement works is some-

---

[34] Note that, assuming we do include a causal relation between experience and
judgement in the complex model as I have suggested we should, it coincides with the
interpretation of McDowell offered by Wright at 1998*a*, pp. 397–9 (2002*a*, pp. 145–7).
In his response to Wright, McDowell objects to the way Wright articulates his model
into temporal stages in a dialectical progression (1998*a*, pp. 425–6; 2002*a*, pp. 286–7):
for in Wright's presentation of the structure the experience–judgement relations are
established before the nature of the world–experience relations has been settled. McDowell's objection to this procedure is that the item labelled 'experience' in the model
cannot be recognized as such at some intermediate stage in the setting up of the model,
before (say) the nature of its relations to the world has been settled; only when the whole
model is in place do we earn the right to label the relevant item 'experience'. But he does
not appear to object to the structure as such, provided it is given all at once, as I am
assuming it to be given. There is an exegetical difficulty here, for at 1998*a*, p. 406,
McDowell appears to reject the complex model, or something like it. I take it that this
apparent rejection is to be read as a rebuttal of any attempt to impute that model to him
as his final position. We must indeed acknowledge that McDowell's *target* position is the
simple model of empirical content; but that does not militate against the possibility (and,
I suggest, fact) that his argumentative *route* to that simple model goes essentially via an
intermediate state at which the complex model is in place. (If that were not the right way
to read this passage, I would have to censure its rejection of the complex model as
disingenuous.)

thing McDowell hopes to explain by means of the transcendental argument to which I have already alluded and which I will examine in detail in Chapter III. For now all we need is the point that, in McDowell's view as I am interpreting him, with the collapse of the complex into the simple model, we entitle ourselves to the thought that 'impressions are, so to speak, transparent'.[35]

What, then, should we say about the 'order of justification'? There is an apparent but not a real difficulty here, I suggest. There is indeed an apparent difficulty, because while it is plausible to suppose that the complex model posits *experiences* as what subjects must point to in ultimate justification of their judgements—for if experience is a relatum, intervening between world and subject, that must surely be where the reach of the mind terminates—the simple model has it that the *world* is the ultimate justifier. The divergent answers given by the models to the question what is ultimate in the 'order of justification' thus reflects the antinomy which, as we have seen, is undeniably present in McDowell's texts on this point. But if we conceive the complex model, as I am proposing, as a *dialectical route* to the simple model, explaining our entitlement to the conduit conception of experience which is embodied in the simple model, the apparent difficulty can be resolved. What is ultimate in the 'order of justification', we might say, is not the world just as such, nor experience just as such, but the *experienced world*. Putting it in this way might appear to reinstate one of the charges of triviality considered in §2: for given that the empirical world is constitutively the world we can experience, how, one might wonder, could empirical thought's directedness at the empirical world be intelligible *other* than in terms of answerability to the 'tribunal of experience'? But in saying that our answerability is not to the world just as such, nor to experience just as such, but to the experienced world, we are doing more than merely unpacking the content of the phrase 'empirical world': we are saying that our answerability is to the world *as accessed in that particular way*, to the world *as* experienced.

A number of texts suggest that that is indeed McDowell's considered position. In one passage, the ultimate justifier is said to be 'the fact observed', and McDowell adds that 'the point of the idea of experience is that it is in experience that facts themselves come to be among the justifiers available to subjects'.[36] Elsewhere, 'how things appear to one' is said to be 'what one goes on in arriving at one's picture of the world'.[37] The phrase 'how things appear to one' can perhaps be glossed, in agreement with my interpretation of McDowell, as 'the world, as it appears to one'. Again, we are told that 'in receiving impressions, a subject can be open to the way things manifestly are'.[38] We are further told that we judge whether things are thus and so 'in the light of whether things are (observably) thus and so'.[39] For my purposes, I think it would be in order to rewrite this phrase by removing the brackets and emphasizing the word 'observably'. Finally, 'for a subject in the best case, the appearance that there is a candle in front of her is the presence of the candle making itself apparent to her'.[40] But is McDowell really entitled to the conduit (as opposed to the interface) conception of experience, as he intends and as the way I have deployed the complex and simple models on his behalf seems to secure for him? As I have mentioned, there are three aspects of McDowell's treatment of experience's part in securing empirical content which raise doubts on this score. I turn first to the role that causation plays in these models.

[36] 1998*a*, p. 430. Cf. 2002*a*, p. 289.   [37] 1994, p. 135 n. 5.
[38] 1996*a*, p. xx.   [39] 1998*a*, p. 405.   [40] 2002*c*, p. 99.

II

Experience and causation

II.1. CAUSATION AND THE COMPLEX MODEL OF EMPIRICAL CONTENT

I have ascribed to McDowell a dialectical progression in which a simple model of empirical content, which is his target position, is reached via a staging-post complex model. The simple model envisages two relata, world and empirical thought (judgement), linked in experience by both rational and causal relations, while the complex model envisages three relata—world, experience, and judgement—with both rational and causal linkages both between world and experience and between experience and judgement. Given the manner in which I am suggesting these two models fit together, we may say that it is in virtue of the way it figures in the complex model that causation figures in the way it does in the simple model. But how does causation figure in the complex model? How, in particular, are we to conceive the causal relation which obtains between world and experience?[1]

McDowell nowhere addresses this question. We are offered, it is true, a number of different causal locutions for the relation in question. In phrases redolent of the British empiricists, experiences are variously styled 'impressions', 'impacts', or 'impingements' (of

---

[1] I focus on this causal relation, as being both more important and more solidly present in McDowell's philosophy of experience than the causal relation connecting experience and judgement.

the world on our senses), 'upshots' (of facts), 'the way the world puts its mark on us';[2] or the Kantian language of intuitions, sensibility, and receptivity is exploited.[3] At one point sensing is said to be 'a way of being acted on by the world';[4] elsewhere we are told that impressions are 'receptivity in operation',[5] and it is confirmed for us, lest there be any doubt on the matter, that 'the concept of receptivity is implicitly causal'.[6] But all these alternative expressions are unhelpful, for none elucidates any of the others: they are simply variant, and essentially equivalent, causal locutions; and none receives any independent explanatory underpinning to enable us to use it as a point of leverage on the others. The absence of any explanation or justification for the involvement of these causal locutions now opens the way for an objector to argue as follows.

Talk of an experience as an impression, in the sense of a causal upshot of the world, goes well beyond anything simply given to us, pre-theoretically, by common sense. On the contrary, the invitation to conceive experiences as impressions[7] is the start of a rudimentary physical *theory* of experience. Indeed, our objector continues, if we

---

[2] Examples of these locutions are so frequent in McDowell's writings that exhaustive citation is unnecessary, but I here refer the reader to a selection of relevant texts. For the language of impressions, impacts, and impingements, see 1994, pp. 9–10, 15, 18, 21, 28–9, 34, 139; 1995a, p. 234; 1996a, pp. xv, xvii; 1998d, p. 443; 1999a, pp. 98, 102. For experiences as the 'upshot' of facts, see 1998c, pp. 388–9; for experiences as 'the way the world puts its mark on us', see 1999a, p. 95; cf. p. 99.

[3] Again, detailed citation is not necessary: the reader who begins *Mind and World* with the introduction to the paperback edition almost immediately encounters the claim that 'our cognitive predicament is that we confront the world by way of sensible intuition (to put it in Kantian terms)' (1996a, p. xii), and from here on in, as well as elsewhere in McDowell's post-1994 writings, Kantian terminology is repeatedly deployed. The sudden and unceremonious appearance of this terminology, accompanied by no explanation or justification, right at the beginning of McDowell's exposition of his position, must surely raise in any reader the question where such Kantian language gets its meal-ticket from. In effect I shall be suggesting (Ch. V) that the answer lies in a deeper—one might say, more sinister—involvement of Kantian metaphysics in McDowell's philosophy than a mere matter of the appropriation of some convenient terminology.

[4] 1994, p. 89.

[5] 1994, pp. 10, 24, 141; 2000a, p. 9.

[6] 2000a, p. 91.

[7] An invitation issued at 1996a, p. xv, though it turns out later to be an invitation we are not permitted to refuse.

are to be 'guided by the etymology of the word "impression" ', as McDowell at one point recommends,[8] the language of impressions will surely point us towards an empiricist theory of experience in quite a substantial sense, one in which (to unpack the metaphor contained in the word 'impression') the world imprints itself on the mind in something like the way a signet ring leaves an imprint of itself on a piece of softened wax.[9] That conception of the relation between world and mind is objectionable, by McDowell's own lights,[10] because the relation between the action of the ring's being impressed on a piece of wax and the imprint it leaves on the wax is a purely external one: but the rational or normative relation between the world and an experience was meant to be an internal one. In other words, so the objector concludes, the language of impressions gives us a transaction in what McDowell calls the 'realm of law' (the subject matter of the natural sciences) when what we wanted was a transaction in the 'space of reasons' (the domain of rationalizing, or justifying, relations). Putting the point in more traditional terms, we might ask how realism about experience—here taking the form of a conduit ('openness') conception of experience—can cohere with a causal theory of perception: for realism requires that experience and its objects be internally related; but causation is surely an external relation.[11] So the objector.

---

[8] 2000*a*, p. 9.

[9] One naturally recalls Plato's use of this image in the *Theaetetus*, at 191c8–e1. But there the image has a quite restricted application: it is invoked to solve a puzzle about false belief, and impressions on the wax tablet of the mind are specifically memory images. See McDowell's comment ad loc.: 1973, pp. 209–10. (The image as applied to experience does capture the epistemological position of the Stoic Cleanthes, though it was rejected by Chrysippus: Sextus Empiricus, *Adversus Mathematicos* 7,227–9 (1983, p. 122).) On the image, in general, of the mind as a wax tablet which receives impressions in a quasi-mechanical way (i.e., in a way which presupposes the availability in principle of a quasi-physical theory of the relevant process of impressing), see Rorty's discussion at 1979, pp. 139–48. Rorty reminds us of the important fact, often forgotten in this context (and ignored by McDowell), that the language of impressions (and impingements etc.), as applied to effects on the mind, is *metaphorical* (1979, p. 143, citing Green 1908, p. 11), and so stands in need of a justification.

[10] Cf. 2000*a*, p. 12.

[11] For an objection along these lines, see Glendinning and de Gaynesford 1998, p. 26.

Now it is indeed one of McDowell's principal aims to insist that impressions, though rightly conceived as 'transactions in nature', are nevertheless within the space of reasons, and hence able to provide a grounding for judgements.[12] And impressions can only provide that grounding if they have conceptual content, the content (to put it schematically) *that things are thus and so*, which is the content of the judgement they ground.[13] Since *that things are thus and so* is also how things (schematically) are in the world, if the judgement is true, there is in general 'no ontological gap' between thought and world.[14] So, given that an experience is partly individuated by its content, the relations between world and experience cannot be purely external. But nor, on the other hand, does McDowell want us to lapse into an idealism according to which the world is just the content of experiences, when these are conceived as mere appearings rather than impressions. For mere appearings need not be linked to the world by causal relations—the obtaining of a causal relation between the world and an appearing, where it does obtain, is not what constitutes the appearing as the kind of thing it is—whereas impressions are constitutively causal upshots of the world. McDowell makes it clear that he thinks that an idealism which tries to construct the world out of mere appearings, so conceived, forfeits the right to genuine empirical content. That is the point of his polemic in *Mind and World* against Sellars and Davidson, who locate experiences, conceived as made up of impressions, items which are constitutively caused by worldly happenings, outside the space of reasons, and so incapable of acting as a tribunal; appearings, on the other hand, which may be taken as the space-of-reasons counterpart of impressions (and so capable of acting as a tribunal), are not conceived to be causally related to items in the world: in effect, appearings are not identified with impressions.[15]

---

[12] See e.g. 1996*a*, p. xx (partially quoted below, §3); 2000*a*, pp. 6–7.

[13] 1994, p. 9; 2000*a*, pp. 9–13.

[14] 1994, p. 27. The phenomenon of falsity raises a problem here, to which I return in Ch. VI below.

[15] In Davidson's case, as McDowell notes, construing appearings as space-of-reasons phenomena requires some licence: 1994, p. 140. As for Sellars, the view of him

Against Sellars and Davidson, McDowell insists that if experiences are to have empirical content to which judgement can be answerable, they must be identified with impressions, conceived as causal upshots of the world. For only impressions, so conceived, can provide judgement with the kind of external constraint it needs to be genuinely about the world; mere appearings, which, unlike impressions, are not constitutively caused by the world, are not good enough to discharge this role.[16] Note that, in the formulation I have just employed, the 'external' constraint exerted by the world on experience is not to be conceived as external in the sense which that word has in the phrase 'external relation'. This is obviously crucial to McDowell's polemic: we might put the point by saying that the worldly constraints exerted on the content of experience are *external* to experience in a non-technical sense of the word 'external'; but when viewed in the context of the technical distinction between external and internal relations these same constraints must be conceived to stand in an *internal* relation to that content. (In order to distinguish the notions we might speak of the external constraint, in the non-technical sense, as an 'exogenous' constraint.) Equipped with the notion of an impression which is both part of the causal order and part of the 'order of justification', McDowell takes himself to be entitled to rebut the charge that he conceives the mind as being like a wax tablet.[17]

II.2. THE THREAT OF ANOMALOUS MONISM

The position is, then, as I have outlined it in the complex model: world and experience are linked by *both* causal *and* rational/

promulgated in *Mind and World* is that he finds no role for impressions in the space of reasons, but McDowell has revised that interpretation in subsequent publications: 1998*d*, p. 441 n. 15; 2000*a*, p. 13.

[16] See 1994, Afterword Part I; 1996*a*, pp. xvii–xviii.

[17] 2000*a*, p. 12.

normative relations.[18] But if the very same things in world and mind are linked by these different relations, we seem to have a problem, which the objector I reported above may be taken to be gesturing at, albeit inchoately. Take an item or event on the subjective end of these world-experience relations: how can it, the very same entity, be linked *both* by realm-of-law *and* by space-of-reasons relations to the world? Is that not just Anomalous Monism, a position which McDowell officially abjures?[19] Remember that, as I noted above, an experience is partly individuated by its conceptual content. (One can—and typically does—have many experiences simultaneously: spatio-temporal criteria will not be adequate to individuate these.) So it is no answer to our difficulty to say that the causal and rational relations have different relata at their subjective end: the experience as spatio-temporal event in the case of the causal relation, and its conceptual content in the case of the rational relation. What is caused is an experience *with that content*; what justifies a judgement (here and now, say), and is correct or incorrect in the light of the way the world (here and now) is, is the content of a *particular* experience (the one I am having here and now).

In his essay 'Functionalism and Anomalous Monism', McDowell censured the doctrine of Anomalous Monism for its misplaced commitment to 'the Prejudice of the Nomological Character of Causality', which he dubbed the 'fourth dogma of empiricism',[20] and his hostility to the doctrine is apparently maintained in *Mind and World*, where at one point he notes that 'it can seem incoherent' to suppose that the operations of sensibility 'are what they are by virtue of their positions in the realm of law' and in addition are 'what

[18] The same goes, of course, for the relata of the simple model, and the difficulties I shall adumbrate below apply just as much to it—and so to McDowell's desired target position—as to the complex model (what I am representing as his starting position). But I shall stick to the complex model in my exposition of these difficulties.

[19] For Davidson's adherence to Anomalous Monism, see his 'Mental Events' (1982, pp. 207–25); McDowell's rejection of the doctrine comes in his essay 'Functionalism and Anomalous Monism' (1998*b*, pp. 325–40). Cf. Putnam's report at 1994, p. 116.

[20] 1998*b*, pp. 339–40. Cf. 2002*b*, p. 178 (quoted below in n. 22).

they are . . . [as] a matter of positions in the contrasting logical space [i.e., the space of reasons]'.[21] But what are we then to say of *the experience that p*? Is it not the fate of this experience, on McDowell's approach, to occupy both logical spaces? And then, since occupancy of a logical space is at least partly constitutive of a thing, will we not have the untoward upshot that the experience that *p* is constituted *both* by its occupancy of the logical space of reasons *and* by its occupancy of the opposing logical space, the realm of law?

This question is rendered the more pressing by the observation that, though McDowell appears to be still officially hostile to Anomalous Monism in *Mind and World*, there is a significant passage in that work where he seems to commit himself to just that doctrine. This is the concluding paragraph of his Afterword polemic against Davidson and Sellars. Here we have a restatement of what I have been calling the complex model:

In the picture I recommend, although the world is not external to the space of concepts, it is external to exercises of spontaneity [i.e., judgement]. Although we are to erase the boundary that symbolized a gulf between thought and the world, the picture still has an in-out dimension. Linkages between what is further in and what is further out stand for the availability of rational groundings, and the world—which is as far out as possible—is ultimate in the order of justification. What I have been urging, against Davidson and Sellars, is that we must find a place for impressions, the deliverances of receptivity, along this in-out dimension. They must figure in the order of justification. Of course there are other dimensions along which we can trace connections between mental items and the world, and we can interpret phrases such as 'the impact of the world on the senses' so as to apply to items [i.e., relations] that stand between minds and the world only along one of these other dimensions. But we must not suppose, with Sellars and Davidson, that that is the only sort of sense we can give to the idea of deliverances of receptivity. (1994, p. 146)

---

[21] 1994, p. 72. I take it that the diffidence of the expression ('it can seem incoherent') masks confidence in the conclusion. Cf. 1994, pp. 74–6, 154 n. 29; Thornton 2004, pp. 226–7.

What this passage seems to say is that a given impression and a given worldly event or state of affairs are linked by two quite different kinds of relation: space-of-reasons relations of rational grounding, and realm-of-law causal relations. The reference to Sellars and Davidson (as well as the insertion of the word 'only' in the penultimate sentence) secures that these realm-of-law causal relations are relations which are *exclusively* located in the realm of law. But it is hard to see how two items could be linked by a space-of-reasons relation without themselves being items in the space of reasons; and similarly it is hard to see how two items could be linked by a realm-of-law relation without themselves being items in the realm of law. And that lands us in the monistic position which McDowell officially rejects, namely one which posits a single item (an impression) residing simultaneously in both logical spaces.[22]

Furthermore, the position falls foul of a criticism of Anomalous Monism which McDowell has just made in the passage immediately before the one quoted. If a single item straddles the two logical spaces in the way outlined, its empirical content (and so its availability rationally to ground judgements) on the one hand, and its capacity to provide an exogenous constraint on mind so as to obviate the threat of Davidsonian coherentism or (in general) an unacceptable idealism on the other, are derived from two different sources: the item's empirical content is derived from its location in the space of reasons, but its ability to provide an exogenous constraint on mind comes from its location in the realm of law. As far as the latter ability is concerned, one might find here an illuminating pun on the two senses of 'external' which I have already mentioned (§1): for the Anomalous Monist, an experiential item (an impression) can provide

---

[22] There is perhaps also a hint of Anomalous Monism at 1998*b*, p. 289, in the concession that a shift to a neurophysiological language for talking about pains 'might succeed in explaining what were in some sense the same explananda'. At 2000*a*, pp. 101–2, McDowell seems to toy with Anomalous Monism without clearly rejecting it: he mentions a rather weak objection to it, and the passage ends inconclusively. But a remark at 2002*b*, p. 178 (evincing an evident lack of sympathy for 'the thought that causal relations between mental activity and the extra-mental world require an ultimate anchorage in physical nature') implies the rejection of Anomalous Monism.

external constraint on judgement, in the non-technical sense of 'external' (that is, an exogenous constraint), only because it is externally related, in the technical sense, to relevant worldly items. But its being identical with a space-of-reasons entity—an appearing—is supposed to ensure that this impression also enjoys an internal relation to the world: the incoherence of this combination is one obvious basis on which one might—and, as we have seen, McDowell does[23]—criticize Anomalous Monism. But his criticism of that doctrine which I am concerned with here is subtler. As McDowell puts it: 'if an item that is an impression [i.e., a realm-of-law entity][24] is credited with empirical content, because it is said to be also an appearing [i.e., a space-of-reasons entity], it is not supposed to be by virtue of being the impression it is that it possesses that content'.[25] So the monistic component of Anomalous Monism is not only objectionable on general grounds of coherence; it also fails to deliver what McDowell finds missing in Davidson's and Sellars's accounts of experience, namely that one and the same experiential item should be endowed with the empirical content it has, and so be something to which judgement can be answerable, *by virtue of its being the impression it is*, that is, by virtue of its having the causal aetiology it has.[26]

We can cast the difference between Davidson and McDowell on this point in terms of the formal distinction popularized in medieval times by Duns Scotus, and the ancestor of 'that distinction of reason' concerning which Hume complained that it was 'so much talk'd of, and . . . so little understood, in the schools':[27] for the doctrine of Anomalous Monism—this fact seems to have escaped its modern exponents—is in fact an application of that notorious distinction.[28]

---

[23] 1994, p. 72, quoted above.

[24] In the context of this quotation McDowell is criticizing Davidson's position, and for Davidson impressions are exclusively realm-of-law entities.

[25] 1994, p. 145; cf. pp. 75–6.

[26] Cf. 1994, p. 141: '. . . the impressions of the world on our senses, the deliverances of our receptivity, are—as such—the appearings [i.e., the space-of-reasons items to which our judgements are answerable]'.

[27] *Treatise*, I.1.7 (1978, p. 24).

[28] For discussion and elucidation of the Scotist background, with reference to further relevant literature, see Bäck 2000 and my 2004.

On Davidson's approach, an appearing (or belief)[29] can be really identical with an impression, but since they will belong to different logical spaces they must be formally distinct: in general, for Davidson, mental events are really identical with, but formally distinct from, appropriate physical events. For McDowell, by contrast, the impression with which we identify a space-of-reasons, tribunal-serving appearing cannot be so much as formally, let alone really, distinct from that appearing, on pain of forfeiting the appearing's empirical content. Now if this formulation is not to send us back into the incoherences we have just rehearsed—that is, of searching for an item which is what it is *both* by virtue of its location in the space of reasons *and* by virtue of its location in the realm of law—one of these affiliations must be jettisoned. It is obvious which one we must relinquish on McDowell's behalf: the latter. For while the project of externalizing the space of reasons offers little hope of success—and is in any case repudiated by McDowell[30]—the suggestion that some causal relations might be internal relations is not, just as it stands, absurd, and is indeed one that he expressly endorses.[31] Hence we should say that, for McDowell, the impression which is endowed with empirical content—which is a space-of-reasons entity fit to serve on the tribunal of experience—by virtue of its being the impression it is (by virtue of having the causal aetiology it has) belongs exclusively to the space of reasons. Hence also the causal relation which makes it the impression it is must be a space-of-reasons causal relation, not a realm-of-law one.

II.3. CAUSATION IN THE SPACE OF REASONS

If this is right, I think we can say that, discounting the passage I quoted in the preceding section as an aberration, McDowell's 'best'

---

[29] Cf. McDowell 1994, p. 140, with n. 15 above.

[30] It is the position which he calls 'bald naturalism': I return to it in n. 65 below.

[31] See e.g. 1994, p. 71 n. 2; 2000*a*, p. 92; 2002*b*, p. 178. So it is wrong to identify McDowell's realm of law with the 'space of causes', as Blackburn appears to do in his 2001.

position is indeed that impressions in the relevant sense—the things by virtue of their identity with which experiences have empirical content—are space-of-reasons phenomena. And it is surely precisely to make this point that he introduces the notion of second nature. One of McDowell's leading ideas is that if we conceive the receiving of an impression as what he calls 'a transaction in nature', we can easily seem to be confined to one of two unappealing options, either a substantial empiricism in which judgements are implausibly grounded in impressions taken as entities or occurrences located exterior to the space of reasons, in the realm of law, or a Davidsonian coherentism in which judgements are cut off from impressions, so conceived, and are accordingly ungrounded in experience. But once we see that a transaction in nature can be a transaction in *second* nature—a transaction within the space of reasons—we can avoid having to make that unpleasant choice:

Once we remember second nature, we see that operations of nature can include circumstances whose descriptions place them in the logical space of reasons, *sui generis* though that logical space is. This makes it possible to accommodate impressions in nature without posing a threat to [minimal] empiricism. From the thesis that receiving an impression is a transaction in nature, there is now no good inference to the conclusion drawn by Sellars and Davidson, that the idea of receiving an impression must be foreign to the logical space in which concepts such as that of answerability function. (1996*a*, p. xx)[32]

In other words, receiving an impression is a transaction in second nature. It seems to me that so long as McDowell insists that the causal relation in virtue of which impressions have the empirical content they have, and so are able to take their place in the 'order of justification', is exclusively a space-of-reasons phenomenon, he can avoid a charge of succumbing to a substantial empiricism when that is motivated by considerations having to do with his treatment of the role of causation in experience. But it is worth noting that, in avoiding that charge in the way I am assuming he must and does

---

[32] Cf. 1995*a*, pp. 236–7.

avoid it, McDowell encounters other difficulties and incurs other criticisms which are just as damaging, in their way, as the charge of succumbing to a substantial empiricism. In the remainder of this chapter I examine these consequential issues.

An immediate and obvious objection to McDowell's account is this. The price of avoiding Anomalous Monism is, I have suggested, that the causal relations between world and experience (and between experience and judgement) in the complex model, and between world and judgement in the simple model, must be conceived as space-of-reasons phenomena; but McDowell tells us next to nothing about how we are to conceive these causal relations, and how they relate to realm-of-law causality. We are told that it is 'scarcely questionable' that impressions are 'occurrences in nature', and that 'it is common ground that impressions of sense are manifestations of sentient life and hence natural phenomena',[33] but we are not told what the thesis that we are not supposed to question and which is common ground actually means. One might have thought that if it is scarcely questionable that impressions are occurrences in nature, that could only be because we are assuming that they are occurrences in *first* nature (the realm of law). If, as it apparently turns out, the impressions we are interested in—the ones we can identify with experiences in order to provide those experiences with the necessary exogenous constraint—are in fact occurrences in *second* nature, we are surely owed not merely an explanation for the surprising turn of events but more fundamentally an account of what it is supposed to mean: what *is* space-of-reasons causation? On this important point McDowell is silent.[34]

---

[33] 1996*a*, p. xxii and 1994, p. 76. Cf. 1994, pp. 87, 89; 1998*a*, pp. 366–7, 407.

[34] Larmore too lodges a complaint on this score, at 2002, p. 205. McDowell responds: '[O]f course, "Reasons can be causes" is only a slogan. The thought it sloganizes would be more accurately expressed by saying that *someone's having a reason* can be causally relevant, for instance to their acting or to their forming a belief' (2002*a*, p. 296). But the formulation which McDowell here substitutes for the slogan, more accurate or not, can hardly be said to be elucidatory. (Similar criticisms attach to B. Williams's expression of this point at 1973, pp. 141–4, and to Brandom's appeal to the slogan in 1994, ch. 4.)

The omission is not one which he would regard as a culpable oversight on his part: on the contrary, when challenged to say more about the nature of space-of-reasons causation,[35] McDowell informs us that, concerning the causal relation between world and experience, 'I see no need to embrace any particular theory of causality', adding that 'the concept of something's being caused to happen is perfectly intuitive'.[36] Elsewhere he objects to

a scientistic hijacking of the concept of causality, according to which the concept is taken to have its primary role in articulating the partial world-view that is characteristic of the physical sciences, so that all other causal thinking needs to be based on causal relations characterizable in physical terms. (2002*b*, p. 178)[37]

But this merely negative elucidation of the notion of space-of-reasons causation cannot be regarded as satisfactory. There are two species of causation in play—realm-of-law causation and space-of-reasons causation—and we have seen that, if McDowell is to avoid an unattractive Anomalous Monism which threatens his position (and to which indeed, in at least one unguarded moment, he appears to succumb), he must insist that the causal relation between world and experience, in virtue of which experience enjoys an exogenous constraint on its content, is a space-of-reasons phenomenon *and not* a realm-of-law one. That claim cries out for elucidation, and the demand for such elucidation cannot simply be rebuffed on the supposed basis that the concept of causation in play 'is perfectly intuitive'. Still, although McDowell himself does not meet the demand for an elucidation of the notion of space-of-reasons causation, there are several things we can say on his behalf, by way of reconstructing what his position must be. On the basis of scattered remarks of his I can think of three ways in which we might at least make a start on filling out McDowell's position in this regard.

In the first place it is presumably a feature of space-of-reasons causation, and something which distinguishes it from realm-of-law

[35] Heßbrüggen-Walter 2000, p. 25.   [36] 2000*a*, p. 92.
[37] Cf. 1998*c*, p. 290.

causation, that it is not nomological: that seems to be an implication of McDowell's rejection of what he calls 'the Prejudice of the Nomological Character of Causality', combined with the fact that realm-of-law causation is by definition nomological. Still less is space-of-reasons causation mechanical.[38]

A second feature, less obvious than the first but one which it seems appropriate to build in to the distinction between the two sorts of causation, is the following. Realm-of-law causation is Humean in the sense that cause and effect are 'logically distinct existences'—that is, a statement of the existence of the cause does not entail a statement of the existence of the effect, or *vice versa*;[39] but this is not so of space-of-reasons causation.[40] Experience is a good case in point. My perception of a ginger cat sitting on a black and white mat, say, has its space-of-reasons cause in that particular cat's sitting on that particular mat (the very fact that, when observed by me, ultimately justifies my judgement that that cat is sitting on that mat), but that cause is not 'logically distinct' from the effect, in the relevant sense, since a statement of the existence of the effect (my perceiving that cat sitting on that mat) entails a statement of the existence of the cause (that cat's sitting on that mat). In other words, as we have already intimated, while realm-of-law causation is an external relation, space-of-reasons causation is an internal relation.[41] There is a standing temptation to resist this consequence by specifying the content of

[38] Cf. 1998*b*, pp. 20–2 with n. 32, 108, 213.

[39] 'All those objects, of which we call the one *cause* and the other *effect*, consider'd in themselves, are as distinct and separate from each other, as any two things in nature, nor can we ever, by the most accurate survey of them, infer the existence of the one from the other': *Treatise*, II.3.1 (1978, p. 405). Cf. 1978, pp. 78–82, 86–7, 161–2, 173. Hume's application of this principle to perception comes in the following passage, for example: 'the relation of cause and effect can never afford us any just conclusion from the existence or qualities of our perceptions to the existence of external continu'd objects': *Treatise*, I.4.2 (1978, p. 216). That is, for Hume perception is exclusively a realm-of-law phenomenon.

[40] On this point cf. Strawson 1966, p. 52; 1979, pp. 51–2.

[41] Cf. McDowell 1998*b*, p. 302, where 'mere causation', which is (unhappily, as I explain below) one of McDowell's ways of talking about realm-of-law causation, is said to be an external relation. For the internal relation between experience and its objects, see e.g. 1998*c*, pp. 388–9, where experiences are held to have the facts of which they are the

the perception in purely general terms, so that having the relevant perception no longer entails the existence of the state of affairs which gives rise to it. But that is not a temptation to which McDowell succumbs: on the contrary, he has been in the vanguard of insisting that the content of perceptual experience cannot be captured in such terms; that is, he insists that in perceptual experience one is cognitively related to one's environment in such a way as constitutively to make the content of one's experience (and of relevant singular thoughts essayed on the basis of one's experience) depend on the existence or otherwise of relevant objects in one's perceptual environment, so that if no appropriate object exists, no experiences with the relevant singular content (and no corresponding singular thoughts) are available.[42]

Thirdly, in the context of a discussion of Gareth Evans's theory of perception, McDowell alludes to Evans's claim that the idea of an object of experience 'cannot stand on its own, stand without any surrounding theory',[43] and he notes that 'the required theory is a theory of the conditions under which something perceptible is actually perceived'.[44] Such a theory is needed to support counterfactuals like 'If the cat had not been sitting on the mat when I turned to look at it, I would not have seen it'.[45] It seems appropriate to incorporate the idea of such a theory into the notion of space-of-reasons causation.

These suggestions are by no means either exhaustive or fully worked out, but perhaps they indicate how we might start to elucidate the idea of space-of-reasons causation—causation where

(sc. causal) upshots as their objects. I return to this important passage in Ch. III, §7 below.

[42] See esp. 1998c, pp. 199–213, 218–19, 225–7 (cf. 252–9), 231–2, 260–74 (cf. 275–91). Cf. 1998b, pp. 342–5. This claim—or rather its generalization to all singular thought and reference—is a fundamental thesis of Evans 1982 (see esp. the passages indexed under 'Russellian thoughts'). For a brief survey of the rise to prominence of the *de re* in the way philosophers conceive the relation between mind and world, see Brandom 1994, pp. 547–52. On McDowell, see de Gaynesford 2004, ch. 11.

[43] Evans 1985, p. 261; cf. 1982, pp. 222–3.

[44] 1994, p. 54 n. 9.

[45] Cf. Grice 1967, pp. 103–4; Strawson 1979, p. 51.

the cause not only *brings about* the effect, but also *rationalizes* it, that is, makes it correct or reasonable in the light of the existence of the cause. One point of terminology is worth noting. When McDowell has the external, realm-of-law kind of causation in mind, he sometimes talks of 'mere' or 'brute' causation.[46] The former of these locutions at least is not happy, for after all space-of-reasons causation, considered just as such and in abstraction from the fact that it rationalizes its effect, is 'mere' causation: if I say that the cat's presence on the mat brings it about that I see it there on the mat, I have so far given expression to a 'merely' causal relation; but the 'merely' causal relation in question, being an item which belongs in the space of reasons, is not capable of being reconstructed out of realm-of-law materials. (This is reflected in the fact, noted above, that in this instance the effect logically contains the cause.) In other words, when we distinguish realm-of-law causation from space-of-reasons causation we do not have to do with a common causal core which comes neat in the case of realm-of-law transactions but sports a rationalizing garb in the case of space-of-reasons transactions—as it were, a 'highest common factor' of the two kinds of causation.[47] Rather, what is (or ought to be) in question when we distinguish between realm-of-law causation and space-of-reasons causation is a dichotomy between *two fundamentally different types* of causation. Of course, if they are genuinely to be species of the same genus—if we are not to be guilty of equivocation in labelling both sorts of transaction 'causal'—they must have something non-trivial in common. But what they have in common cannot be a shared core of realm-of-law causation, as though space-of-reasons causation were constructed out of realm-of-law causation plus something extra. (I do not expect McDowell to dispute this: my point is that the dichotomy between the two types of causation is not well captured by referring to one of them as 'mere' causation. Still less, of course, is the dichotomy captured if that qualification is just dropped, and not

---

[46] 1994, pp. 8, 71 n. 2, 133; 1998*a*, p. 366; 1998*b*, pp. 144 (with n. 42), 239, 281, 302 (cf. 276); 2002*b*, p. 178. Cf. 1994, p. 68.

[47] On the 'highest common factor' conception of experience, see Ch. III, §7 below.

replaced by a more appropriate epithet. This remark applies, for example, to a passage in the essay 'Non-Cognitivism and Rule-Following', where it is implied that a causal account of how value-experience relates to the world is not, as the dichotomy would require, to be subdivided into an—acceptable—space-of-reasons account of the relation, appealing to internal relations, and an—unacceptable—realm-of-law account, appealing to external relations, but is simply to be identified with the latter.)[48]

A parallel point applies to nature. Before he hit on the distinction between first and second nature, McDowell was prone to think of the former—the topic of the so-called 'natural' sciences—as 'pure' nature,[49] and even after he had made the distinction he continued to call first nature 'mere' nature.[50] But such terminology suggests a misleading 'highest common factor' conception of the natural, according to which second nature is construed as analysable into a 'pure' core—common to first and second nature—together with a detachable normative surround, the normative component being related merely externally to the core it surrounds. Or, in an alternative locution which McDowell uses in this phase of his thinking, first-natural facts are conceived as a 'substratum' on which second-natural facts are 'constructed':[51] again, this image

---

[48] 1998*b*, pp. 217–18; cf. 1986, p. 380. Note also 1998*b*, pp. 186–7, where realm-of-law causation is simply called 'causation', and the existence of a space-of-reasons species of causation is not recognized: see here Larmore's apposite criticism at 2002, p. 208 n. 22. By contrast, McDowell's remark that 'there is nothing normative about the causal nexus as such' (1998*b*, p. 335) can perhaps be allowed to stand, taken as a remark about the genus of causation, which subdivides into space-of-reasons and realm-of-law species. (Perhaps some of McDowell's references to 'mere' or 'brute' causation, or equivalent, can be subjected to a similar interpretation, and so saved from the criticism I deploy in the text, but I do not think this will work in all cases, e.g. in the case of the passage from 1998*b*, p. 302 referred to in n. 41 above.)

[49] So in his essay 'Are Moral Requirements Hypothetical Imperatives?', at 1998*b*, p. 84.

[50] See e.g. 1994, pp. 72, 183 n. 2.

[51] 1998*b*, p. 283: the context involves a claim to the effect that pre-linguistic awareness can, without persisting into the 'life of concept-involving awareness', nevertheless serve as a 'substratum on which the capacity for concept-carried awareness is

suggests a merely external relation between substrate and superstructure. But that is not McDowell's mature conception of second nature: on this conception, the ascent to second nature involves not the mere imposition of a second-natural superstructure on an essentially unaltered first-natural base, but rather a 'transformation' of, or 'evolution' out of, first nature.[52] The idea behind the terminology of transformation and evolution must indeed be that, wherever the transformation or evolution has been successfully effected, the unity of the product will be such that it will be impossible to factorize it into distinct and merely externally related components, into a neutral core of first nature on the one hand and a normative appendage on the other. It follows that McDowell should not call first nature 'pure' nature, any more than he should call realm-of-law causation 'mere' causation.[53] I said that this was a point of terminology: but it opens out into two much more substantial problems affecting the way McDowell wishes to deploy both the notion of space-of-reasons causation in contrast with realm-of-law causation, and the corresponding distinction between second and first nature. I examine these problems in §§4–5 and §6 respectively.

constructed'. But if the claim succeeded in this limited context, it would presumably be legitimate to apply its moral to the relation between first nature and second nature quite generally.

[52] 1994, pp. 125, 183 n. 2; 1998*a*, p. 412. Cf. 1996*b*, p. 106.

[53] Still less, of course, should he call first nature simply 'nature', as he perhaps does in his essay 'The Role of *Eudaimonia* in Aristotle's Ethics', where he speaks (at 1998*b*, p. 19) of the 'causal and enabling role' which 'human nature' (clearly meaning our first nature) can play in the context of ethical reflection (cf. 1998*b*, pp. 35, 190; 1994, pp. 109–10). (But note that in the same place he allows that the expression 'human nature' *can* be given a 'value-loaded' application—and this application is further elaborated in the footnote to this passage at 1998*b*, pp. 19–20 n. 27—so that already in this early essay McDowell is implicitly moving towards recognizing at least human nature as constituting a genus with first-natural and second-natural species.) Again, the claim at 1996*b*, p. 106 that acquired values 'can have a sort of autonomy with respect to what naturally appeals to human beings' needs sympathetic handling: the autonomy in question is achieved with respect to our first nature, not to human nature in general.

II.4. NATURE AND SUPERNATURE

The first of these problems is that, although there may be prospects for making sense of causation in the space of reasons along the lines suggested in the previous section, there remains the question how it fits together with realm-of-law causation. We must ask: what is the non-trivial common genus under which both species of causation are to be found? This is essentially the same problem as the problem how first nature and second nature fit together. In that case too, we are impelled to ask: what is the non-trivial common genus under which both species of nature are to be found? McDowell is keen to 'point to the dualism of nature and reason as the source of the merely apparent difficulties confronted by traditional philosophy',[54] and he is quick to observe that 'it would be a cheat, a merely verbal manoeuvre, to object that naturalism about nature [that is, refusing to recognize a second nature] cannot be open to question';[55] but what evidently escapes him is the futility, for purposes of overcoming philosophy's traditional dualism, of extending the label 'nature' to the materials of (what we are then entitled to call) second nature. Of course McDowell would contest my characterization of what he is doing as 'extending' the label 'nature' to the materials of second nature. He would prefer a characterization along these lines: recognizing (recalling) that the label 'nature' does anyway apply to these materials.[56] But nothing turns here on whether the application of the label 'nature' to second nature is an extension of the term's proper usage or a recognition of that usage, for nothing is gained by insisting that we have to do with the latter rather than the former: if the former, the problem is how to make sense of the extension; but if the latter, the problem is merely transmuted into a requirement to

---

[54] 1994, p. 153. See also, on this theme, his essay 'Two Sorts of Naturalism', 1998*b*, pp. 167–97.

[55] 1994, p. 77.

[56] 1995*a*, p. 291: 'Remember... that second nature, which brings the ideal into our view by opening our eyes to the demands of reason, is nature too'; cf. 1998*e*, pp. 122–3.

explain how the term 'nature' can be applied univocally to both first and second nature. Or is a sense of philosophical puzzlement assuaged by simply adverting to facts of usage? What if that usage embodies an equivocation? If there is anything we need to be reminded of hereabouts it is surely Hume's wise remark that 'nature' is a word 'than which there is none more ambiguous and equivocal'.[57]

In permitting or recognizing the materials of second nature to be 'natural', we 'overcome' the dualism of reason and nature, but the victory is a pyrrhic one, for we are left with a distinction which is the same, in substance, as the one we started with, only now relabelled a distinction between reason and law. And what we are left with is more than a *distinction*: it is a *dualism* in the philosophically loaded sense. As Brandom puts it:

A distinction becomes a dualism when its components are distinguished in terms that make their characteristic relations to one another ultimately unintelligible. (1994, p. 615)

If the original problem was how to fit reason into a world understood *naturalistically* (giving this word its traditional gloss, by adverting to facts of exclusively first nature), the redescribed problem is how to fit reason into a world understood *nomologically*—in Kantian terms, how to fit *Sollen* into a world of *Sein*.[58] Merely assuring us that the rational, as well as the nomological, ought to be regarded as—or is anyway—natural goes no distance at all towards addressing the underlying problem.

We can bring out the essential emptiness of McDowell's manoeuvre by focusing on the residual dualism of law and reason with which he leaves us, and noting that this dualism in fact invites the deployment of a replica of the alleged solution to the original dualism, that of nature and reason. For the concept *law* does not apply to just one side of the residual dualism, understood as

57 *Treatise*, III.1.2 (1978, p. 474).
58 *Kritik der reinen Vernunft* (*KrV*), A547/B575.

McDowell intends us to understand it:[59] as well as the descriptive laws of nature (as we call them), such as the laws of physics, there are also such normative or prescriptive laws as the laws of Scotland or the laws of Rugby Union.[60] Descriptive laws tell us how things do behave, not how they ought to behave; prescriptive laws, on the other hand, tell us (by laying down guidelines for behaviour) how things (people) ought to behave, not how they do in fact behave.[61] We might call descriptive laws 'first laws' and prescriptive laws 'second laws', in recognition of the fact that the so-called first laws are temporally and counterfactually prior to the so-called second laws: that is, first laws preceded second laws in time, and could exist in the absence of second laws (but not *vice versa*). But is anything explained by these moves? Not if what we started with was the problem how, in a world governed in the first instance by first laws, there can be such things as second laws. To explain *that* we need an account of how second laws *emerge* from first laws: we need a *genealogy* of the normative. The genealogy need not, like Nietzsche's genealogy of Christian morality, be a debunking one.[62] In fact, unless the position which McDowell calls 'bald naturalism'— the view that the space of reasons is not *sui generis* but can captured in first-natural terms—is true, it had better not be debunking: rather, it should be what Bernard Williams has called a 'vindicatory

---

[59] Cf. de Gaynesford 2004, p. 76.

[60] Kant offers us an assimilation in the opposite direction, when he styles as 'rules' not only normative principles, but also laws of nature: see e.g. *KrV*, A52/B76, A112–14, A549/B577. But this is a misapplication of the notion of a rule.

[61] Cf. Frege 1983, p. 157 (cited by Brandom 1994, p. 12). We must be careful in our handling of the descriptive/prescriptive dichotomy. I have no wish to deny the general principle that, as McDowell puts it, 'that some vocabulary belongs in the logical space of reasons—that our employments of it are constitutively governed by the ideal or norm of rationality—does not . . . warrant saying that statements employing that vocabulary are not descriptive' (1998a, p. 424). McDowell perhaps has in mind the point that, for example, a morally charged characterization of a situation is not shown to be non-descriptive merely by virtue of the fact that it is motivationally normative. That point is correct. But as far as the present issue is concerned, I think it is reasonable to say that prescriptive *laws* are not, as such, descriptive.

[62] See here Geuss 1999, ch. 1.

genealogy',[63] such as Hume's celebrated genealogy of justice or Sellars's 'myth of Jones'.[64] But McDowell not only does not begin to show us how to construct such a genealogy; he even rejects the need for any such thing.[65]

---

[63] 2002, ch. 2. Such a genealogy would presumably make use of materials drawn not (or not exclusively) from the 'hard' sciences, but from the 'softer' natural and social sciences. (Cf. Putnam's criticism that McDowell is wrong to ignore these distinctions: 2002, pp. 186–7.)

[64] Hume *Treatise*, III.2 (1978, pp. 477–573); *Enquiry concerning the Principles of Morals*, III and app. III (1975, pp. 183–204, 303–11); Sellars 1956, §§48–63 (1997, pp. 90–117).

[65] 1994, pp. 123–4; 2000*a*, p. 99. McDowell is also dismissive of the need to refute bald naturalism, the view that the space of reasons can be constructed out of realm-of-law materials: 1996*a*, p. xxiii (cf. 1998*a*, p. 428 n. 13). Actually, this dismissal (in the introduction to the paperback edition of *Mind and World*) does not (*pace* 1995*a*, p. 238) square with the 1994 text of the lectures, where McDowell states or clearly implies, in a number of passages, that he thinks that bald naturalism is *false*: 1994, pp. 75, 77–8, 81, 84, 87–8 (so too at 2000*a*, pp. 6–7). But to stigmatize a position which is in addition conceded to have a certain philosophical sophistication (1996*a*, p. xxi; 1994, pp. 88–9 n. 1) as false is surely to incur the obligation to argue against it, something that McDowell refuses to do (cf. Quante 2000, p. 959). In fact it is not very difficult to offer at least a *prima facie* refutation of bald naturalism, on the basis of an argument to the special and irreducible nature of the intentional: Wright draws attention to some germane considerations at 2002*a*, pp. 143–4, as indeed did McDowell himself in his early essay 'Physicalism and Primitive Denotation: Field on Tarski', §7 (1998*c*, pp. 149–54; cf. 1998*b*, pp. 83, 288–9; 1998*b*, p. 29; Pettit and McDowell 1986, pp. 12–13). But whether these considerations are decisive or not, the main point is that it matters a great deal to the project of understanding the place of the normative in the world whether bald naturalism is true or false (so, rightly, Putnam 2002, p. 190 n. 36). Interestingly, the clash between McDowell's 1994 attitude to bald naturalism and his later, more insouciant approach is paralleled by a tension in his essay 'Some Issues in Aristotle's Moral Psychology', concerning the relation between an ethical outlook and a purported external validation of it. Having first assured us that 'an external validation of the correctness of a specific ethic would be enormously significant' (1998*b*, p. 35), McDowell goes on to remark that 'we ought to be suspicious of our tendency to suppose genuine objectivity would require something more than Neurathian [=internal] reflection' (1998*b*, p. 37; cf. p. 40). The latter remark seems to point to McDowell's preferred position in this essay (and elsewhere: cf. 1994, pp. 81–3; 1995*b*; 1998*b*, p. 189), and harmonizes with his post-1994 nonchalance about the status of bald naturalism: for why, one might ask in the spirit of that nonchalance, should it matter to the internal point of view from which a moral stance is properly and relevantly validated if, independently of any such internal endorsement, that stance can *also* be validated from an external point of view? But I think his first intuition was correct: the availability of any such external validation would indeed be of great significance—perhaps not for ethical practice, but certainly for philosophical reflection on that practice.

It is true, as McDowell observes,[66] that second nature is something we can be educated into possessing, by undergoing a process of initiation into the space of reasons (*Bildung*, enculturation).[67] But the observation that we are so educable does not, in itself, help: for the fact that we can be educated into possessing a second nature, and into recognizing facts of second nature, is the explanandum, not the explanans. Just so far, nothing has been said to undermine the possibility that what we are educated into possessing is a realm not of *second* nature but of *super*nature (that is, of something which is *not* natural).[68] Perhaps that is a potential which human beings simply have (or have as a divine dispensation): such an idea may strike many of us now as absurd (McDowell describes it as 'hard to take seriously'),[69] but it has by no means always struck all people as absurd. In any case, McDowell provides us with nothing to support our intuition of absurdity, assuming we have it—nothing to reassure us that we are not simply equivocating when we call both the realm of (first) law and the space of reasons 'natural'. In effect, for McDowell it is just *definitional* that the fact that we can be educated into inhabiting the space of reasons shows that we are not peculiarly bifurcated beings, with one foot in a supernatural camp.[70] But this terminological policy—though in itself unobjectionable: the natural construed as simply what happens—does nothing to diminish our sense of puzzlement over the fact that the world apparently contains

---

[66] 1994, p. 92: I discuss this passage below. Cf. Larmore 2002, pp. 195–6.

[67] McDowell despairs of finding a short English equivalent for *Bildung* (1994, p. 84): I offer him 'enculturation'. Some writers use 'acculturation' in the relevant sense, but the *OED* makes a distinction (corresponding to the different prefixes) between initiation into one's first culture (enculturation), and initiation into a second or subsequent culture (acculturation), and it seems to me that this distinction is worth preserving. Actually, in view of the individualistic connotations of *Bildung* (cf. Geuss 1999, ch. 2), I wonder whether 'enculturation' does not *better* capture the notion McDowell intends to introduce than *Bildung*, although, ironically enough, I shall in due course (Ch. III, §§6–9) be directing a charge of individualism against McDowell's treatment of the relation between experience and judgement, so that it may be that his choice of the German word turns out to be apt after all, for a reason that he did not anticipate.

[68] Cf. Wright 2002a, pp. 150–6.

[69] 1998b, p. 177.

[70] Cf. 1994, pp. 78, 88.

two natures, first nature and second nature, and correspondingly *two* kinds of causation, realm-of-law causation and space-of-reasons causation. Overcoming a dualism of nature and supernature represents no intellectual advance, if what we are left with is a notion of nature which is itself dualistic in just the way that made the dualism we have supposedly overcome mysterious.[71]

In fact the position is even more serious than this objection suggests. The problem is not just that we seem merely to have replaced one dualism with another, equally mysterious dualism, but more fundamentally that we have no guarantee that we have even achieved so much as that—no guarantee, that is, that the dualism we have substituted *is* genuinely distinct from the one we have supposedly overcome and discarded. Of course the terminological policy I have mentioned gives us a superficial guarantee that the dualisms in play are distinct: but that merely definitional assurance can do little to assuage our sense of unease here. For, aside from that definitional stratagem, what ensures that the dualism of first and second nature we are left with is not, *au fond*, a dualism of nature and supernature? It is hardly sufficient to be told that

the only unity there needs to be in the idea of the natural, as it applies, on the one hand, to the intelligibility of physical and merely biological phenomena . . . and, on the other, to the intelligibility of rational activity, is captured by a contrast with the idea of the supernatural—the spooky or the occult. (2000*a*, p. 99)[72]

For McDowell nowhere elucidates the notion of the occult.[73] Presumably it, and the idea of the supernatural in general, is to be

---

[71] See on this point Gubeljic, Link, Müller, and Osburg 2000, pp. 44–9; Greenberg and Willaschek 2000. The passage I quote in the next paragraph is taken from McDowell's reply to the former of these essays. In his response to the latter, McDowell in effect concedes that he owes us an account of 'how the law-governed and the free [in McDowell's rationalist sense, i.e., the rational: on this see Ch. III, §2 below] are related, especially given how plausible it is that natural law holds sway at least over the subpersonal machinery that underlies our ability to act and think' (2000*a*, p. 102). At least, he concedes that anyone who rejects Anomalous Monism owes us such an account: and, as I have suggested (§2 of this chapter), his own 'best' position, in spite of a certain wavering on the question, involves a rejection of that doctrine.

[72] Cf. 1994, p. 83.   [73] Cf. Strobach 2000, p. 57.

understood negatively, as what *is not* (in any sense) natural. But for that construal to work, we need to have a clear grasp of the positive idea of the natural—of what *is* (in some sense) natural. And now the crucial point is this: unless something is said to elucidate the dualism of first and second nature, as a necessary preliminary to overcoming that dualism—unless, that is, we are told what exactly distinguishes first and second nature, and what despite their differences warrants applying the label 'nature' unequivocally to both—it will follow that the envisaged contrast of both natures with the supernatural lacks sufficient determinacy of content to give us the confidence that, in being presented with a distinction purportedly between first and second nature, we are really being offered a distinction which falls *under* the overall rubric of the natural, as opposed to a distinction *between* nature and something *other* than nature.

It has been suggested by Axel Honneth and Martin Seel that McDowell's invocation of the notion of *Bildung* in connection with the idea of second nature must be intended to do more than merely rehearse the fact that we can be subjected to a process of enculturation:[74] rather, the idea must be, they conjecture, that there is a *continuity* between human first nature and the second nature which that process forms in us. That is certainly the position implied in *Mind and World*,[75] but the sequel to the passage I quoted in the previous paragraph, from a later publication, shows McDowell resisting any such commitment to a doctrine of continuity, with its concomitant suggestion of an unavoidable explanatory task: 'I need only the bare invocation of *Bildung*—not . . . a detailed story about how what happens in *Bildung* connects with phenomena characterizable in terms of conformity to natural law'. Once again McDowell fails to register that, in the absence of the detailed story he so resolutely refuses to give, the 'bare invocation' of a notion such as *Bildung* (or of the notion of space-of-reasons causation, or of a purported contrast between nature and supernature) not merely

---

[74] 1998, p. 14.   [75] See e.g. 1994, p. 84.

lacks adequate warrant, but more seriously lacks sufficient determinacy of content to do philosophical work for him.

II.5. RAMPANT AND NATURALIZED PLATONISMS

This point connects with McDowell's polemic in *Mind and World* against what he calls 'rampant platonism', a position which seems to have much in common with what McDowell elsewhere simply calls 'platonism'; but in *Mind and World* he wishes to distinguish an acceptable version of platonism, which he calls 'naturalized platonism', from an unacceptable version, which attracts the pejorative soubriquet 'rampant'.[76] It is not an entirely straightforward operation to extract from *Mind and World* a precise definition of either rampant or naturalized platonism. Similar difficulty attaches to formulations of platonistic positions which McDowell gives us elsewhere in his writings. For example, in his essay 'Wittgenstein on Following a Rule' McDowell characterizes a (rampantly) platonistic position as follows:

A genuine fact must be a matter of the way things are in themselves, utterly independently of us. So a genuinely true judgement must be, at least potentially, an exercise of pure thought; if human nature is necessarily implicated in the very formation of the judgement, that precludes our thinking of the corresponding fact as properly independent of us, and hence as a proper fact at all. (1998*b*, p. 254)[77]

But it is not obvious what exactly is being said here. What is it, on the view which McDowell wishes to attack, for a fact to be constituted

---

[76] This distinction was anticipated in 'Non-Cognitivism and Rule-Following' (at 1998*b*, pp. 215–16).

[77] Cf. 1998*b*, p. 63: 'The [rampant platonist's] illusion is the misconception of the deductive paradigm: the idea that deductive explicability characterizes an exercise of reason in which it is, as it were, automatically compelling, without dependence on our partially shared "whirl of organism" '. See also 1998*b*, p. 210.

'independently of us'? What is an 'exercise of pure thought'? What is it for human nature to be 'implicated' in the formation of judgement?[78]

In his response to the charge, levelled by Crispin Wright, that he has abandoned the paths of analytic philosophy, McDowell repudiates the suggestion that 'analytic philosophy prohibits imagery except for rare special effect, and precludes letting the full import of a term...emerge gradually in the course of using it, as opposed to setting down a definition at the start'.[79] I do not find Wright's accusation compelling; but the moves which McDowell makes in response to it can hardly be regarded as satisfactory, and this is a convenient place to say why. The objection to the use of imagery is not to its use as such, but rather to the use of unexplained imagery which is nevertheless clearly intended to be load-bearing: that objection nets the use, in the passage I quoted in the last paragraph, of the metaphor of implication (as well, as we have seen in §1 of this chapter, as the metaphorical use of the word 'impression'). The policy of allowing the full import of a term to emerge gradually is not in itself objectionable, but it is a highly risky one, the risk being that the author will not command a clear sense of how he or she is using the term, which may in consequence be crucially ambiguous: in fact I believe that this lack of clarity significantly—and damagingly—attaches to McDowell's own use of the term 'non-conceptual content', as I explain in the final section of this chapter.

To return to the polemic against rampant platonism in *Mind and World*, we are told that, according to that position, the space of reasons is pictured 'as an autonomous structure—autonomous in that it is constituted independently of anything specifically

---

[78] Some of Putnam's characterizations of the opposition between the doctrines he calls internal realism and metaphysical realism—a distinction which corresponds closely to that between naturalized and rampant platonisms—prompt similar questions: see e.g. 1981, pp. 49–50, 54, 128; 1992, pp. 57–9; 1994, p. 352; 1999, p. 63. For some apposite criticism of Putnam on this score, see Schantz 1996, pp. 331–40.

[79] 2002*a*, p. 291. For the charge, see Wright 2002*a*, pp. 157–8.

human',[80] whereas for its naturalized congener 'the structure of the space of reasons is not constituted in splendid isolation from anything merely human';[81] in the particular case of the space of moral reasons, 'the rational demands of ethics are not alien to the contingencies of our life as human beings'.[82] But, again, what do these characterizations mean? The remark in *Mind and World* which comes closest to giving us a usable definition of either rampant or naturalized platonism is the comment that, for naturalized platonism, 'the demands of reason are *essentially* such that a human upbringing can open a human being's eyes to them';[83] in the particular case of the rational demands of ethics, we are told that 'they are *essentially* within reach of human beings'.[84] What these characterizations suggest is that the rampant platonist claims that it is, in general, *not essential* to the demands of reason that our upbringing can open our eyes to them.[85]

This interpretation of what McDowell means by 'rampant platonism' is supported by a passage in his essay 'Values and Secondary Qualities', where he remarks that a (sc. rampantly) platonistic conception of values makes the mistake of assimilating them to primary qualities,[86] which are (unlike secondary qualities) not *constitutively* connected to the responses of our human sensibility. Again, he implies in his essay 'Projection and Truth in Ethics' that to construe a property suitable for projectivist treatment as 'a property some things have intrinsically or absolutely, independently of their relations to us' is to treat it as a primary quality. For the idea of 'a reality that is wholly independent of our subjectivity and set over against it'

---

[80] 1994, p. 77. Cf. p. 92: 'In rampant platonism, the rational structure within which meaning comes into view is independent of anything merely human, so that the capacity of our minds to resonate to it looks occult or magical'.

[81] 1994, p. 92; cf. p. 88.

[82] 1994, p. 83.

[83] 1994, p. 92, emphasis added. Cf. p. 28: 'perceptible facts are essentially capable of impressing themselves on perceivers', and 'facts in general are essentially capable of being embraced in thought'.

[84] 1994, p. 84, emphasis added.

[85] See here again Wright 2002*a*, at p. 155.

[86] 1998*b*, p. 147.

is the idea of something that is *definitionally prior* to our subjective responses, in just the way that is characteristic of primary qualities.[87]

But there is a complication. McDowell sometimes writes as though the rampant platonist were asserting not the idea that it is not essential to the *demands of reason* that our upbringing can open our eyes to them, but the converse idea, namely that it is not essential to *us* (as living, biological beings) that our eyes can be opened to those demands of reason:[88] although we can indeed respond to those demands, we do not do so *qua* natural beings but by the grace of a 'gift from outside nature'.[89] That suggests that, if we are to arrive at a consistent interpretation of McDowell's various pronouncements on the matter (and assuming that we can rule out the possibility of a simple confusion between 'It is essential to *A* that it have *B*' and its converse), we should take it that the rampant platonist denies *both* that it is essential to us (living, biological beings) that we can have our eyes opened by our upbringing to the demands of reasons, *and* the converse, that it is essential to the demands of reason that our upbringing can open our eyes to them. The naturalized platonist will then presumably *assert* both these conjuncts (and will accordingly adopt a position which is the contrary, not the contradictory, of rampant platonism).

A more recent characterization of rampant platonism which has been offered by McDowell, according to which 'it just so happens that we can acquire abilities to take in the relevant facts', and our ability to become aware of the relevant stretch of reality 'takes on the look of a fortunate contingency',[90] can perhaps, without undue strain, be interpreted in such a way as to conform to my suggested definition of the rampant platonist's position. In the same place, the contrasting position, that of the naturalized platonist, is held to involve the claim that neither the relevant stretch of reality (the space of reasons) nor our means of access to it is prior to the other, in the sense that 'neither is intelligible independently of

---

[87] 1998*b*, pp. 151, 159.   [88] See e.g. 1994, pp. 115, 123.
[89] 1994, p. 88.   [90] 2000*a*, pp. 103–4.

the other',[91] which fits neatly with my conjunctive reconstruction of that position, according to which it is essential to the space of reasons, and essential to us (living, biological beings), that we can engage with it by being educated into responding to its demands.

I will return to the issue of McDowell's attitude to these platonisms in Chapter V below. The point which is relevant here is the following. While it is no doubt true that a naturalized platonism, defined as I have presumed it must be defined, is incompatible with the thesis that we are, in any interesting sense, partly supernatural beings, by setting out the positions in this way nothing has so far been done to vindicate the naturalized platonist's (and so McDowell's) claim that we engage with reasons *as living beings*—as a matter of our *biological* constitution. What has to be justified is the claim that

the idea of a subjectively continuous series of states or occurrences in which conceptual capacities are implicated in sensibility—or, more generally, the idea of a subjectively continuous series of exercises of conceptual capacities of any kind, that is, the idea of a subjectively continuous series of 'representations', as Kant would say—is just the idea of a singled out tract of a *life*. (1994, p. 103, emphasis added)[92]

And, once again (cf. §4), the problem is really more serious than is implied by this objection, serious though that is. For even more fundamentally, we lack an account of what exactly the naturalized platonist's claim (in particular the part encapsulated in the passage I have just quoted) *means*. But we require both that account and that vindication if naturalized platonism is to be sustained. I do not insist on any priority here—that the explanation of the meaning of the naturalized platonist's thesis be given before, as a precondition of the possibility of giving, its vindication. No indeed: it is quite likely— and we can contemplate this prospect with equanimity—that a narrative which achieves either of these objectives will only be

---

[91] 2000*a*, p. 104.

[92] Cf. 1998*e*, p. 123: 'We are nothing but living beings, not beings whose careers include, over and above manifestations of life, some goings-on that cannot be understood to be part of something as natural as life would have to be.'

able to do so while, and in virtue of, achieving the other. But one way or another the story must actually be told: it cannot simply be taken as read. For the question presses: what does our biology as such—what does life as such—have to do with responsiveness to reasons? In considering this issue it is perhaps fair to grant McDowell a broad construal of what, in this context, constitutes the domain of the living, and of the biological. He himself remarks, in connection with his appeal to these notions ('Of course it had better not be that our being in charge of our lives marks a transcendence of biology'),[93] that it is made 'without prejudice to the possibility of synthesized life'.[94] That suggests, what one anyway suspects, that the claim that (sc. all) demands of reason are essentially within reach of *human* minds (minds belonging to our particular animal species) goes too far: for surely there could be non-human beings endowed with cognitive equipment at least to some extent unlike ours, and so sensitive to at least some demands of reason to which we have no access. And McDowell indeed acknowledges, as we have already noted (Chapter I, §1), that there might be secondary qualities detectable by Martians but not by us.[95] Still, there must be limits—indeterminate ones, no doubt—on the extent to which we can recognize alternative ways of responding to demands of reason to which we are insensitive: candidate alternative responders must be recognizable by us *as* genuine subjects of thought, and of experience, if we are to grant them their alternative ways of responding to demands of reason.[96] Taking these points into account, we might revise our definition of naturalized platonism so that it holds the demands of reason to be essentially accessible not *exclusively* to human beings, but *centrally* to human beings—for in our understanding of what a demand of reason is we naturally start from our own case—and *derivatively* to beings who may be unlike us in a number of respects, but who are at least living, embodied beings, and whose mode of life, and manner of responding to demands of reason

---

[93] 1994, p. 115.   [94] 1998*b*, p. 282.
[95] 1994, p. 123 n. 11; 2000*a*, p. 95.   [96] See my 2001*c*, pp. 208–10.

which are debarred to us, are sufficiently close to our human mode of
life and our human manner of responding to the demands of reason
that we would be right to acknowledge such beings to be rational.[97]
But that of course invites the further question: what counts as being
sufficiently close?

Elsewhere, in a discussion of platonism,[98] McDowell refers with
approval to Wittgenstein's remark that even God can settle a mathematical question only by doing mathematics:[99] but his naturalized
platonism casts doubt on the possibility that God can so much as do
mathematics, given that God is, on most traditional accounts, not a
biological being, not even in an extended sense of that term which
admits non-human ways of living and of being embodied. Again,
McDowell's naturalized platonism about ethics seems to have the
consequence that God could not be sensitive to the demands of
morality. For we are told that ethical second nature 'could not float
free of potentialities that belong to a normal human organism'.[100]
No doubt we must adjust this claim in line with the revision we have
made to naturalized platonism, so as to allow non-human, but
sufficiently similar, beings to participate in ethical reflection and
action: but however the issue raised at the end of the last paragraph
is settled, it is hard to see how a being like God, who is traditionally
conceived not to be (even in an extended sense) an organism,
let alone embodied, could on an approach such as McDowell's
participate in the ethical. Furthermore, it is hard to see how McDowell could allow a being such as God to have perceptual experience.
For, as we are assured in the continuation of the previously quoted
passage:

The idea of a subjectively continuous series of 'representations' could no
more stand alone, independent of the idea of a living thing in whose life

---

[97] See McDowell's remarks at 2000*a*, pp. 96–7, where he appeals to Davidson and
Wittgenstein for support.
[98] 1998*b*, p. 232.
[99] *Remarks on the Foundations of Mathematics* VII, §41 (1978/1989, p. 408).
[100] 1994, p. 84.

these events occur, than could the idea of a series of digestive events with its appropriate kind of continuity. (1994, p. 103)

Finally, we are told that 'a thinking and intending subject is a living animal'.[101] Even given the necessary adjustment to this statement in the light of our revision to the doctrine of naturalized platonism, there seems no escaping the conclusion that, for McDowell, God, as traditionally conceived, is incapable of engaging in mathematical or ethical reflection, of perceiving, and indeed of having any thoughts at all; an upshot which is surely tantamount to a disproof of his existence.[102]

The crux of the disproof would be the claim that to allow that beings such as God (as traditionally conceived) might engage with normativity would undermine our confidence that our engagement with normativity depended in any essential way on our status as living, embodied beings, on 'our way of actualizing ourselves as animals'[103]—ultimately on our biology, broadly construed—as opposed to accruing to us supernaturally. Perhaps a disproof of God's existence can be constructed on the basis of some such piece of reasoning: I certainly do not wish to rule out the possibility. (At least, the reasoning would secure the non-existence of a divine being who inhabited the space of reasons: a more mystical—perhaps a deist—conception of divinity would be less affected by these considerations.) But clearly that would require an elucidation and vindication of (revised) naturalized platonism. So far as I am aware, however, McDowell nowhere offers to make good the promissory note implicitly contained in his assertion of naturalized platonism: the alleged connection between normativity and biology hangs in the air without support, and, still more damagingly,

---

101 1994, p. 104.
102 Cf. too 1994, p. 125: 'It is not even clearly intelligible to suppose that a creature might be born at home in the space of reasons'—and still less intelligible, presumably, to suppose that a being might simply exist in the space of reasons without having come into existence.
103 1994, p. 78.

we lack an account of what life in the relevant sense (that is, broadly construed) is.

Alternatively, I can imagine McDowell seeking to obviate the obligation to undertake a disproof of theism, as traditionally conceived, by making a move which, as we have begun to see in this chapter and will see in more detail in due course, is highly characteristic of his thinking: he might divide normativity, taken as a genus, into biologically-based and non-biologically-based species. I have already pointed to the vacuity of this kind of strategy—at least in the absence of any explanatory underpinning—in the case of parallel taxonomic moves which McDowell makes in respect of the categories of causation (§3) and nature (§4), where as we have seen he recognizes realm-of-law and space-of-reasons species of these categories taken as genera, and I will have more to say by way of censure of the strategy when we come to consider McDowell's treatment of infant and animal 'experience' in Chapter IV below.

Whichever strategy McDowell adopts—whether he takes the tough line which we can sloganize as 'no biology, no normativity', or the tender line which permits non-biological beings to engage with normativity of a different species from the one with which we engage—he is confronted with the problem how to elucidate the claimed connection, whatever its scope, between biology (in the broad sense) and normativity. The worry here is, of course, that in attempting to define biology in the broad sense, we will be forced to appeal to the notion of the space of reasons itself, or in other words that the more liberal conception of biology which McDowell needs for his purposes will not be constitutively independent of normativity. And that will threaten the thesis that we engage with the space of reasons as a matter of our biology, broadly construed, with triviality. In that case, too, our human engagement with the space of reasons will not be guaranteed to be biological in the narrow sense, but will risk transcending our human kind of biology just as the rampant platonist says it does. Moreover it is, for McDowell, a crucial constraint on any elucidation and vindication of the alleged connection between normativity and biology that these tasks be executed without lapsing into bald naturalism. The connection, in other words, is to be constitutive, but not (in either direction) reductive: McDowell's failure to provide an account of how this combination is possible, and of what exactly it means, is a substantial deficit in his philosophy.[104]

II.6. REALM-OF-LAW CAUSATION AND THE MYTH OF THE GIVEN

The second problem affecting the way McDowell wishes to deploy the notion of space-of-reasons causation and the contrast with realm-of-law causation is that there is a serious unclarity attaching to the notion of realm-of-law causation in McDowell's account. Kant's point against Hume, made principally in the Second Analogy,[105] was that, as McDowell puts it, we should 'understand causation as something that operates within the empirical world',[106] and that 'the ordinary empirical world, which includes nature as the realm of law, is not external to the conceptual'.[107] We might approach the point in this way. Things that interact causally are essentially things of certain sorts—things that already fall under defining or sortal concepts—and the sorts under which things fall determine their causal dispositions, so that the causal regularities we observe in the empirical world are not independent of our original conceptions of substances with the relevant dispositions, but are rather the explicable products of things' essential empirical natures. As P. F. Strawson puts it:

It is not that we first acquire the concepts of types of thing and only then, and only by repeated observations of similar conjunctions of events or circumstances, come to form beliefs about what kinds of reaction may be expected of such things in what ranges of antecedent conditions. Rather,

---

[104] I return to this point in Ch. IV, §9 below. On bald naturalism, cf. n. 65 above.
[105] *KrV*, A189/B232–A211/B256. Cf. A106, 126–8, A277/B333, A766/B794.
[106] 1994, p. 42. Cf. 1998*b*, p. 183.
[107] 1994, p. 97. Cf. 1998*b*, pp. 178–9, 306.

such beliefs are inseparable from our concepts of the things. . . . There is no point, in our self-conscious existence as beings aware of a world of objects and events, at which we are equally prepared, or unprepared, for anything to come of anything ... (1985, pp. 126–7)[108]

There are two complementary aspects to the anti-Humean polemic. Not only is it the case that our primitive concept of a concrete, empirical thing is the concept of something which already comes equipped, at the ontological ground level, with causal dispositions; it is also the case, conversely, that we do not conceive of the activation of causal dispositions as yielding, in the first instance, regularities which could in principle arise between any two things. A given sort of thing essentially has the causal dispositions it has; and those causal regularities arise essentially from that sort of thing.[109]

It follows that, if we are considering where to locate the realm of law, which contains the causal regularities we observe in (first) nature, in a dualism consisting of the conceptual on the one hand and something non-conceptual on the other, we must locate it firmly on the conceptual side of the divide. To locate the realm of law on the non-conceptual side of the line would be to assimilate it, incoherently, to the Kantian noumenal realm, where we are supposed to find not things of certain empirical sorts, but bare things-in-themselves. (Or perhaps we should say 'thinginess-in-itself', since plurality is one of the Kantian categories,[110] and the noumenal realm is said to be extra-categorial.[111] But thinginess-in-itself still falls under the category of unity: the familiar upshot is that we cannot talk about the noumenal realm at all.) Now in the context of the second of the two passages I quoted at the beginning of this section, McDowell shows awareness of the need to accommodate, as he puts it, 'the Kantian thought that the realm of law, not just the realm of meaningful doings, is not external to the

---

[108] Cf. 1966, pp. 145–6; Hume *Treatise*, I.3.15 (1978, p. 173: 'Any thing may produce any thing'); Kant *KrV*, A765/B793.
[109] Cf. Kant *KrV*, A198–9/B243–4.
[110] *KrV*, A80/B106.
[111] *KrV*, A253, A286–7/B342–3, A478/B506 n., A696/B724.

conceptual'.[112] But unfortunately this insight enjoys as precarious a position in McDowell's metaphysical economy as it does in Kant's:[113] elsewhere, as I shall now try to show, he commits himself to the assimilation which I have just branded as incoherent.

In the first lecture of *Mind and World* McDowell attacks what (following Sellars) he calls the 'Myth of the Given', the idea that justificatory relations can extend outside what he calls 'the space of concepts' and be grounded in bits of raw input—'bare presences that are the ultimate grounds of judgements'.[114] The Given[115] is introduced into the dialectic as offering us one superficially attractive way to provide an exogenous grounding for something recognizable as empirical thought (judgement), and so avoid the spectre of 'frictionless spinning in a void' which is the nemesis of Davidsonian coherentism. But, McDowell argues, the Given cannot satisfy our just demand for an exogenous constraint on judgement. For nothing which is no more than a non-conceptual 'bare presence' is fit to ground judgement. Now in what sense does McDowell intend us to understand the non-conceptuality of the Given? In the third lecture of *Mind and World* (and in the Afterword, Part II), McDowell attacks the idea that experience might have non-conceptual content in the sense of possessing representational content which is unavailable to the subject's critical and reflective activity— unavailable to 'active thinking, thinking that is open to reflection

---

[112] 1994, p. 97; cf. p. 82.

[113] Although Kant does not strictly allow law-governed behaviour to extend to the noumenal—there is, strictly speaking, no such thing as transcendental causation *(KrV,* A677–9/B705–7)—he does hold that an analogue of such behaviour operates outside the sphere of the conceptual: A678/B706, A696–700/B724–8, A772/B800. For noumena are said to be the causes, in the analogous sense (they are not subject to law and not in time: A551–2/B579–80), of *Erscheinungen*: A278/B334, A288/B344, A372, A390–3, A491–7/B519–25, A537–58/B565–86, A696/B724. Indeed, causation between the noumenal and the sensible is held to be necessary in order to ground the accidental (A566/B594) and freedom (A536–7/B564–5). On the consequential incoherence of Kant's position, see Strawson 1966, pp. 40–1.

[114] 1994, p. 18; cf. p. 9.

[115] The word is capitalized to indicate that a special sense is in question: 1994, pp. 4, 10; 1998*a*, p. 427 n. 12.

about its own rational credentials'.[116] He implies there that the sense of 'non-conceptual content' in question in this polemic is continuous with what was in question when the Myth of the Given was discussed in the first lecture.[117] But I do not think that this can be so. Rather, in the first lecture the Given was stigmatized as being nonconceptual, or extra-conceptual (both phrases are used), in the much more radical sense that it has no articulated or articulable empirical content at all: it really is just *bare*, 'an ineffable lump, devoid of structure or order'.[118] That the Given does not even have representational content in the sense later allowed to so-called 'non-conceptual' content is implied by the remark that we should understand experience

not as a bare getting of an extra-conceptual Given, but as a kind of occurrence or state that already has conceptual content. In experience one takes in, for instance sees, *that things are thus and so*. That is the sort of thing one can also, for instance, judge. (1994, p. 9)

Unless a great deal is being packed into the final sentence of this quotation—to be exact, unless that sentence is supposed, despite its rather innocent appearance, to introduce the third-lecture notion of the conceptual, according to which the subject not only *can* but also *must be able to* judge that things are thus and so, if he or she is to count as enjoying an experience with that content—the implication of this passage is surely that the content which is contrasted with the Given is representational content *tout court* (content that can be captured by a 'that' clause), not some special *kind* of representational content (content that must additionally be available to a critical and reflective faculty possessed by the subject). As Charles Larmore puts it, the 'Given' implied by the passage I have quoted is something 'to

---

[116] 1994, p. 47.

[117] That is an implication of his remark that the 'unqualified claim that the content of perceptual experience is conceptual will have been raising some eyebrows since my first lecture' (1994, p. 46). Cf. 1998*a*, pp. 365–7 (a précis of *Mind and World*), which seems to have been drafted with the third-lecture notion of conceptual content in mind.

[118] 1998*b*, p. 178. Cf. Brandom 1995*a*, p. 254.

which we could only point, speechlessly as it were'.[119] (Larmore's phrasing nicely recalls T. H. Green's formulation: 'As Plato long ago taught—though the lesson seems to require to be taught anew to each generation of philosophers—a consistent sensationalism must be speechless'.)[120]

That the Given is so conceived by McDowell is further confirmed by the role it plays in his argumentation: his point, as I have noted, is that the extra-conceptual Given cannot serve to ground or justify judgements, and this point would not go through if the Given, though not enjoying conceptual content in the richer sense later exploited in the third lecture, were nevertheless being allowed to enjoy some less demanding kind of representational content. The argument will only work if the Given is utterly *bare* of representational content: for any bit of the world, or experience of the world, which has the representational content *that p*, in however attenuated a sense, will ground or justify the judgement *that p*, whether or not anyone is in a position to make that judgement. A further indication that McDowell conceives the Given as utterly bare is his assimilation of it to the target of Wittgenstein's Private Language Argument.[121] His point in making the assimilation is to suggest that, even if a friend of the Given were to concede that 'language could not embrace the supposed items she insists on'[122]—this being indeed one way of making her point that empirical thinking must be constrained from outside the conceptual—she would still need 'bare presences' to function as items capable of grounding

[119] 2002, p. 197. Cf. Christensen 2000, p. 892.

[120] 1908, p. 36: Green here alludes to Plato's *Theaetetus*, esp. 177c6–186e12. The point was indeed, we may surmise (partly on the basis of Aristotle's report in the *Metaphysics* concerning the doctrines of Plato's teacher Cratylus), a principal motivation behind the introduction of the theory of forms, which can plausibly be seen as an ancestor of the Private Language Argument, on McDowell's reading of that (see next note). See further on this topic my 1996, §II.

[121] 1994, pp. 18–19. See also his essay 'One Strand in the Private Language Argument', 1998*b*, pp. 279–96; and cf. 1998*b*, pp. 309–13.

[122] 1994, p. 19. Cf. 1998*b*, p. 312 with n. 34, where we are told that 'there is no making sense of how any concepts ... could get a grip on' an item that is merely 'a brute presence in consciousness'.

judgements. Against this attempt to preserve a residual role for 'bare presences', McDowell's Wittgenstein applies the general moral that 'a bare presence cannot be a ground for anything'.[123] For our purposes, the point that the friend of the Given is taken to concede establishes that, as McDowell conceives it, the Given is utterly bare of representational content: for if language does not 'embrace' the Given, that can only mean that it is devoid even of the attenuated degree of representational content granted to the less austere kind of non-conceptual content introduced in the third lecture of *Mind and World*.

The argumentation of the previous paragraph seems to me decisive in fixing the sense which 'the Given' must have in McDowell's thought. Or perhaps I should say 'ought to have'. For there is no denying that, if my interpretation is correct, we are forced to find some confusion in McDowell's texts on this point.[124] For example, in the first lecture of *Mind and World* McDowell talks of the rational relations which warrant judgements, such as implication and probabilification, as holding between 'potential exercises of conceptual capacities',[125] which suggests the more demanding notion of the conceptual prominent from the third lecture onwards. One's attention is drawn to the phrase I have just quoted by its striking inaccuracy: for relations such as implication and its congeners do not hold between *exercises* of anything, but between propositional *contents* (or rather the linguistic bearers of such contents). McDowell is here trying to squeeze the argument into a form that will fit the later progress of the dialectic; and in fact in the third lecture, although it is conceded that relations such as implication and probabilification hold between (sc. linguistic) possessors of representational content—indeed we are informed in the Postscript to the third

---

[123] 1994, p. 19. Cf. 1998*b*, p. 280: 'What is pre-conceptually given has to be outside the space of reasons, since it is not in conceptual shape and therefore not capable of standing in rational relations to anything'.

[124] So too in Brandom's statement of the Myth of the Given at 2002, p. 93.

[125] 1994, p. 7.

lecture that this is a routine thought[126]—the claim is made that that relation can only hold between items both of which are available to a critical and reflective faculty possessed by a (single) judging subject.[127] Somewhat similarly, in one of his replies to his critics, McDowell remarks that 'the problem [sc. of the Myth of the Given] is at least in part with the idea that episodes of sentience, present independently of a subject's conceptual capacities if any [that is, present independently of a subject's critical and reflective faculty], could stand in rational relations to anything'.[128] In response to this one must insist that, provided the relevant relata are in the right propositional form, there is no difficulty about how one of them might imply or probabilify another, and that quite regardless of the question of their availability or otherwise to a judging subject:[129] the cogency of the attack on the Myth of the Given derived its force—*all* its force—merely from the assumption that the Given is not a vehicle for propositional content of *any* kind.

A further confusion which we will be forced to find in McDowell's treatment of the non-conceptual concerns his attack on Evans in the third lecture of *Mind and World*. In effect he takes Evans's deployment of the notion of non-conceptual content to have been undermined in advance, as it were, by the first-lecture refutation of the Myth of the Given.[130] But Evans is committed to a notion of non-conceptual content not in the sense of the Given—that is, of utterly bare presences—but in the sense introduced at the beginning of McDowell's third lecture, that is, of items which may possess representational content but which are unavailable as such—as non-conceptual states—to the subject's critical and reflective faculty (they become available, in Evans's view, as a result of a process of conceptualization).[131] And, contrary to what McDowell appears to

---

[126] 1994, p. 162.
[127] 1994, p. 53.
[128] 2002*a*, p. 290 with p. 304 n. 19.
[129] Cf. Byrne 1995, p. 265 with n. 9; Heck 2000, pp. 505–11.
[130] 1994, p. 51.
[131] This is abundantly clear from Evans's discussion of non-conceptual content in 1982, chs. 5–7: see esp. pp. 122–3, 226–7, 239–40. The unavailability of non-

suppose, there is no automatic implication to the existence of non-conceptual content in the former sense (the existence of utterly bare presences) from its existence in the latter sense (the existence of states with representational content which are nevertheless unavailable, as such, to the subject's critical and reflective faculty). So to refute the cogency of the latter notion of non-conceptual content it does not suffice to refute that of the former. The attack on the Given—the refutation of the possibility that 'bare presences' might ground judgements—is quite limited in its scope: it cannot be converted into an attack on the notion of non-conceptual content in the sense sponsored by Evans.[132]

Taken in a properly restricted way, the argument that the extra-conceptual Given cannot serve to ground or justify judgements is indeed cogent; but (this brings us back to our point of departure in this section) when he presents the argument, McDowell allows that the Given may impinge on subjects *causally*, so at least excusing, though not justifying, their judgements.[133] But if what I have said about the way the Given ought to figure in McDowell's thinking is right, it cannot be correct to allow that the Given might impinge causally on anything. For if the Given is external to the conceptual, it is external not only to the space of reasons but also to the realm of law, as McDowell in effect concedes when discussing Kant's attack on Hume. Hence the right thing to say about the Given is this: not only can it not give us justifications, it cannot give us exculpations either,

conceptual content to the subject's critical and reflective faculty is mirrored in the fact that, as Evans sees it, such content need not conform to the Generality Constraint: 1982, pp. 104 n. 22, 158–9. Cf. Heck 2000, pp. 486–8.

[132] In his attack on Evans, McDowell adduces in support Sellars's claim that seemings are conceptual: 1994, p. 166 n. 3 (cf. 2000*a*, pp. 9, 12), with reference to Sellars 1956, §§10–20 (1997, pp. 32–46). But Sellars's leading contention concerning seemings is that they should be characterized 'as, so to speak, making an assertion or claim . . . as containing propositional claims' (1956, §16; 1997, p. 39), that is, that they are not Given in the radical sense—they are not 'bare presences'—which is compatible with their being given to subjects in the sense intended by Evans, that is, presented to subjects, but actualized in them, as such (as seemings with representational content), at a level below the threshold required to activate what critical and reflective capacities (if any) those subjects possess.

[133] 1994, p. 8. Cf. 1998*b*, p. 181; 2000*a*, p. 12.

for it cannot interact with us (or with anything) in any way at all. Supposing that the Given might enter into causal interactions is tantamount to expelling the realm of law from the sphere of the conceptual, and so is tantamount to retracing the steps of Kant's advance on Hume, something which, officially at least, McDowell does not want to do.

But whatever his official position, my claim that McDowell does indeed succumb to the temptation to think of realm-of-law causation as being outside 'the space of concepts'—the claim that he is inclined to assimilate the realm of law to the Kantian noumenal realm—is unfortunately confirmed by a not insignificant number of texts. At one point, McDowell apparently agrees with the suggestion that 'it can seem incoherent to suppose that [operations in the realm of law] might be shaped by concepts'.[134] Elsewhere, it is suggested that if nature were identified with the topic of the natural sciences (that is, identified with first nature), 'the fact that something is a happening in nature would be a ground for supposing that—at least in itself, viewed as the happening in nature it is—it is "without concepts" '.[135] McDowell imputes the urge to deconceptualize nature, understood in terms of a denial of the intelligibility of law to nature, not only to Hume,[136] where the charge has some plausibility (though one should probably add, as McDowell perhaps wishes to add, that its operation in him was subconscious),[137] but also to W. V. Quine (and Davidson), where the charge has less plausibility. This further imputation is evidenced by McDowell's criticism of Quine's epistemology as embodying 'a naturalism that cheerfully casts experience as "intuitions without concepts" '.[138] Again, we are told (in a passage I have already quoted in part) that the disenchantment of nature, that is, the treatment of nature as exclusively a realm of law,

---

[134] 1994, p. 72.
[135] 1999*a*, p. 99; cf. p. 100, where the wrong conception of nature as exclusively first nature is held to be committed to a construal of experiences as 'intuitions without concepts'.
[136] 1994, p. 97.
[137] 1998*b*, pp. 174–6.
[138] 1999*a*, p. 101; cf. p. 102 on Davidson.

'can seem to point to a conception of nature as an ineffable lump, devoid of structure or order'.[139] McDowell indeed goes on here to affirm his official line, that the realm of law is conceptually structured; but the fact that he is willing to entertain, even momentarily, the contrary claim—his concession that, if nature were exclusively a realm of law, that could so much as *seem* to imply its being devoid of structure or order—perhaps helps explain why there is some confusion in several of his texts on this matter.[140]

In this connection we may usefully, in closing this chapter, examine a remark which Davidson makes in response to an essay of McDowell's.[141] In characterizing the difference between them, Davidson states that

> I think the interface between our bodies and the world is causal and nothing more, while McDowell holds that the world directly presents us with propositional contents. McDowell sees no trouble in accounting for the contents of perception, since nature provides these. (2005, p. 321)

Davidson here misrepresents the difference between himself and McDowell, concealing his misunderstanding under a slide from 'our bodies' to 'us'. McDowell does not deny that the interface between *our bodies*—on a suitably objectivistic understanding of that phrase—and the world is causal (in the realm-of-law sense) and nothing more; further, one can legitimately talk of an interface in this context, for our skin forms just such a boundary between world and body, and it is no part of McDowell's project to deny that the transactions across that boundary are exclusively causal (in the realm-of-law sense). (Of course, no interface in any philosophically pregnant sense is in question: our skins constitute an interface in a merely biological sense.) By contrast, the propositional contents that the world presents to us are presented not to our bodies, in that objectivistic sense, but to *our minds*; and here McDowell will insist that it would be quite wrong to talk about an interface—and quite impossible to locate a boundary: that is, it would be wrong in principle to go looking for one—between a given individual mind (let alone the mindedness of a community) and the world. As he puts it: 'Where mental life takes place need not be pinpointed any more precisely than by saying that it takes place where our lives take place'.[142]

But, having ironed out Davidson's misreading of McDowell's position, we can now see how there might be a temptation to think that the acknowledged causal transactions between the world and our bodies are, by virtue of their distinctness from the world's presenting of propositional contents to our minds, somehow 'without concepts'. Of course no such thing really follows, if by 'without concepts' we mean to allude to a deconceptualized vision of nature as 'an ineffable lump, devoid of structure or order'. The causal transactions between world and body—on Quine's, Davidson's, or indeed anyone's approach—are conceptually structured in the contrasting sense to the one exploited by the deconceptualized vision: that is, they have conceptual content in McDowell's first-lecture sense—they are propositionally structured—and that simply by virtue of the fact that we can characterize them in language. For Quine and Davidson, like everyone else, think that it is possible for us to study and describe these connections. It is true that the contents we employ in so describing them may not be available as such (or at all) to the subject who is on the receiving end of the causal transactions in question: in that—third-lecture—sense those contents may well be non-conceptual. But, as we have seen, it is a mistake on McDowell's part to try to conclude from the non-conceptuality of a content in the latter (third-lecture) sense to its non-conceptuality in the former (first-lecture) sense: there is no such entailment. Why does McDowell so readily suppose otherwise? The answer is, I think, that he conceives experience—to focus on the transaction between world and mind which interests us here—individualistically and intellectualistically, in the sense that he holds that an experience's possession of content is conditional on that content's being essentially available for introspection and verbal articulation by the experience's subject. In the next chapter I turn to consider this aspect of McDowell's thinking.

III

Experience and judgement

III.1. McDOWELL'S TRANSCENDENTAL ARGUMENT

A second feature of McDowell's thinking which raises the suspicion that his empiricism is more than minimal is his handling of the relation between experience and judgement. According to the reconstruction that was offered in Chapter I, we can reconcile McDowell's various and superficially inconsistent pronouncements on the 'order of justification' if we see him as offering, in the first instance, a complex model of empirical content which is articulated into three relata—world, experience, and judgement—with both rational and causal relations running both between world and experience and between experience and judgement. With that model in place, we are entitled, so McDowell proposes on my reconstruction, to move to a simple model of empirical content, in which experience is conceived not as a relatum, as the complex model had it, but as a relation, mediating between the world and judgement: it is constitutive of that relation that it is both rational and causal in nature. With the simple model in place, we supposedly entitle ourselves to conceive of experience not as an interface between mind and world, but as a conduit, enabling minds to be open to the world, to reach out and embrace it in judgement. The supposed entitlement to move from the complex to the simple model of empirical content is earned, I suggest, by a transcendental argument which McDowell offers in several places.

The ostensible aim of the argument is to reconcile what McDowell calls the 'freedom of judgement'—the fact that, in making a judgement one has to, and is free to, make up one's mind what to think—with the objective purport of judgement. The argument proceeds as follows:

Capacities of the sort one wants to see as freely exercised, in what one wants to be entitled to see as judgement, are also actualized in sensory consciousness; these actualizations in sensory consciousness are occurrences of a kind that can be understood, partly by virtue of the involvement in them of capacities that are also freely exercised in judgement, as cases of having objective reality directly in view. This way, we enable ourselves to make sense of a consciousness that is capable of both being intuitionally in touch with objective reality and making judgements about it. We make sense of a consciousness as having each of those capacities only because we see it as also having the other. (1998a, p. 427)

The last sentence is the crucial one: we might encapsulate its thought by saying (to put it in the Kantian terms which McDowell often adduces) that the faculties of spontaneity (judgement) and receptivity (perception) are interdependent.[1] As Kant himself put it: 'thoughts without content are empty; intuitions without concepts are blind'.[2] Actually, the Kantian slogan goes too far by McDowell's own lights, in two respects.

In the first place, while he frequently stresses that *receptivity* does not make an even notionally separable contribution to its co-oper-

---

[1] There are many passages in *Mind and World* which contain more or less complete statements of the transcendental argument. For the dependence of the (empirical) judgements issued by a faculty of spontaneity on engagement with receptivity see e.g. 1994, pp. 4–5, 10, 42; for the dependence of experience of objective reality on involvement of conceptual capacities contributed by a faculty of spontaneity, see e.g. 1994, pp. 9, 11–13, 24, 29, 31–3, 40–1, 47, 51, 58; for the dependence in both directions, see 1994, pp. 33–4, 66–7. But the clearest statements of the transcendental argument come in subsequent publications. Apart from the version quoted in the text, note the following: 1998a, pp. 365–8, 407, 410–13; 1998d, pp. 440 n. 14, 462–6; 2002a, p. 287; 2002b, pp. 172–3.

[2] *KrV*, A51/B75, cited by McDowell at 1994, pp. 3–4 (cf. 1999a, pp. 87–8). Cf. *KrV*, A67–9/B92–4, A239/B298.

ation with spontaneity,[3] McDowell nowhere says that *spontaneity* does not make a notionally separable contribution to the co-operation; and indeed it is a crucial feature of his position that spontaneity's contribution to the co-operation with receptivity is at least notionally—and presumably actually—separable,[4] because his view is that experience is a *passive* actualization of capacities whose core actualization is *active*, namely their exercise in judgement.[5] Of course, McDowell is probably committed, as we have seen (Chapter I, §1), to the thesis that the possession of a faculty of spontaneity requires or involves the possession of a faculty of receptivity, as well as to the claim (Chapter II, §5) that only biological beings (in a broad sense) can be endowed with a faculty of spontaneity, but these points, difficult as they are, do not undermine his commitment to the notional (and actual) separability of the contribution made by spontaneity to its co-operation with receptivity *at the level of individual exercises of judgement*. They simply require him to maintain that the separability in question goes no further than that: in particular, McDowell must claim that a *faculty* of spontaneity is not available to a being who does not also possess a faculty of receptivity, even though not all *exercises* of spontaneity involve exercises of receptivity. (Perhaps he would also wish to claim, along Hegelian lines, that the faculties of spontaneity and receptivity are connected in the more intimate sense that exercises of judgement, though individually available independently of exercises of receptivity, are structured in a way which is constitutively dependent, in general, on deliverances of receptivity. The thought here would be the anti-Kantian one that our forms of cognition do not have a necessary nature knowable *a priori*, but are historically and culturally embedded products of the contingent interplay

---

[3] 1994, pp. 9, 41, 46, 51. In fact, despite his slogan, Kant regularly writes in such a way as to presuppose that receptivity does indeed make a notionally (and perhaps even actually) separable contribution to its co-operation with spontaneity: see e.g. *KrV*, A89–91/B122–3, A111–12, B129–30, B137, B145, A156/B195, A166/B208, A374.

[4] *Pace* de Gaynesford 2004, p. 94.

[5] See e.g. 1994, pp. 10–12; 1998*a*, pp. 367, 426; 1998*d*, p. 440.

between the faculties of spontaneity and receptivity, and so are infected with the *a posteriori*.)[6]

The second respect in which the Kantian slogan goes too far for McDowell is that he is willing to concede that we can make sense of a kind of faculty of receptivity which does not involve actualizations of conceptual capacities: namely the kind of perceptual sensitivity to their environment enjoyed by infants and animals. But the claim is that any such inchoate faculty of receptivity endows its possessors with something less than experience of objective reality.[7] I shall postpone discussion of this matter until the next chapter. Here I wish to focus on problems that arise for the slogan in the cases where McDowell sees it as having unrestricted application—in the experience and empirical thinking of mature humans.

My suggestion is, as I have stated, that the transcendental argument offered by McDowell is best seen as intended to underwrite our entitlement to move from the complex to the simple model of empirical content. If experience, as that figures in the complex model, is essentially structured by the conceptual capacities involved in judgement, and if (empirical) judgements are answerable to the deliverances of experience, so conceived, that seems to license the claim that experience mediates between world and judging subject not as an intermediary or interface, blocking the subject's direct view of the world, but as a conduit, securing the subject's answerability, in empirical judgement, to the way the world is.[8] That is how McDowell hopes to win through to a conduit, as opposed to an interface, conception of experience; but there are several obstacles in his thought to his achieving this goal.

[6] See on this point Sedgwick 2000.

[7] Cf. 1994, p. 114. The incompatibility of the unrestricted Kantian slogan with McDowell's treatment of infant and animal mentality is noted by Willaschek 2003, p. 280 n. 328.

[8] Recall the passage already quoted from 1994, p. 26: '[T]he idea of conceptually structured operations of receptivity puts us in a position to speak of experience as openness to the layout of reality. Experience enables the layout of reality itself to exert a rational influence on what a subject thinks'.

III.2. JUDGEMENT AND FREEDOM

The first of these obstacles is implicit in the ostensible motivation for the transcendental argument. The immediate aim of the argument is to secure objective purport for the empirical judgements issued by a faculty of *spontaneity*, that is, by a faculty which is *free* to make up its mind what to think. In effect McDowell follows Kant in identifying the possession of a faculty of spontaneity, which constitutively involves a capacity to act freely, with the possession of a capacity to make judgements. The connection between spontaneity and freedom is etymologically obvious, but that between spontaneity and judgement is not at all obvious, and by applying the label 'spontaneity' to the faculty which issues judgements, Kant and McDowell in effect insinuate by sleight of hand the thesis that the capacity to make judgements is at least dependent on, and perhaps even identical with, the capacity to act freely, in a philosophically pregnant sense. The thesis is encapsulated in a slogan which McDowell offers us: 'the space of reasons is the realm of freedom'.[9] My purpose in this section is to examine the credentials of this slogan.

Now McDowell's view is that not only are we free, by virtue of our possession of a faculty of spontaneity, to make up our minds what to think; it is also the case that we are under a 'standing obligation' to do so.[10] He is at some pains to stress that, after experience has presented the subject with an appearance, the subject both *can* and *must* decide whether 'to take the experience at face value'.[11] He is impressed by the existence of visual illusions, such as the Müller–Lyer illusion, which continue to present their illusory appearance after the subject

---

[9] 1994, p. 5. Cf. 1998*b*, pp. 319, 321; 1998*d*, p. 434. Cf. Brandom 1979; 1999, p. 166 with n. 2.

[10] 1994, pp. 12, 39–40, 126. As Kurbacher and Heßbrüggen-Walter remark, self-criticism seems, for McDowell, to be a 'condition of the possibility' of spontaneity: 2000, p. 62.

[11] 1994, p. 26. Cf. 1998*a*, pp. 367, 405; 1998*c*, p. 398; 1998*d*, pp. 462, 471; 2000*a*, pp. 11–12.

has decided not to take that appearance at face value: such cases serve as a warning against a naïve identification of appearances with the judgements we can form on the basis of those experiences.[12] McDowell concedes that we do not usually question appearances in the way the Müller–Lyer illusion forces us to do—we normally make empirical judgements, without reservation, simply on the basis of the fact that things *look* a certain way[13]—but he claims that when we make a judgement on the basis of our experience we must always be prepared, in principle, to question the veridicality of our senses.[14] Hence even if one has not actively reflected on the credentials of a given judgement, the fact that one forms one's judgements under a standing obligation to be prepared, if necessary, to scrutinize their credentials has the effect of fixing on the subject what we might, borrowing a piece of legal terminology, call *constructive responsibility* for the judgement in question.[15] Judgement differs in precisely this respect from experience: in experience the involvement of conceptual capacities is involuntary, in the sense that one cannot be held responsible for the content of one's experiences; in judgement, by contrast, the involvement of conceptual capacities is held to be—whether 'expressly' or 'constructively'—voluntary, in the sense that one can be held responsible for one's judgements. As McDowell puts it: 'How one's experience represents things to be is not under one's control, but it is up to one whether one accepts the appearance or rejects it'.[16] McDowell registers this point, as we have noted, by saying that the conceptual capacities which are drawn on in both judgement and experience are *exercised* (that is, actively drawn on) in judgement, whereas they are merely *actualized* (that is, passively drawn on) in experience.

This stress on the freedom of judgement is very prominent in McDowell's thinking, and, as I have indicated, it forms the backdrop to his transcendental argument. But at one point he appears to

---

[12] 1994, p. 11.
[13] I return to this important point in §§6–7 below.
[14] 1994, p. 60. Cf. 1998*c*, pp. 385–6, 398; 1998*d*, p. 434.
[15] On the issue of constructive responsibility, see 2000*a*, pp. 92–3.
[16] 1994, p. 11.

express the distinct and indeed opposing position according to which empirical judgement is not free, but constrained by experience:

Suppose ...there is an inclination to apply some concept in judgement. This inclination does not just inexplicably set in. If one does make a judgement, it is wrung from one by the experience, which serves as one's reason for the judgement. (1994, p. 61)[17]

In this passage we are told that *the inclination to apply a concept in an empirical judgement*, so far from being the upshot of a free act, is wrung from one by the experience. (The position is offered as an interpretation of Evans, rather than put forward *propria voce*: but I think it is clear from the context that McDowell himself endorses it.) Does it follow that the *judgement itself* is wrung from one by the experience? It is not evident from the passage I have cited whether McDowell intends us to make this inference:[18] if he did so, the corollary would be in tension with his official line, according to which subjects are always, at least in principle, free to accept or reject the deliverances of their senses. For the official line opens a deliberative gap between experience and judgement which the metaphor of the judgement's being wrung from the subject closes. That presents us with a dilemma: do we want to follow the official line, or rather take the metaphor of wringing as our guide?

It seems obvious that in offering his official line McDowell has been excessively influenced by epistemologically peripheral phenomena, and that the opposing suggestion, if he intended to make it, that experiences wring judgements from subjects, without allowing them freedom of movement, is correct. If McDowell did not intend us, in the passage I have cited, to infer that empirical judgements themselves—as opposed to mere inclinations to apply concepts in

---

[17] The phraseology here is derived from Sellars (1956, §16; 1997, p. 40), though the use to which Sellars puts it is distinct: see McDowell 1998*d*, p. 440.

[18] I assume (with Brandom, 2002, p. 95) that, in the phrase 'it is wrung ...', the antecedent of the pronoun 'it' is intended to be 'This inclination' (from the previous sentence), and not 'a judgement' (from the previous clause). Of course if McDowell in fact intended the latter (as Alweiss supposes: 2000, pp. 266 and 268), the inference would be trivial.

judgements—are wrung from subjects by their experiences, my point becomes this: he *ought* to have taken the line that experiences wring judgements, and not merely inclinations to apply concepts in judgement, from the subject (regardless of whether the former is an implication of the latter or not).[19] In general, McDowell's persistent identification of what freedom we enjoy with freedom to make judgements is surely a mistake: our freedom, insofar as we have it, is freedom not to *judge* on the basis of experience but to *act* on that basis; it is not as subjects of experience, and as thinkers who can base judgements on our experience, that we enjoy freedom, if and to whatever extent we do, but as agents.[20]

Of course, to the extent that the issuing of a judgement is a public act—as, for example, the promulgation of a legal judgment is a public act—recorded in speech (including 'inner' speech, and 'outer' speech directed solely to oneself) or in writing (including what one writes to oneself), it counts as an action for which we can legitimately be held responsible, and that regardless of the basis on which it is made, so that judgements publicly issued on the basis of experience are indeed voluntary acts. But though such publicly made judgements are, as such, voluntary acts for which one is accountable, we must distinguish within these acts between a voluntary and an involuntary component. The voluntary component of publicly made judgements, for which one may be held responsible, is not the bare *formation* of a judgement on the basis of experience (as it might be, the thought 'He went that way', as one witnesses a chase), but its *communication*, whether to oneself or to others (as it might be, to the fugitive's pursuer). In experience one finds oneself simply saddled with beliefs about the layout of the world, and these beliefs can be thought of as warranting judgements with the same content as

[19] For some further texts drawn from *Mind and World* which may suggest that McDowell did occasionally, despite his official policy to the contrary, take the line I say he ought to have taken, see Larmore 2002, p. 200.

[20] McDowell offers a better (but regrettably isolated) picture of the location of freedom in our lives in his essay 'Two Sorts of Naturalism': 1998*b*, p. 170. Cf. also Rorty 1998, p. 150, who points out, rightly, that McDowell's conception of freedom does not engage with the conception of it which 'we invoke when ascribing moral responsibility'.

the underlying beliefs and experiences.[21] But just so far there is nothing voluntary in the transaction for which the subject may be held accountable; only when (if) the subject advances to the distinct act of issuing a public judgement do we enter the domain of free and responsible action.

If we supposed freedom to be located where McDowell wants to locate it, between experiences and the judgements which are based upon those experiences, it would be impossible to see how the subject might rationally exploit that freedom. Subjects are presented with appearances, and supposedly have to decide whether to take those appearances 'at face value': but how are they to decide that?[22] The transcendental argument closes one gap, a *conceptual* gap— it secures the objective purport of empirical judgements, by virtue of their engagement with receptivity, so that to that extent judgement is not unconstrained[23]—only to open a distinct but equally serious gap—a *practical* gap this time, between the materials on the basis of which we make judgements, on the one hand, and the judgements themselves, on the other. The new gap is, in its own way, every bit as devastating as a conceptual gap would have been, for while a decision is required of subjects there is no principle to guide them in making it. McDowell's experiencing and judging subjects are, like the forlorn agents of existentialist theory, exiled from rationality because condemned to a freedom which they have no rational means of exploiting. Rather than imposing this strange form

---

[21] Evans held that a belief-state is 'a disposition to have certain thoughts or to make certain judgements' (1982, p. 236), and his view is noted, apparently with approval, by McDowell (1994, p. 60). Such an account of the connection between belief and judgement strikes me as quite implausible: one should surely give (and I would have expected McDowell to prefer) a normative rather than a dispositionalist story linking them. Hitherto I have ignored belief in my exposition of the 'order of justification': I introduce it in the present chapter in order to conform my discussion to the terms employed in the base texts I shall be considering. I do indeed think that belief-formation is a distinct moment in the 'order of justification' from judgement-formation, though they are closely connected (in the normative sense I have specified); but I shall not be further concerned with the details of their relation to one another.

[22] Cf. Kern 2000, p. 930.

[23] See here again McDowell 1994, pp. 66–7; 1998*a*, pp. 410–11.

of punishment on the subject, we should say that the space between experience and judgement is not a locus of freedom: the formation of beliefs and judgements based on experience is, contrary to McDowell's official doctrine, not voluntary.[24] (This was recognized by Hume—at least for the case of belief—in spite of the implausibility of his general account of the nature of belief.)[25]

There is, of course, an intimate connection between freedom and reason, and it is no part of my project to deny that such a connection exists. As we have noted, McDowell's attempt to adumbrate the connection takes the form of the slogan 'the space of reasons is the realm of freedom'.[26] But, in view of what we have said, that slogan cannot be right. It is certainly a substantial insight—one which we owe to the rationalist tradition—that freedom presupposes rationality; but in embracing this insight we must not allow to disappear from view the obvious point that freedom also involves the subject's having a genuine choice among alternatives. Of course, what exactly *constitutes* genuine choice is a matter of ancient and continuing controversy. But the details of that debate are not to the point here: for present purposes, we can adopt a position which, while refusing to abjure freedom, is maximally modest, metaphysically speaking, in the way that it construes freedom, namely one of agreeing with Hobbesian compatibilists that genuine choice among alternatives does not require anything so strong as liberty of indifference, as Kant still required. Rather, freedom should be identified with a rationally constrained version of what Hume called, etymologically appropriately, 'liberty of spontaneity'.[27] For it is plausible that the incompatibilist's search for a metaphysical freedom trans-

---

[24] Cf. McDowell 1998*a*, p. 426. Contrast B. Williams 1973, pp. 147–9. Williams makes the (constitutive) point that belief-formation cannot be thought of as voluntary on pain of undermining our entitlement to conceive the mental state so produced as one of *belief*; i.e., one whose aim is to track the truth (as opposed to cohering with other projects the subject might have).

[25] *Treatise*, I.3.12 (1978, pp. 140–1).

[26] See above, n. 9.

[27] Hume *Treatise*, II.3.2 (1978, p. 407). 'Liberty of spontaneity' is the freedom to do what one wants: Hume half-recognized that such liberty needs to be subject to a

cending the mere ability to make rational decisions among given options on the basis of (largely given) desires and motivations is unrealistic and ill-conceived. Still, trimming our metaphysical pretensions in the direction of compatibilism does not in any sense absolve us from the need to incorporate an element of genuine choice in our understanding of the nature of freedom.

But what that means, given that the space between experience and judgement is not a locus of choice, is that the space of reasons extends more widely than the realm of freedom: the space of reasons is not *coextensive with* the realm of freedom, as McDowell's slogan has it, but *properly includes* that realm. And once we have firmly located freedom where it belongs, between the formation of judgement and action (under which latter soubriquet we should include the act of communicating a judgement we have formed), we can recognize the space between experience and judgement for what it is, as a locus—within the space of reasons, by all means— not of freedom but of constraint. In epistemologically peripheral cases such as that presented by the Müller–Lyer illusion, we should say that the (incorrect) judgement which the experience constrains us to form is, or can be (in the knowing subject), cancelled by a second-order judgement, itself constrained by further experiences. There is no call to accommodate such cases by opening, quite generally, a deliberative gap between experience and judgement.

McDowell is aware that the constitutive connection he draws between freedom and 'responsiveness to reasons'[28] is likely to arouse opposition, and in one of his replies to his critics he shows sensitivity to the charge that he espouses a 'wild-eyed voluntarism'.[29] He concedes that the appeal, in his discussion of the Müller–Lyer illusion, to 'the language of decision and its being up to one what

---

rationality constraint if it is to constitute genuine freedom, but did not make enough of this point. On the connection between freedom and rationality, see Wolf's excellent discussion in her 1990.

[28] 1996*a*, p. xxiii.   [29] 2000*c*, p. 334.

to judge ... is perhaps dangerous',[30] but his reply to the charge that he embraces an unwarranted voluntarism is unsatisfactory. He reminds us that free actions can be—or can at least seem to their agents to be—forced:

> Was Luther saying his action was not free when he said 'I can do no other'? ... Decisions can be forced, as Luther said his was; and he was not denying that it was up to him whether or not to act as he did. (2000*c*, p. 334, p. 342 n. 9)

But the implied analogy with judgements made on the basis of experience fails. There is a metaphysical sense in which Luther's action was free: in that sense he certainly could have done otherwise. The sense in which the stand he took was forced and he could 'do no other' was, broadly speaking, a moral one. There is no analogy to this collocation of metaphysical freedom and moral compulsion in the case we are interested in, namely the connection between experience and judgement. Here the deliberative situation is, so to speak, one-dimensional rather than, as in the case of Luther's decision, two-dimensional. In deciding whether to take one's experience at face value—the quandary in which McDowell places the experiencing subject—there could be nothing like a metaphysical freedom to withhold assent from it combined with a moral compulsion to regard the experience as veridical, or *vice versa*. For the moral dimension of assessment can only be in place if there is metaphysical freedom of movement: we might say that it is definitive of genuine action that both metaphysical and moral dimensions are indeed in place. But in the case we are concerned with one of the necessary conditions for genuine action is not met, since the metaphysical dimension admits of no freedom of movement: the judgement which a subject makes on the basis of an experience is metaphysically constrained by the experience's propositional content.

---

[30] 2000*c*, p. 342 n. 9.

III.3. KNOWLEDGE AND THE OPPORTUNITY TO KNOW

McDowell's erroneous location of freedom between experience, on the one hand, and belief or judgement, on the other, is suggestive of a substantial empiricism, one which conceives experience as an interface rather than as a conduit; and it is of a piece with this empiricism that McDowell, in a number of passages, construes appearances—even veridical appearances—as providing the subject not with knowledge *tout court*, but merely with an *opportunity* to know, which the subject may or may not take: 'seeings are not, as such, non-inferential knowings or acquirings of knowledge ..., but rather opportunities to know, which may not be taken'.[31] This is the second point at which an obstacle emerges in McDowell's thinking to his being entitled to claim whole-hearted endorsement of the conduit conception of experience. For if subjects are presented, in experience, not with knowledge as such, but merely with an opportunity to know, which they may or may not take, experience as such is not connecting them with the world. To take (or refuse) the opportunity for knowledge offered by experience calls for a decision on the subject's part, a decision for the making of which, as I have urged, the subject has in general no principled basis. McDowell opens this implausible gap between experience and knowledge because he is impressed by cases in which, for example, although one's senses are in fact functioning perfectly, one has good reason to believe that they are malfunctioning, so that it would be doxastically irresponsible to trust them.[32] But once again this represents the ill-conceived promotion of what are in fact epistemologically peripheral phenomena to a position where they are driving the application of fundamental concepts. In order to cater for these phenomena, McDowell has again introduced a deliberative gap

---

[31] 1998*d*, p. 437 n. 10. Cf. 1998*c*, pp. 39, 390 with n. 37; 2002*a*, p. 289.
[32] Cf. 1998*c*, p. 430 with n. 25.

between experience and judgement which is disastrous for subjects, who are thereby encumbered with a freedom they cannot rationally exploit. What we should say in such cases is that, if one's senses are functioning normally and one seems to see that *p*, then one does see, and *eo ipso* know, that *p*.[33] That knowledge may, however, be prevented from feeding into action (including the issuing of a judgement) by a higher-order belief—which, depending on the circumstances, it may indeed be doxastically responsible to entertain—that one's senses are malfunctioning and hence that one's relevant first-order beliefs are unreliable.[34]

Contrast the case of testimony, where the question of doxastic responsibility bears not, as in the case of experience, on one's second-order knowledge, but on one's first-order knowledge. In his essay 'Knowledge by Hearsay', McDowell imagines the case of a tourist who asks the inhabitant of a town he is visiting where the cathedral is.[35] Here it seems clear that any good reason the tourist has to doubt the reliability of the answer he receives will affect his first-order knowledge of the cathedral's whereabouts, not merely his second-order belief (and so knowledge) that he has first-order knowledge of its whereabouts.[36] That is because receiving testimony, unlike having an experience, is genuinely being faced with an intermediary, an emissary from the world, and not with the relevant bit of the world itself.[37] McDowell writes:

One cannot count as having heard from someone that things are thus and so, in the relevant sense, unless, by virtue of understanding what the person

[33] There is a certain wavering in McDowell's texts on the question whether, in cases where one's senses are in fact functioning normally but it would be doxastically irresponsible to trust them, one counts as perceiving but not knowing, or as not even perceiving. In at least one passage (2002*a*, p. 289; cf. 1998*d*, pp. 437 n. 10, 474) he seems to endorse the former idea, but in others (1998*c*, pp. 390 with n. 37, 430 with n. 25) he appears to prefer the latter.

[34] Since in another context McDowell rightly rejects the so-called *KK* principle—the principle that if you know, you thereby know that you know—he should have no difficulty accepting the possibility of scenarios having this structure: see 1998*c*, p. 419 n. 10.

[35] 1998*c*, p. 417.

[36] This point is clearly implied by McDowell at 1998*c*, pp. 434–5.

[37] Cf. 1998*c*, pp. 45, 417.

says, one is in a position to know that things are indeed thus and so. (1998*c*, p. 434)[38]

Here the retreat from ascribing simple *knowledge* to the hearer to crediting him or her with merely *being in a position to know* seems appropriate.[39] But the case of testimony is precisely unlike that of experience in this respect.[40] McDowell is of course officially hostile to the idea that experience might function as a mere emissary.[41] But his mislocation of the role of doxastic responsibility, in the case of experience—his assumption that it bears on the epistemic status of experience, rather than on the status of beliefs about experience—and his assimilation (in effect) of the case of the experience to that of testimony, show that his rejection of the emissary model of experience is at best half-hearted. Officially McDowell no doubt wishes to distance himself from anything that smacks of 'the testimony of the senses', literally construed; but unofficially he appears to commit himself to just that notion.

III.4. KNOWLEDGE AND INFALLIBILITY

A third respect in which McDowell's unconditional acceptance of the conduit conception of experience is compromised is his

---

[38] Cf. 1998*c*, pp. 46, 417 with n. 6.

[39] Cf. 1998*c*, p. 436 on the case of the boy who cried 'Wolf', where McDowell suggests that a stranger who hears the cry on an occasion when it is really an expression of knowledge has 'an opportunity for the acquisition of knowledge' which 'is closed to those who know too much' (i.e., who are familiar with the boy's past lies). In Horace's version of the fable (*Epistles* 1.17.58–62), villagers who have been repeatedly duped by a vagabond pretending to be crippled pointedly tell him to address his pleas to a stranger.

[40] Cf. 1998*c*, p. 407 n. 17: 'when one learns something from someone else, the cognitive transaction is of course not a sort of perception of the state of affairs one is told about'. A suggestion that McDowell endorses elsewhere (and which is enthusiastically seconded by Putnam: 1978, p. 98), that 'in communication knowledge rubs off on others like a contagious disease' (1998*c*, p. 336 n. 51) risks undermining this important difference between perception and testimony as ways of acquiring knowledge. (McDowell credits the suggestion to Evans: cf. Evans 1982, pp. 310–11.)

[41] 1994, p. 143.

endorsement, in his essay 'Singular Thought and the Extent of Inner Space', of the coherence of a position which, following Myles Burnyeat, he ascribes to the ancient sceptics.[42] According to this position, 'ancient scepticism did not call our possession of a world into question; its upshot was, less dramatically, to drive a wedge between living in the world and (what is meant to seem dispensable) knowing about it'.[43] In concert with a principle of acquaintance which Russell formulated—that in order to entertain a singular thought about an object one must know which object one's thought concerns[44]—the position ascribed to the ancient sceptics seems to yield the result that insofar as we can entertain singular thoughts about objects (and we must be able to entertain some such thoughts, if we are to be thinkers at all), these objects are, for all we know, 'inner' objects. That result traps subjects behind their experiences: such experiences can no longer be conceived by subjects as constitutively conferring on them openness to the world, but must be conceived by them as, for all they know, blocking their access to the world.

Now McDowell accepts Russell's principle of acquaintance; but he also detaches it from Russell's own Cartesian epistemology and applies it to our thinking about ordinary objects of perception,[45] which makes his acceptance of the coherence of the ancient sceptical position, as reported by Burnyeat, strange, to say the least, given the consequence which that position, together with Russell's principle of acquaintance, seems to have. Indeed the incongruity deepens when we note that, in the same passage as the one in which McDowell appears to admit the coherence of supposing that we might 'possess'

---

[42] 1998c, pp. 237–43.

[43] 1998c, p. 238.

[44] Russell 1912, p. 91 (1967 edn., p. 32); 1918, pp. 219–21 (1963 edn., pp. 209–11). Cf. Evans 1982, ch. 4. McDowell rightly remarks that the principle, as thus formulated (using 'know which' in the sense of *savoir/wissen* rather than *connaître/kennen*), is not well styled as a principle of *acquaintance* (1998c, pp. 164–5, 230–2; cf. 1990, p. 257), but provided we are aware of the grammatical conflation, that conflation can be, as McDowell says, theoretically suggestive.

[45] 1998c, pp. 230–2; cf. pp. 214–27.

the world without knowing about it, he attacks Cartesianism for refusing to allow us 'to depend on our possession of the world for knowledge that we are not dreaming'.[46] If our possession of the world gives us such a means of rebutting Cartesian scepticism about the so-called 'external' world, how can the position imputed to the ancient sceptics really be coherent?

In spite of his official rejection of Cartesian epistemology, McDowell apparently accepts, in the same essay, one feature of that epistemology which, while perhaps not strictly inconsistent with his officially adopted direct realism, sits ill with it: the subject's infallibility about how things seem to him of her.[47] Actually, elsewhere both in this essay and in other writings McDowell is clear that infallibility cannot extend to the subject's beliefs about his or her own *de re* mental states,[48] that, to echo Evans (who puts the point in linguistic terms), 'in general thoughts associated with Russellian singular terms are such that the subject cannot infallibly know that he has one'.[49] (Russellian singular terms are singular terms whose possession of sense depends upon their having reference.)[50] But in the passages where McDowell claims infallibility for the subject, there is no suggestion that the subject's infallibility does not extend to *de re* mental states,[51] so that the conflict is left unresolved. Since, in general, one's beliefs about one's own *de re* mental states will include beliefs about how things *seem* ('It seems to me that *that*

---

[46] 1998*c*, p. 239; cf. pp. 408 n. 19, 419 n. 10. For some apposite criticism of McDowell's Moorean appeal to our 'possession of the world' in the debate with the sceptic, see Pritchard 2003, esp. §2.

[47] 1998*c*, pp. 242–5. Cf. Macarthur 2003, pp. 178–9.

[48] 1998*c*, pp. 204–9, 227 n. 42, 231–2, 236. Connectedly, 'scepticism about the existence of the objects of seeming singular thoughts is equally scepticism about the layout of the mental realm' (1998*c*, p. 255). Cf. 1998*d*, pp. 475–7.

[49] Evans 1985, p. 311 n. 21 (=1982, p. 196 n. 4). Cf. 1982, pp. 44–6, 199–200, 201–2.

[50] Evans 1982, p. 12.

[51] So, too, apparently, at 1994, p. 26, where McDowell writes: 'Certainly one can be misled, at least in the case of "outer experience" ', a formulation which (given the absence of any explicit signal to the contrary) suggests that McDowell thinks one cannot be misled in the case of 'inner experience'.

wall is green', pointing—or taking oneself to point to—a seen or purportedly seen wall), we have it that subjects are not, in general, infallible about how things seem to them to be, and hence that McDowell is mistaken in his claim that 'the uncontentiously legitimate category of things that are the same' across the cases of veridical and non-veridical perceptual experiences which are indistinguishable from the subject's point of view 'is the category of how things seem to the subject'.[52] In the veridical case subjects will be in a position to entertain a fully *de re* belief about how things seem to them to be, whereas in the non-veridical case they will not, there being, in the non-veridical case, an absence of *de re* content in at least part of the experience's content—the part in which it is non-veridical—and a corresponding absence of singular content, therefore, to form the matter of the relevant belief. From the fact that, on a given occasion, a subject cannot tell whether an experience is veridical or not, it does not follow—and it would not be correct to say in such a case—that our specification of how things seem to the subject will be indifferent to the issue of the experience's veridicality.[53]

In fact the position that subjects are infallible about how things seem to them is unacceptable not merely for *de re* beliefs but for general beliefs too, and that for a reason made familiar by the later Wittgenstein. The relevant point applies just as much to singular as

[52] 1998*c*, p. 248. At 1998*d*, p. 476 McDowell secures content for an illusory appearance of a red cube by restricting that content to a claim expressible by the words 'There is a red cube *there*'. Now this claim is *de re* only in its employment of the spatial demonstrative 'there', and if we do not suppose that subjects are under an illusion about their location in public space, the general and existential thought conveyed by the claim is uncontentiously available to them (as would be the thought expressed by 'There seems to be a red cube there'). What would not be available to subjects in our envisaged scenario, however, is a thought with its purportedly *de re* content in the same place as the illusion, such as a thought with the purported content that *that red cube is F*, or that *it seems to me that that red cube is F*.

[53] McDowell remarks, in the continuation of the passage I have quoted in the text, that 'the legitimacy of the category of how things seem is consistent with the essentially disjunctive conception of the state of seemingly entertaining a singular thought [i.e., the conception according to which one is either entertaining such a thought or merely seeming to do so]': 1998*c*, p. 248. But what is not consistent with that disjunctive conception is the category of how things seem when this is construed, as McDowell does construe it, as being *the same* across veridical and non-veridical cases.

to general beliefs, and constitutes the fundamental reason why any claim of infallibility for the judging subject about any tract of reality—no matter how 'inner'—must be rejected. A subject's beliefs about any subject matter, including his or her own mental states, are necessarily expressible in language, and language is a public phenomenon, in the sense that what words mean is a matter not of the individual's say-so, but of how these words are used by the community. As McDowell himself puts it, in the context of a discussion of an individual's initiation into a shared language,

> the primary form of the ability to mean something by verbal behaviour is the ability to mean what one's words mean, independently of the particularity of one's communicative situation—that is, what they mean in the language, in the ordinary sense, that one is learning to speak. (2002*b*, p. 187)[54]

It follows that no individual has infallible knowledge of what words mean, either in general or on any particular occasion of use, and so no individual has infallible knowledge of the correct way to characterize in words any mental state he or she may be in (or anything else): which is as much as to say that no individual has infallible knowledge of which mental state he or she is in (or of anything else). The attempt to secure the subject's infallibility about his or her own mental states, against the background of the publicity of language, only drives us back to the incoherent notion of a private object, in Wittgenstein's sense, that is, an object which can—and must—be thought and talked about in a language which is supposedly exempt as a matter of logic from the publicity requirement.[55]

Wittgenstein's would-be private linguist, trying to keep a record of his sensations in a private language (he uses 'S' as a name of the

---

[54] This passage occurs in an attack on the later Davidson's idiolectic approach to linguistic understanding. The point of the rider 'primary' is to concede to Davidson that, in a secondary sense, one can on occasion utter words with the intention of meaning by them something other than what they mean in the shared language. That is correct, of course, but does nothing to undermine the basic point that speakers are not infallible about what their words mean: it is not as if one could secure that infallibility simply by using one's words to mean something *other* than what they mean in the public language.

[55] Wittgenstein, *Philosophical Investigations* I, §243.

sensation whose repeated occurrence he is trying to track), is forced into a hopeless retreat:

> What reason have we for calling 'S' the sign for a *sensation*? For 'sensation' is a word of our common language, not of one intelligible to me alone. So the use of this word stands in need of a justification which everybody understands.—And it would not help either to say that it need not be a *sensation*; that when he writes 'S', he has *something*—and that is all that can be said. 'Has' and 'something' also belong to our common language.—So in the end when one is doing philosophy one gets to the point where one would like just to emit an inarticulate sound.—But such a sound is an expression only as it occurs in a particular language-game, which should now be described. (*Philosophical Investigations* I, §261; 1958, p. 93)

Of course individuals very often do know what mental state they are in, and they are often (though by no means always)[56] in a better position to tell that than a third party; but there is no level of generality or depth of innerness at which a subject knows *infallibly* what mental state he or she is in, even when the mental state in question is one with maximally modest content—a mere matter of how things *seem* to the subject to be.

The Cartesian 'I think, I exist' no doubt constitutes a limited exception to this claim, in the following sense. If it genuinely *seems* to me—if I genuinely do *think*—that I, the thinker of this very thought, exist (as the thinker of this very thought), then I am guaranteed to be right about that.[57] For in this case the sheer supposition that I am genuinely thinking *eo ipso* guarantees my existence as a thinking thing, regardless of *what* I am thinking (even if I do not know the meanings of the words in which my thinking is conducted). But this degenerate case has the status of a mere epistemological curiosity:[58] it cannot, as Descartes supposed,

---

[56] As McDowell himself notes, with reference to Freud, 'there are aspects of one's subjectivity that are not transparent to one' (1998c, p. 252 n. 43).

[57] I think we can safely discount Evans's curious idea that the attempt to entertain such a thought might be liable to reference-failure: 1982, p. 253. For if the thought is essayed, someone must be essaying it: cf. McDowell 1990, p. 261.

[58] Cf. Brandom 1994, pp. 294–5.

provide a sound basis for the construction of a dualistic metaphysics. For, as McDowell stresses, relying on prior work by Strawson and Evans,[59] even if I am able to think about myself (the thinker of this very thought) in a way which abstracts from context and environment, that merely *epistemological* achievement does not suffice to yield the *metaphysical* conclusion that features of that context and of my environment—and, in particular, my existence as an element of the objective, spatial order, and one which traces a continuous spatio-temporal path—play no essential role in constituting me as a conscious being.[60]

But, aside from this degenerate case, it remains the case that there is no level of generality or depth of innerness at which a subject knows *infallibly* what mental state he or she is in. To drive the point home, we can make it in terms of what is often taken to be the paradigm of an 'inner' state about which the subject is infallible: being in pain. I can be wrong not only about whether or not I am in pain, but also about whether or not it seems to me that I am in pain. There may be empirical reasons why I can be wrong on both of these counts, but the fundamental reason which concerns us here—a distinctively philosophical one—is that I do not have infallible knowledge of the meaning of the word 'pain', or of any other words which I may care to use in characterizing my mental state. I may have sufficient grasp of the language to ensure that the thought *that I am in pain*—or *that it seems to me that I am in pain*—can indeed be certified as the thought I am essaying; but I may have temporarily forgotten the meaning of the word 'pain', or mistake its

---

[59] McDowell 1994, pp. 99–102. Cf. Strawson 1966, p. 165; Evans 1982, *passim* e.g. p. 176 and ch. 7 esp. pp. 252–3. Some passages in Kant support the Strawson/Evans line: e.g. *KrV*, A359–60, B426–7. But there are also contra-indications, as McDowell points out, esp. in the first edition of *KrV*: e.g. A362–4, A381–2, A400–1.

[60] See 1994, pp. 101–2; 1998*b*, pp. 361–6, 376–7; 1998*f.* As I have indicated already (Ch. II, §5), it is a substantial question, unaddressed by McDowell (although he depends heavily on a favourable verdict), what would suffice to show (and what it means to claim) that my embodiment *as a biological being* is essential to my constitution as a conscious being, inhabiting the space of reasons.

meaning in some other way which does not undermine the hypothesis that it is that very word I aim to employ, that (to echo Evans)[61] it is that very linguistic counter I mean to put forward. And, as Wittgenstein reminds us in the passage quoted above, it will not save the subject's prospects for infallibility if he retreats from the claim that he has (or seems to have) *a pain* to the claim that he has (or seems to have) *something*: that claim too is (necessarily) expressed in a public language, and so leaves a hostage to fortune—to the vagaries of what words actually mean in the public language, a matter on which the subject can of course be an authority, even a very eminent authority, but by no means an infallible one. McDowell is clear that 'the capacity to know *someone else's* meaning that partly constitutes command of a language is fallible'.[62] What has escaped him is the fact that exactly the same fallibility attaches to my capacity to know *my own* meaning.[63]

It is of a piece with McDowell's mistaken ascription of infallibility to subjects in respect of how things seem to them that he claims that 'no distinction between "seems right" and "is right" opens up, with respect to the obtaining of these states of affairs, from the subject's point of view'.[64] If no such distinction opens up from the subject's point of view, that might seem to license the thought that 'inner' objects sit closer to the experiencing subject than 'outer' objects, and that in turn might seem to license the ascription of infallibility to subjects about how things seem to them to be. But if what I have said

---

[61] 1982, p. 69.

[62] 1998*c*, p. 100 n. 33; emphasis added.

[63] Even the following goes too far: 'If one is to have a feasible assertoric project, one needs to be certain of the ability to recognize, not that one has succeeded in saying something true, but that one has succeeded in saying what one intends to say' (1998*c*, p. 323 n. 24). Poor speakers of a language cannot be certain of having that ability; but it would be unacceptable to deny them feasible assertoric projects on that basis. Their capacity to engage in assertoric projects can perfectly well rely on the ability of *other* speakers to recognize whether they have succeeded in saying what they intended to say: this point has the same general structure as one I urge against McDowell below in this chapter and in the next chapter. It represents a form of externalism, and is opposed to an internalist strand which we find in McDowell's writings quite generally.

[64] 1998*b*, p. 311.

so far in this section is correct, this claim must be mistaken, even when its scope is restricted, as it is in the final phrase of the quotation, to the subject's own point of view. The subject's point of view on any state of affairs, including his or her own 'inner' goings-on, is just one point of view on a state of affairs to which others also, necessarily, can have access. This point is acknowledged by McDowell, who agrees that a 'seems right'/'is right' distinction opens up, with respect to states of affairs of the relevant kind, from the 'necessarily thinkable second-person or third-person point of view',[65] and that 'I myself must be able to think of my being thus and so as a case of someone's being thus and so'.[66] But what guarantees this multiplicity of access to 'inner' states of affairs is the fact that our access to any sector of the world is essentially linguistic.[67] That, taken together with the publicity of language, guarantees that a 'seems right'/'is right' distinction opens up quite generally, so that even from the subject's own point of view, contemplating an 'inner' state, the question arises (even if the subject in question is not able to raise it) whether what seems to be a state of affairs with such-and-such a character really is so.

We do not need to be worried that if we relinquish the notion of epistemologically privileged access, in the sense of a circumscribed domain where the subject is guaranteed to be right, we thereby lose the special interiority of (some of) the mental, in the sense that I can know 'from the inside' that I am (for example) in pain, and do not acquire that knowledge in the way I come to know that (for example) I need a haircut. Knowing that you need a haircut is a piece of knowledge acquired 'from the outside', in just the way in which a third party comes to acquire that knowledge of you;[68] and it is certainly plausible that there are many mental states, such as that of being in pain, which I

---

[65] Ibid. Cf. 1994, pp. 37–8; Strawson 1966, pp. 100–1.

[66] 1998*b*, p. 312 n. 31. Cf. 1998*f*, p. 134.

[67] But transcendentally so: that is, cognitive access to any sector of the world requires merely the possibility of (someone's) expressing in (some) language how things are in that sector. This point will be important in much of the rest of this study.

[68] Cf. McDowell 1998*b*, p. 312 n. 33; 1998*f*, p. 131.

can know I have not on the basis of the sort of observation of my appearance or behaviour which would in principle be available to someone else, but rather in a special 'interior' way. But all that this interiority can legitimately amount to is that I know that I am, for example, in pain *by virtue of having the pain*, something that is not true of observers of my pain, who see my pain (and they can indeed *see* it) by virtue of seeing it *expressed in pain-behaviour*. The special status of the interior, so understood, is not threatened by deconstructing the Cartesian conception of privileged access.[69]

One might raise the question whether, despite his express words, McDowell seriously intends the claim of infallibility. Two weaker formulations in the passage from the essay where the claim of infallibility is lodged may suggest that he does not. We are told that how things seem to the subject is 'knowable in a way that is immune to familiar sceptical challenges',[70] and is 'knowable in a way that is immune to the sources of error attending one's capacity to find out about the world around one'.[71] Both of these claims are mistaken in a way that should now be clear: the first because one of the 'familiar' sceptical challenges (it is the challenge posed by Kripke's Wittgenstein)[72] is that we do not know the meanings of the words we use, and our knowledge of how things seem to us is not immune to that challenge (which is not to say that we should in practice be worried by it: my claim has not been that individual subjects do *not* know the meanings of their words, but that they do not know them *infallibly*); the second because, relatedly, although our knowledge of how things seem to us may be immune to *some* sources of error which attend our capacity to find out about the world around us, it is

---

[69] Cf. 1998*b*, pp. 314–19, where McDowell suggests that one knows one's own intentions (perhaps not a case where McDowell would wish to defend the subject's infallibility, but I think the point applies quite generally to the interior in the relevant sense) not by performing an act of inner observation, or by waiting to see what one does (cf. Wittgenstein, *Philosophical Investigations* I, §197), but simply 'by forming them'. Cf. 1998*f*, pp. 141–3.

[70] 1998*c*, p. 242.

[71] 1998*c*, p. 245.

[72] Kripke 1982.

not immune to *all* such sources, as McDowell's formulation implies, for it is not immune to the source of error which consists in failure to know the meanings of one's words. But the fact that these weaker claims are both mistaken in the same way as the claim of infallibility suggests that we may as well take the claim of infallibility as indeed seriously intended by McDowell.[73]

III.5. AYER ON PERCEPTUAL ERROR

Before we move on, it is interesting in this connection to note a shift which occurred in A. J. Ayer's thinking between the 1940s and 1950s. In *The Foundations of Empirical Knowledge*, published in 1940, and in the introduction to the second edition of *Language, Truth and Logic*, published in 1946, Ayer argues that there are propositions about our 'immediate' experience which are incorrigible in the sense that 'it is impossible to be mistaken about them except in a verbal sense'.[74] He distinguishes between 'verbal' and 'factual' error. Of course, he concedes, it is in one sense a question of fact whether one is using words correctly. But, he continues,

the point is that whereas, in the case of most empirical propositions, it would still be possible to doubt them even if there were no doubt that the relevant words were being correctly used, this possibility does not extend to the class of propositions about sense-data that I have been considering. (1969, p. 84)

But when he comes to publish *The Problem of Knowledge* in 1956, Ayer has changed his mind on this point: he now thinks that I can be 'factually', not merely 'verbally', mistaken in the way I describe my

---

[73] Perhaps McDowell has been influenced in this connection by Rorty, who, in his book *Philosophy and the Mirror of Nature* (a work which has played a formative role in McDowell's thinking: cf. 1994, pp. ix–x), despite deconstructing the Cartesian inheritance in so many ways, strangely leaves in place the claim that 'nothing can overrule [the subject's] own sincere report' that he or she is, for example, in pain (1979, pp. 109–10).

[74] 1976, p. 13; 1969, pp. 80–4.

experience.[75] If, for instance, I am shown two lines and asked to say which of them looks longer to me, I can reasonably be in doubt about which answer I should give. In such a case it is hardly plausible to suppose that I am hesitating about the meaning of the English expression 'looks longer than'. I know the meaning of this expression, and my hesitation concerns rather the question of fact: which line *does* look longer? Presumably I can give a wrong answer to this question, and in that case I have made a 'factual', not a 'verbal', mistake about my experience.

Ayer is surely right to revise his position in this way, at least given that he is maintaining his initial distinction between 'verbal' and 'factual' error: but a better revision would have been the more radical option of overthrowing that distinction, and it is a way of putting the point I urged against McDowell in §4 to say that the distinction is ill-grounded. For the price of trying to isolate a class of propositions that can be known with a certainty which is liable to, at most, merely 'verbal' error is—this is the lesson of *Philosophical Investigations* I, §261, and of the Private Language Argument in general—that such propositions will lack content. Indeed this point is conceded by Ayer in his introduction to the second edition of *Language, Truth and Logic*, where he remarks that the propositions to which incorrigibility in the requisite sense attaches do not convey any information either to the individual subject or to anyone else.[76] But that is just to say that they have no content, or, as we should rather put it—taking propositions to *be* contents (of declarative sentences), rather than to *have* content (which would imply that they are merely vehicles for content)—that there are no such propositions. If making a mistake about the meanings of the words which one uses to characterize one's experience is not allowed to count as a factual error, precipitating misdescription of the experience in as thoroughgoing a sense of misdescription as we have, and one which certainly suffices to undermine a claim of incorrigibility or infallibility, then the content of the

---

[75] 1956, pp. 52–68.   [76] 1976, p. 14.

experience itself which one is trying to describe, and about which one is allegedly infallible, evanesces. For we cannot be infallible about something that we cannot infallibly describe: in seeking to preserve infallibility, while conceding the risk of misdescription, one will be compelled to attenuate the content of the relevant speech act, in just the way Wittgenstein so eloquently charts, until that content crumbles to nothing in one's hands. This evanescence of content is attendant upon any attempt to *describe* the experience in the context of a claim of incorrigibility or infallibility, while if one seeks to circumvent the obligation to describe the experience one will be forced back to the humiliating position in which one can do no more than utter a sound which purports to *point* at the experience in question: but 'such a sound is an *expression* only as it occurs in a particular language-game, which should now be described'.[77]

Oddly enough, this consequence had been clearly recognized by Ayer in the main text of *Language, Truth and Logic*, first published in 1936, in a passage to which he explicitly alludes in the part of the subsequently written introduction to which I have been referring. In the fifth chapter of the main text Ayer remarks of the position in question, namely that there exist 'basic propositions' which are incorrigible in virtue of their modestly seeking to do no more than characterize the subject's immediate experience, that such a position

appears to involve a contradiction in terms. It implies that there could be a sentence which consisted of purely demonstrative symbols and was at the same time intelligible. And this is not even a logical possibility. A sentence which consisted of demonstrative symbols [sc. as the propositions in question would have to do, if they are not to risk going beyond the subject's immediate experience] would not express a genuine proposition. It would be a mere ejaculation, in no way characterizing that to which it was supposed to refer. (1976, p. 121)

---

[77] In quoting again the final sentence of *Philosophical Investigations* I, §261 (1958, p. 93), I have placed an emphasis on the word 'expression' in accordance with von Savigny's helpful comment on the text (1994, p. 317).

And he continues:

> The fact is that one cannot in language point to an object without describing it. If a sentence is to express a proposition, it cannot merely name a situation; it must say something about it. And in describing a situation, one is not merely 'registering' a sense-content; one is classifying it in some way or other, and this means going beyond what is immediately given. (1976, p. 121)

This splendid passage was written, it is instructive to remind oneself, over a decade before the publication of *Philosophical Investigations* made the thought it contains commonplace.[78]

Why, when he came to publish the second edition of *Language, Truth and Logic* in 1946, did Ayer resile from his earlier position? Why does he now think that a 'basic proposition', though admittedly incompetent to convey any information, either to the subject who purportedly entertains the proposition or to anyone else, may nevertheless still be said to be 'verified' by the experience it allegedly reports, and indeed conclusively verified, so that in allegedly entertaining the proposition the subject cannot be mistaken, except in a merely 'verbal' sense, about the nature of the experience? How can his earlier insight—that a 'proposition' with no content is quite unable to discharge this, or indeed any, epistemological role—have escaped Ayer ten years after he had displayed such a sure grasp of it? I do not know the answer to these questions. It is of course no explanation, but it may perhaps offer some relevant historical contextualization, to note that the later Wittgenstein is himself not entirely immune to confusion on the point at issue: in a passage in his *Remarks on the Foundations of Mathematics* he claims that I am entitled to regard myself as an infallible guide on which colour is correctly called 'red'. The interlocutor rightly queries this expression of hubris: 'But could I not be under an illusion and be calling the wrong colour "red"?', he asks. Wittgenstein replies confidently 'No', but then a little later adds that 'I can of course even in this case

---

[78] See esp. *Philosophical Investigations* I, §49. See further my 1996, esp. §II.

assume a slip of the tongue, but nothing else'.[79] So what I am infallible about is not what I *say*—since I may make a slip of the tongue—but what I *mean* to say: the prospects of this retreat are, as Wittgenstein himself has made so familiar, hopeless.[80] Even Evans's more cautious remark that 'when the subject conceptualizes his experience in terms of some very elementary concept, such as a simple colour concept like "red", it is not easy to make sense of his making a mistake',[81] plainly goes too far: though it is no doubt true that such mistakes occur relatively infrequently, there is, as I have shown, no difficulty in *making sense* of a mistake in this sort of case.[82]

III.6. EXPERIENCE AND SELF-CONSCIOUSNESS

As we have seen, there is for McDowell a rational connection between experiences and judgements. Such a claim does not, just as such, have to be understood either individualistically or intellectualistically, but McDowell makes it clear in many texts that the rational connection in question must both obtain at the level of the individual's experience and judgement (individualism), and be available to introspection and verbal articulation by the individual for whom an experience serves as a reason for a judgement—that in order to have an experience which justifies a judgement one must be able to state, with understanding, what the justification is

---

[79] *Remarks on the Foundations of Mathematics*, VI, §28 (1978/1989, p. 329).

[80] Note that even if we waive the standard Wittgensteinian objection to any claim to infallibility about what one's words mean, there are straightforward empirical objections to the claim, illuminatingly explored by Reichenbach 1952. Cf. Putnam 1994, pp. 128–9.

[81] 1982, p. 229.

[82] Evans offers an argument (1982, p. 229) for 'such infallibility as there is' in judgements made on the basis of experience, but it involves a slide from (i) its being 'a necessary condition for the subject to possess ... simple observational concepts [like "red"] that he be disposed to apply them when he has certain experiences' to (ii) its being a necessary condition of one's making a judgement with a certain content [e.g., 'That looks red'] that it be a response to a state (the relevant experience) with just that content. The latter (infallibility) does not follow from the former (a weak form of behaviourism).

(intellectualism).[83] In the 'order of justification', the experiences which function (in the first instance in the complex model) as justifiers for judgements are individual appearances, and, so McDowell thinks, one is entitled to demand at least a minimal level of self-consciousness about the relevant experiences, and an at least rudimentary ability to verbalize that self-consciousness, if the 'order of justification' is to be in place and, concomitantly, if thought is to enjoy a sufficient degree of objective purport to render nugatory fears of a free-wheeling, coherentist disengagement from the world.[84] So, for example,

suppose one asks an ordinary subject why she holds some observational belief, say that an object within her field of view is square. An unsurprising reply might be 'Because it looks that way'. (1994, p. 165)[85]

The requirement on subjects that they be able to articulate their reasons for an observational judgement at least to the minimal extent captured in this quotation—the requirement that, as McDowell puts it elsewhere, 'observational authority must be self-consciously possessed'[86]—is a requirement, distinctive of the rationalist and idealist traditions, to the effect that it is a constraint on a subject's being conscious that he or she be self-conscious;[87] and, again, McDowell makes it clear in numerous texts that he endorses this entailment.[88] These requirements have unacceptable implications for infant and

---

[83] See e.g. 1994, pp. 162–6; 1995a, pp. 292–6; 1998a, pp. 408–9; 2000c, p. 335, 2002c, pp. 100–1. Cf. 1998c, p. 427 (on knowledge) together with p. 418 n. 7: 'If knowledge is to be a standing in the space of reasons, someone whose taking things to be thus and so is a case of knowledge must have a reason (a justification) for taking things to be that way', and 'we lose the point of invoking the space of reasons if we allow someone to possess a justification even if it is outside his reflective reach'. On McDowell's individualism, cf. Brandom 1995a, pp. 256–7; 1995b, pp. 901–6; 1998, pp. 373–4.

[84] See here Christensen 2000, pp. 894–5.

[85] Cf. 1994, p. 135 n. 5; 1995a, p. 299; 1998c, pp. 385, 407 n. 18, 434 n. 30; 1998d, p. 439; 1998f, p. 48.

[86] 2002c, p. 101.

[87] See e.g. Kant *KrV,* B131–2 (and throughout the Transcendental Deduction, in both A and B versions); Hegel *Phänomenologie des Geistes,* §III (1988, pp. 118–19).

[88] See e.g. 1994, pp. 47 n. 1, 54, 99–104, 114, 165; 2001, pp. 183–4.

animal mentality, which we will address in Chapter IV; here I wish to focus on the position in its own terms.

III.7. THE 'HIGHEST COMMON FACTOR' CONCEPTION OF EXPERIENCE

If individual lookings, or in general individual appearings—appearings to individual subjects—are pivotal in the 'order of justification', one might ask how the position distances itself from what McDowell has famously called the 'highest common factor' conception of experience. According to this conception, we are confronted, in experience, not directly with features of the world, but with mere proxies for such features, 'inner' appearings whose status and content are not dependent on the veridicality or otherwise of the associated experiences: in other words, we are confronted with the 'highest common factor' of a veridical experience, on the one hand, and an illusory experience which the subject cannot distinguish from a veridical experience, on the other.[89] This conception of experience has been integral to traditional epistemology, and, as I have noted (Chapter I, §3), McDowell has been one of its most vigorous opponents. Against that conception, he has insisted that, in veridical perception, the mind does not stop short at mere proxies, but reaches out and embraces the world. Of course I may be subject to illusion or hallucination, and in such cases it may be reasonable to think of my experience as constituting an intermediary or obstruction, blocking my direct access to the world.[90] But it does not follow from that fact that we have to conceive my access to the world, even in veridical cases, as essentially indirect, dependent on epistemic intermediaries. Rather, when I seem to see (to put it neutrally) that such and such is the case, my mental state is *either* one of really seeing that such and such is the case, *or* of merely seeming to do so.[91] That disjunctive

---

[89] See 1998c, pp. 385–6.   [90] 1994, p. 143.   [91] 1998c, pp. 386–7.

characterization is held to be fundamental: it does not supervene on
a more basic characterization in terms of a 'common core' of experience, supplemented in the veridical case by some relational fact
about the subject's placing in his or her environment. That is, the
left-hand disjunct is not to be conceived as constructed out of the
right-hand disjunct together with some such relational fact.[92]

The question I posed at the beginning of this section acquires
some urgency in the context of a passage in which McDowell first
claims that 'when I see that things are thus and so, I take it that things
are thus and so on the basis of having it look to me as if things are
thus and so', which reads like an endorsement of the 'highest
common factor' conception of experience, but then goes on in
effect to reject a position according to which 'the true starting
point in the space of reasons', from which the subject moves to
factive mental states, must be something common to veridical and
non-veridical appearances, 'like having it look to one as if things are
thus and so'.[93] The apparent antinomy in this passage is mirrored in
a terminological uncertainty present in some of McDowell's writings
on the question whether we should regard experience (specifically
seemings) as *mediating* between world and subject: in one passage
our cognitive contact with the world is held to involve 'the mediation
of seeing that things are thus and so by having it look to one as if
things are thus and so';[94] but elsewhere we are told that experience is
an 'unmediated openness' to the world.[95] Which is it?

Now the reader will recall that I mentioned the mediating role of
experience in the context of my discussion of the simple model of
empirical content in Chapter I (§4): I suggested there that, in
McDowell's view, experience does function as a *mediator* in the
simple model, but not as an *intermediary* or *interface*—not as something that would render the subject's access to the world indirect.
And when I came to discuss McDowell's seeming uncertainty on the
question what is ultimate in the 'order of justification' (§§5–6), I

[92] 1998*c*, p. 284. Cf. my 1995*a*, §1, and Willaschek 2003, pp. 217–30.
[93] 1998*c*, pp. 396–7.   [94] 1998*c*, p. 434 n. 30.   [95] 1998*c*, p. 392.

suggested that McDowell could resolve his apparent indecision between two candidates—the world and experience—by insisting, as he indeed does insist in a number of passages, that neither the world as such, nor experience as such, constitutes the ultimate justifier of empirical judgement, but rather the *experienced world*. Given my strategy in Chapter I, it is natural to ask: why can we not apply a similar approach here, and resolve the verbal tension between the texts I have quoted by saying that McDowell's formulations are really intended to capture the position I expressed at the beginning of this paragraph, that is, the position put by saying that experience is a mediator but not an intermediary? Mediation in general can be either direct or indirect: if we have the indirect kind of mediation in mind, it will be wrong to cast experience as mediating between world and judging subject; but so long as we insist that the mediation in question is of the direct sort, it will be right to say that experience mediates between world and judging subject. Surely, we might aver on McDowell's behalf, there is no difficulty here.

But unfortunately this irenic strategy, though its counterpart worked in Chapter I, will not work here. The reason why it worked in the earlier discussion was that there we were simply considering the *general shape* of McDowell's model of experience: the question of its detailed interpretation had not yet been raised. Specifically, we had not raised the question whether or not the model should be interpreted *individualistically*. But we now have raised this question, and answered it in the affirmative (§6). That puts the simple model of empirical content in a completely new light. We have noted that McDowell agrees, as he must, that veridical and illusory experiences may be indistinguishable from the subject's point of view, from which it follows that a subject's assessment of which sort of experience he or she is enjoying is essentially fallible.[96] Further, McDowell concedes that although subjects may in some cases be able to decide whether an experience enjoyed on any particular occasion is veridical

---

[96] 1998c, pp. 240–1, 385–6.

or illusory, they are not *in general* able to make that judgement.[97]
Given, now, that the 'order of justification', glossed individualistically, requires each and every subject of experience to be able to make,
and justify, observational judgements on the basis of individual
appearances, the question presses: how can we *avoid* casting these
appearances in the role of a 'highest common factor'?

In order to make progress with this question we need to set down
exactly what McDowell's objection to the 'highest common factor'
conception of experience is. In his essays 'Reductionism and the First
Person' and 'Criteria, Defeasibility, and Knowledge', McDowell
suggests that such a conception forfeits any entitlement to the *content*
of the appearance which allegedly forms the common core of veridical and illusory experiences.[98] It is not that we cannot form a
conception of a common core; the point is rather that any such core
will not be metaphysically basic. The idea is that we should not think
of any such common core as having a proprietary content which
comes neat in the illusory case and is supplemented in the veridical
case by a relation to an extraneous fact. Rather, the veridical case is
the metaphysically basic case, in the sense that the content of an
appearance, whether veridical or illusory (and so the content of the
common core), is to the effect that things are, in the world, as the
appearance represents them as being, that is, that things are, in
the world, as they would be if the appearance were veridical. The
content of the common core is *derivative* of the notion of a veridical
experience, and not *vice versa*. The general point here is expressed by
Brandom thus: 'Purporting to represent is intelligible only as purporting to represent *successfully* or *correctly*'.[99] The metaphysical price
of trying to start from a common core conceived as having its own
autonomous content is, in McDowell's view, that we deprive it of
content, and a corollary of that deprivation is that the 'order of

---

[97] See here 1994, p. 113; 1998*c*, pp. 386, 390 n. 37, 404–8.
[98] 1998*b*, pp. 373–4; 1998*c*, p. 388. Cf. 1994, pp. 112–13 with n. 2; 1998*c*,
pp. 242–3, 284.
[99] 1994, p. 72.

justification' will collapse: for a common core which lacks content is not competent to justify an observational judgement.[100] What are we to make of this argument (which I shall call the 'metaphysical argument'), and does it go far enough for McDowell's purposes? We may note immediately that there is a tension between, on the one hand, McDowell's allowing that veridical and illusory cases share a common core, whose content is to the effect that things are, in the world, as the relevant appearance represents them as being and, on the other hand, the doctrine of the *de re* nature of perceptual experience, that is, the doctrine that in perceptual experience one is cognitively related to one's environment in such a way as constitutively to make the content of one's experience (and of relevant singular thoughts one might essay on the basis of one's experience) depend on the existence or otherwise of relevant objects in one's perceptual environment, so that if no appropriate object exists, no experiences with the relevant singular content (and no corresponding singular thoughts) are available (cf. Chapter II, §4). The tension emerges as follows. A veridical perception of a ginger cat on a black and white mat, to revert to our earlier example, will have the representational content that *that* cat is sitting on *that* mat (the demonstratives here picking out the cat and the mat in question). But this content is not available to serve as the putative common core—common to a veridical experience and a

---

[100] Cf. 1998c, p. 407 n. 18, where I take it that substantially the same point is being made (albeit less satisfactorily) in the following passage: 'Our being able to count as, say, seeing that things are thus and so depends on our being properly sensitive (where "properly" expresses a rational assessment) to how things look to us. But it is a mistake to think this dependence is a matter of the appearance's functioning as a starting-point in the space of reasons, with the status of seeing how things are supposedly reconstructed in terms of a sufficiently cogent argument with the appearance as a premise. If the additional premises we can appeal to are restricted to what is available to reason on the interiorized conception of it, no such argument will be sufficiently cogent ....' The passage is faulty because the mistake McDowell wishes to censure does not occur in the sentence beginning 'But it is a mistake ...': that sentence contains a claim (that 'this dependence is a matter ...') which is unobjectionable by McDowell's lights, for it indeed expresses his minimal empiricism (it tells us what it is to 'take experience at face value'). The alleged mistake comes rather in the following sentence, and lies in the interiorized conception of the space of reasons (a conception which is tantamount to taking the 'common core' of veridical and non-veridical experience to have 'autonomous' content).

good illusion. For in the non-veridical case (supposing there is no cat and no mat) there is no such singular content. So the illusory case cannot precisely match the content of the veridical case. The most that can be common to the two types of experience, in respect of the cat and the mat, is a *general* content, to the effect that a cat of such-and-such a description is sitting on a mat of such-and-such a description. Of course the common core will not entirely lack singular content, for it will (at least) represent the cat and the mat as being located somewhere in the subject's egocentric space (we must suppose that the subject is not under an illusion about his or her location in public space: I shall return to this point shortly), and features of that space will necessarily be available to our otherwise deluded subject as potential targets for singular thought. But the point is that whatever degree of singular content the common core has, it will always fall short of the degree of singular content which the relevant veridical experience has, and so cannot precisely match the content of that experience.

But if that is right, it is quite unclear, in the first place, that the general content of the common core, as I have specified it, cannot be autonomous in the sense denied by McDowell. For this general content is *not* exactly as a veridical experience with the same general content represents its objects as being: as I have noted, a veridical experience with that general content also has a fully singular content—for instance, it is not just about *a* cat but about *that* cat, not just about *a* mat but about *that* mat—and so has *more* singular content than the common core, which matches the veridical experience, in at least some crucial respects, only generally. And, in the second place, it is also unclear that, so long as the general content of an experience has appropriate singular anchorage, it cannot serve as a platform on the basis of which the experience's subject may essay a justification for a judgement with fully singular content. In the veridical case the subject can succeed in this endeavour, for in that case the experience will have fully singular content matching the content of the judgement. (I will return to the importance of a match in content between experience and judgement in §8.) In the non-veridical case, by contrast, the endeavour will fail, no judgement with the required singular content being available. By requiring 'appropriate singular anchorage', I mean to exploit the familiar thought that, for subjects to enjoy contentful experiences, whether veridical or non-veridical, they must be able to situate themselves in public space, and that in turn will require them to locate themselves with respect to a range of objects, of which they have direct (*de re*) cognitive grasp, in that space.[101] Even hallucination is a sophisticated cognitive achievement which has to be earned: Macbeth's capacity to hallucinate a dagger—his entitlement to enjoy an experience with *that* (non-veridical) content—depends on his having a direct and largely veridical cognitive grasp of a sufficiency of the objects in his immediate environment, and (relatedly) a grasp of his location in that environment.

Where do these considerations leave the metaphysical argument? The transcendental requirement of what I am calling 'appropriate singular anchorage' does guarantee the metaphysical priority, in one sense, of veridical experience over the common core. The existence and availability of a common core, which can serve as 'fall-back' content for a non-veridical experience, depends, as we have said, on the singular anchorage of the general content of that core in the subject's immediate environment. It follows that the common core depends on veridical experience in the following sense: any experience whose content can be characterized (in the case of non-veridical experience, we will be able to say: can *at best* be characterized) in 'common core' terms—that is, any experience whose content is, at least in part, purely general—will also be, in part, both veridical and singular. But this dependence, in one sense, of the common core— the item available to serve as an experience's content should that experience turn out to be non-veridical—on veridical experience does not derogate from the autonomy of that core, in another sense, at the level of individual experiences. At that level, though an experience characterized in terms of the common core (for

---

[101] Cf. McDowell 1998c, p. 267 n. 11, with reference to Evans 1982, chs. 6 and 7.

example, an experience as of *a* ginger cat on *a* black and white mat) is not independent of veridical experience *tout court* (for the experience is in part constituted by a transcendental dependence on appropriate singular anchorage, and is guaranteed to be veridical to the extent that it has that anchorage), it is independent of the *corresponding* veridical experience—the experience which not merely has 'common core' content but is saturated with singular content (in the case of our example, that would be the experience of *that* ginger cat on *that* black and white mat, with appropriate referential anchorage for the demonstrative expressions).

It follows that, though in one sense the metaphysical argument does establish the metaphysical priority of veridical experiences over the common core, there is an important distinct sense in which it does not. For the fact that there is a logical gap between, on the one hand, the content of the common core under any reasonable conception of it—and any such conception will certainly need to invest the common core with appropriate singular anchorage in subjects' thoughts about themselves and their spatial location, but it will in a number of crucial respects leave the core's content purely general— and, on the other hand, the fully singular content of a particular corresponding veridical experience, guarantees *both* that the content of the common core will be independent of the content of that corresponding veridical experience, *and* that the subject, in having an experience with (at least) the content of the common core, may seek to justify a fully singular thought on that basis, the justification and the thought only succeeding if the relevant experience is veridical, and so imbued with fully singular content.

The metaphysical argument purported to demonstrate the metaphysical priority of veridical experience over the common core—the content common to that experience and a good illusion. But its failure to undermine the autonomy, in the sense I have specified, of the common core represents an epistemological as well as a metaphysical failure. For, given (i) the logical gap I have alluded to between the common core, whose content is, at least in part, purely general, and the fully singular content of the corresponding veridical experience; and given (ii) what I have claimed this gap guarantees, that is, not only the autonomy of the common core, in the specified sense, but also the availability to the subject of an experience with 'common core' content of the option to essay an empirical judgement with fully singular content, purportedly justified on the basis of that experience (but actually justified only if the experience is veridical); and given (iii) the individualistic construction which McDowell puts on the 'order of justification'; it follows that we have been offered no adequate reason, just so far, to rebut an empiricism which holds that, even in veridical experience, minds are confronted in the first instance not with the world but with 'common core' proxies. Indeed the individualistic construction put on the 'order of justification' surely makes that form of empiricism the most natural one for McDowell to adopt.

Of course, as we have seen, there is a transcendental requirement on 'common core' experience that it have (veridical) singular anchorage. So it will be said that the sense in which we have agreed that veridical experience does have metaphysical priority over the common core ensures that a *radical* gap between experience and the world is avoided: surely there is no question of our being trapped in individual private theatres; surely, it will be said, nothing in McDowell's position, as I have interpreted it, commits him to anything so extreme as that. Be that as it may (let us bracket the point for a moment), I do not see that McDowell is entitled, on the basis of the metaphysical argument, and in view of the supplementary considerations I have adduced, to disavow a less radical, but still substantial, empiricism holding that subjects of experience are confronted, in the first instance, not directly with tracts of the world, but with percepts or similar mental intermediaries purportedly representing the world. The content of those percepts, so we are assured by the transcendental requirement, is guaranteed to be at least in part singular and in part veridical, but, from the point of view of the individual subject of experience, that content is not guaranteed to be *fully* singular and *fully* veridical. As they figure in the 'order of justification'—and I stress again that the 'order of justification' must, according to

McDowell, be in place *in toto* at the level of the *individual* subject of experience—a subject's experiences have a content which is, for all he or she knows, at least in part purely general. The transcendental requirement does indeed assure the individual subject that any genuine experience cannot have *exclusively* general content. But there is no transcendental assurance for the individual that any given experience has *more* than 'common core' content; hence there is no transcendental assurance that any fully singular judgements which the subject essays on the basis of his or her experience are going to succeed. And that consequence is enough to introduce an indirectness—not, perhaps, the most radical and worrying kind of indirectness we can think of, but still an indirectness—into the individual subject's dealings, in perception, with the world.

It is worth emphasizing that the point here is not that individual subjects must always reckon with the possibility of their being mistaken; that they must always admit the possibility that a given experience might be at least to some extent non-veridical. This point is agreed on all sides: it is uncontroversial that, for an individual subject, experiential error is always a possibility, however remote that possibility may sometimes seem (and be) in practice. The issue is rather what the status of this concession is; the question we must ask is how the concession impacts on our epistemology. If, like McDowell, one insists that the 'order of justification' has to be in place *in toto* at the level of the individual subject of experience, one cannot avoid the unsettling (if not yet quite devastating) epistemological upshot I have registered. For, to repeat, given that 'common core' content is autonomous in the specified sense, and given that there is no transcendental guarantee, for the individual subject, that he or she is, on any given occasion, enjoying an experience with more than 'common core' content—with fully singular content—it follows that, by insisting that each individual subject establish, or actualize, the 'order of justification' at the point of his or her individual experiential engagement with the world, McDowell in effect (and unintentionally, of course) traps the individual subject behind experiential proxies which, though they are (so we are assured) transcendentally guaranteed, via the requirement of appropriate singular anchorage, to be at least in part veridical, are not guaranteed simply to disclose the world.

But if this is right, we may well suspect that the extreme consequence I temporarily bracketed above cannot, after all, be so easily avoided by McDowell as the line of thought we have rehearsed seems to grant him. Catastrophe is threatened by the presence of a small but vital qualification which must be written into the transcendental guarantee. The reader may have noticed the give-away: a proviso I included without explanation or comment in a sentence which occurred in my last paragraph but one. I said: 'The transcendental requirement does indeed assure the individual subject that any genuine experience cannot have *exclusively* general content.' Reread this sentence with the emphasis shifted to the word 'genuine'. The point is then this: only a *genuine* experience—not just anything that the subject might *take* to be an experience—comes within the purview of the transcendental guarantee. But if the 'order of justification' is to be set up at the level of the individual subject, it is clear that, at that level, there can be no assurance, transcendental or otherwise, that a given mental state, however much the subject would like it to count as an experience, really is an experience. Macbeth's hallucination, we said, had to enjoy appropriate singular anchorage even to merit so much as the title of a hallucination. But individual subjects have, in general, no individually constituted guarantee that their purported experiences even succeed in being hallucinations, let alone anything of a cognitively more secure nature. That is, *from the perspective of McDowell's individual subject*, struggling to establish or actualize the 'order of justification' at the point of his or her (purported) engagement with the world, in order to advance to the making of judgements, there can be no assurance that any given mental state is an experience of any kind, even nonveridical. And of course, ultimately, even so much as the availability of a thought with the content, whether true or false, *that one has an experience* is not something that can be constituted by the individual working on his or her own; even so much as the existence of a mental state *of any kind* is not within the remit of an individual to constitute on his or her own. It follows that McDowell's insistence that we locate the 'order of justification' at the level of the individual subject of experience has, it seems, as an unhappy consequence not merely that the task of establishing that very order cannot be completed: worse, it cannot even be begun. The insistence precipitates a Cartesianism which is exposed to a scepticism of the most destructive sort. The radical gap between experience and world which we temporarily averted on McDowell's behalf above cannot, it seems, ultimately be avoided by him.

So far as I am aware, the closest McDowell comes to addressing the epistemological issue which examination of his metaphysical argument renders pressing is in the following passage in his essay 'Criteria, Defeasibility, and Knowledge':

Suppose someone is presented with an appearance that it is raining. It seems unproblematic that if his experience is in a suitable way the upshot of the fact that it is raining, then the fact itself can make it the case that he knows that it is raining. But that seems unproblematic precisely because the content of the appearance is the content of the knowledge. And it is arguable that we find that match in content intelligible only because we do *not* conceive the objects of such experiences as in general falling short of the meteorological facts. That is: such experiences can present us with the appearance that it is raining only because when we have them as the upshot (in a suitable way) of the fact that it is raining, the fact itself is their object; so that its obtaining is not, after all, blankly external [sc. to the mind]. (1998c, pp. 388–9)[102]

I say that this is the closest McDowell comes to addressing the epistemological issue; but evidently it does not come very close. In fact it comes no closer than telling us what would have to be argued if the epistemological claim—the claim that the objects of experience do not, in general, fall short of the worldly facts—were to be made good. What would have to be shown, to put it in the terms I have been using, is, first, that we have a transcendental guarantee that we

---

[102] Cf. 1998c, pp. 242–3.

do indeed, in general, enjoy genuine—contentful—experiences; and secondly that these experiences do not, in general, have merely 'common core' content, or in other words that their content does not, in general, fall short of fully singular content.

The most promising way, in my view, to supply these desiderata would be to address the second one directly, in the (surely reasonable) expectation that if we are able to satisfy that desideratum, the first one will thereby be met *ambulando*. My suggestion on the score of meeting the second desideratum is that we invigorate the transcendental requirement (the requirement on 'common core' experience that it have veridical singular anchorage), on the basis of an argument from the nature of communication. We can, I think, strengthen the import of the transcendental requirement by reminding ourselves what holds it in place. The rejection of a Given element in experience brings in its train a general requirement on experiential content that it be conceptual, in the more modest of the two senses available to this word in context of the present study (Chapter II, §6), that is, in the sense that the content of any experience must be expressible in language (not in the sense that that content must be available to a critical and reflective faculty possessed by the subject of the experience, and be articulable by that subject). Now language, as Wittgenstein taught us, is essentially a public means of communication, and it is plausible that the operation of this constraint on language presupposes the availability of a world of entities fit to serve as common objects of reference, including genuinely singular (*de re* or essentially object-involving) reference, and thereby to ground mutual understanding between communicators. For a shared language imports shared truths, shared truths are (in the first instance) shared true sentences, and the semantic analysis of sentences necessarily deploys a referential relation between subsentential linguistic expressions and objects of reference. If this line of thought (which would clearly need to be expanded in a full account)[103] is

---

[103] I will say more about the theoretical status of the reference relation in Ch. VI, §2 below.

correct, its effect is surely to transform the mere requirement that experiences with 'common core' content have appropriate singular anchorage into a requirement that experiences have, in general (to the extent that is necessary to ground the possibility of communication on their basis), world-involving and fully singular content.

That, at any rate, is what I take to be the most fruitful line to pursue if one is engaged in the project of closing the epistemological gap between subject and world (or of ensuring that no gap opens up in the first place). But no such strategy is followed by McDowell, and the fact that his metaphysical argument is open to the objections I have raised in this section suggests, in the context of the individualism in his position which we have noted, that, official intentions notwithstanding, the individual appearings which figure pivotally in the 'order of justification', as McDowell construes that, are epistemic intermediaries in something like the sense embraced by the 'highest common factor' conception of experience, a consequence which, by McDowell's own lights[104] as well as by mine, can hardly be regarded as satisfactory. On the alternative strategy that I have briefly sketched, by contrast, there is, crucially, no requirement that the 'order of justification' be established at the level of the individual subject of experience: on the contrary, the Wittgensteinian considerations I deployed, insisting as they do on the essentially shared nature of language, are thoroughly anti-individualistic in tendency. So the radical scepticism which, as we have seen, hangs over McDowell's unwitting but for all that real commitment to Cartesianism is simply not in the offing for my alternative strategy. It is ironic in this context that McDowell claims an advantage for his doctrine of disjunctivism over its more traditional rivals in the debate with an epistemological sceptic; for, in view of his individualistic approach to the 'order of justification', it has actually turned out that he is in the same boat as his traditionalist rivals, epistemologically speaking, and accordingly that he embraces, as much as they do, a position which is wide open to a devastating scepticism. How, given this upshot,

[104] See here again 1998*b*, pp. 373–4; 1998*c*, pp. 369–94, esp. 392–4; pp. 396, 402 n. 10.

disjunctivism is supposed to turn the tables on the sceptic is obscure to me. But I do not want to take that issue further here.[105] My main concern here is to elaborate the individualistic interpretation I have offered of the way in which McDowell connects experiences and judgements: to that I now turn.

III.8. McDOWELL'S INDIVIDUALISM

I have claimed that McDowell understands the rational connection between experiences and judgements individualistically and intellectualistically, but more needs to be said about this, if only because the soubriquet of individualism is one which McDowell himself rejects.[106] McDowell does insist that a subject's reason for a judgement must be available to introspection and verbal articulation by that very subject (the position which I am calling intellectualism); but he also takes it that the possession of these conceptual capacities requires the subject to have been initiated into a communal tradition and shared language.[107] That initiation 'can transform the capacities of an individual considered just as such'.[108] To that extent McDowell's position has an externalist flavour—individual subjects have to be constituted as such by membership of a linguistic community—

---

[105] The main difficulty in seeking to deploy disjunctivism against epistemological scepticism is that the sceptic can simply shift the focus of attack: the problem is no longer (to put it compendiously) how to get from appearance to reality, but how to satisfy oneself that one is located on the veridical disjunct (on which, *if* one is located there, one's contact with reality is assured). No doubt the disjunctivist would come off better from the scrap with the sceptic if McDowell were right that his traditionalist rivals could not make out an entitlement to the *content* of the proxy mental states with which, on their view, the subject is confronted in the first instance. But it is at just this point that, as I have indicated, there is a lacuna in McDowell's argumentation; and, as we have seen, it turns out that his own position faces precisely the sceptical meltdown which confronts his rivals, and for the same reason. In all this, disjunctivism seems to me to do no more than furnish an idle epicycle. On this and the other topics of this section see further: Brueckner 1993; my 1995*a*, esp. §IV; Christensen 2000, pp. 899–900; Kern 2000, pp. 928–32; Wright 2002*b*; Pritchard 2003.

[106] 1995*a*, pp. 292–6; 1998*a*, pp. 408–9; 2002*c*, pp. 104–5.

[107] 1994, pp. 124–6, 184–7; 2002*b*. Cf. 1986, pp. 381–2.

[108] 1998*a*, p. 409.

but it remains internalist to the extent that it insists that the individuals so constituted must have fully self-conscious and verbalizable access to every stage of the 'order of justification'. His view is that the 'order of justification' cannot be parcelled out between individuals; rather, where an individual participates in any stage of that order (has a justifying experience, or forms a justified judgement), the order must be in place, *in toto*, within that individual, in such a way as to grant that individual fully self-conscious and verbalizable access to it.

McDowell explicitly opposes a Davidsonian brand of externalism, which simply bypasses individual experiences as justifiers of judgements, and locates the rationality of observation reports in the possibility of their certification as such from the theoretical perspective of the radical interpreter.[109] (An alternative, Heideggerian account would trace empirical content to the individual's actions in the world, rather than individual experiences.)[110] McDowell complains that the absence of individual experiential justifiers from Davidson's picture—the repudiation, that is, of an even minimal empiricism—makes it a mystery how observational judgements can have empirical content. Davidson's well-known transcendental argument that a system of beliefs must be mostly true 'comes too late', by McDowell's lights, because it presumes—what it has not yet earned the right to presume—that observational beliefs or judgements do indeed have empirical content.[111]

The issues here are delicate, and we need to distinguish two questions. First, there is the question whether McDowell is right about the need for some individual experiences to figure in the 'order of justification'; that is, whether he is right that it is unacceptable to suppose that observational judgements might be rationally sensitive

[109] This kind of externalism is urged, against McDowell, by Brandom in his 1995*a*; 1995*b*; 1998; 2002; and is set out at length in his 1994 (see esp. ch. 4).

[110] See here Glendinning and de Gaynesford 1998; Habermas 1999, pp. 40–8; Denejkine 2000, §III.

[111] See 1994, pp. 16–17, 68, 112 n. 2, 144; 1995*a*, p. 287; 1999*a*, pp. 95–7. McDowell has a fondness for objections of the 'too late' form: see e.g. 1994, p. 186; 1998*c*, pp. 251, 405, and 442. I will comment on the significance of this objection in the present context shortly.

to the layout of reality without requiring that that sensitivity be routed via individual experiences. In effect this is the question whether he is right that it is philosophically incumbent on us to adopt some form of empiricism. To anticipate, I shall answer this question affirmatively. But secondly, there is the question what follows from an affirmative answer to the first question, assuming that it is correct: does it follow that any degree of self-consciousness or verbal articulacy is called for in any given individual who enjoys such justifying experiences? In other words, should we, as theorists, follow McDowell in putting an internalist construction on these individual experiences, or should we instead look favourably on a position which combines some form of (no doubt minimal) empiricism with externalism? I shall endorse the latter option.

On the first question, it is indeed hard to see how an observational judgement that things are thus and so could be rationally grounded in the way the world is if it were not based on an act of perceiving that things are thus and so, which, as we have agreed (§7), is a conceptual state in the modest sense, that is, it is endowed with the (schematic) propositional content *that such and such is the case*.[112] But as soon as it is conceded that a subject's *seeing* (say) that things are thus and so plays an epistemological role in the 'order of justification' of (a range of) observational judgements, it is surely plausible that a correlative notion of the seen object's *looking* thus and so must equally be granted epistemological significance. And, as McDowell remarks, 'the concept of something's looking thus and so to one is not the concept of the thing's being such that on looking at it one becomes inclined to say that it is thus and so'[113]—in general: the concept of something's *appearing* thus and so is not the concept of the thing's being such that on *perceiving* it one becomes inclined to say that it is thus and so (taking the appearing/perceiving pair to be the generalization, applicable to any sense modality, of the specifically visual looking/seeing pair)—for any such dispositionalist

[112] McDowell 1994, pp. 9, 26.
[113] 1995*a*, p. 298. Cf. 1994, pp. 61–2.

account omits the normativity governing the relation between something's appearing thus and so and the judgement that it is thus and so. There must be a normative connection, at the level of individual experiences and judgements, between experiences and the judgements which they justify.[114]

Now it might be held that the reason why it is so evident that the first question must be answered in this way is that the connection between question and answer is an essentially trivial one. For, it might be said, the answer simply spells out what it is for a judgement to be *observational*; or, as McDowell puts it, 'experience is *simply the way in which* observational thinking is directly responsive to facts'.[115] That is, it is just definitional of observational judgement that its rational responsiveness to empirical facts gets routed via experience. But I do not think that this suggestion can be quite right. For, as well as accommodating a normative connection between experiences and corresponding judgements, we must acknowledge that the relation constituted by that connection is an internal, not an external, one.[116] That is, it is not enough, if subjects' judgements are to be *based on* relevant experiences (whether enjoyed by them or not: the need for this rider will become clear shortly), that those judgements should merely reliably covary with features of reality to which these (or other) subjects have access through one or more of the sense modalities, and that our subjects should know that their judgements so covary with such features, and so know that the normative connection obtains— know that they ought, given certain experiences, to make certain

---

[114] The *locus classicus* for the rejection of dispositionalist reconstructions of normativity is Kripke 1982, pp. 22–37. Cf. McDowell 1998*b*, pp. 226, 328–32; Brandom 1994, pp. 28–9.

[115] 1998*a*, p. 406, emphasis added. Brandom agrees that insofar as one has a reason for an observational judgement that things *are* thus and so, it is 'that things *are* thus and so, or, more carefully, that one can *see* that things are thus and so' (1995*a*, p. 257): this is in effect to grant McDowell's point (cf. Brandom 2002, p. 99). But, as I go on to indicate in the text, the admission that experience figures, in this sense, in the 'order of justification' does not tell us whether we should interpret these justifying experiences internalistically (as McDowell wants) or externalistically (as Brandom and I would prefer, though in different ways, as I shall explain below).

[116] See here Brewer 1999, esp. chs. 2–3.

judgements. If that is the best our subjects can do, their knowledge of how things are in the world would be merely operational or instrumental.[117] To secure suitably direct—not merely instrumental—experience-based knowledge of the layout of reality, the relevant experiences—and correlatively also the appearances presented by reality—must have *subjectively available contents* matching the contents of the corresponding justified judgements.[118] Otherwise experiences would be, as McDowell puts it, 'opaque' rather than 'transparent', in the following sense: if one knew enough about one's causal connections with the world, one could no doubt *infer* the layout of the world on the basis of one's experiences, so conceived, but the experiences would not themselves *disclose* the world to one; rather, they would 'have an epistemological significance like that of bodily feelings in diagnosing organic ailments'.[119]

In Wittgensteinian terminology, to characterize experiences as opaque in the objectionable sense would be classify them as *symptoms*, merely externally related to the world and requiring a theory to reconstruct their aetiology, rather than as *criteria*, internally related to the world and thereby essentially disclosing it.[120] But it is surely essential to experiences that they disclose the world to us in the

---

[117] Cf. Brewer 1999, pp. 218–19.

[118] I am here in effect siding with McDowell in the debate he conducts with Brandom about the notorious 'chicken-sexers', who allegedly possess the ability reliably to classify chickens as male or female, though not on the basis of male or female 'looks'. McDowell's view is that any such ability does not equip its possessor with the kind of observational knowledge which one acquires when, for example, one judges, on the basis of its visual appearance, that an object is red: McDowell 1995*a*, pp. 296–8; 2002*a*, pp. 279–81. Brandom disagrees: 2002, pp. 97–100. Wright in effect sides with Brandom when he states that 'justification accrues [sc. to empirical belief or judgement] in virtue of (one's being aware of) something's happening which one is entitled to take as an indicator of the truth of the candidate belief, and it is all the same whether that something is a McDowellian experience that *p* or, say, a loud noise' (2002*a*, p. 170). Wright's claim is that there need be no internal connection—no match of content—between justifying experience and justified judgement, but that an external relation, provided it both is and is known to be sufficiently reliable, is enough; and that is what I think we must deny.

[119] See 1994, p. 145.

[120] Cf. McDowell 2000*a*, p. 12. I have formulated this sentence in such a way as to remain aloof from the major exegetical crux facing the interpreter of Wittgenstein's views on criteria, namely the question whether he took them to be defeasible or not. On this

criterial sense—by virtue of a match between their subjectively available content and the world—and, equally, that they achieve this disclosure by virtue of being conceptually (in the modest sense, i.e., propositionally) structured: this much we may legitimately salvage from the wreckage of McDowell's transcendental argument (§1). Experiences disclose the world to us by virtue of the fact that, as Wittgenstein put it, 'we understand their language'.[121] Their disclosure of the world is untheoretical and immediate, not mediated by theory. Acquiring experience is a matter of having one's eyes opened to the world; it is not a matter of mastering a theoretical discipline such as a natural science.

An alternative way of expressing the necessary point might exploit the traditional distinction between nominal and real essence: for one can say that, on the view to be rejected, according to which we can at best infer the layout of the world on the basis of our experiences, experiences are being conceived to have content as a matter of their real, not nominal, essence. That is, their content—what they tell us about the layout of the world—is conceived on this view to be fixed by the nature of our (realm-of-law) causal connections with the world, something which is up for (and requires) empirical investigation; correspondingly, our grasp of that content could be no better than inductively based. But, as McDowell correctly observes, it is a mistake to conceive experiential content in this way: the truth is rather that experiences disclose the world to us not by dint of having a concealed content which it takes scientific effort to uncover, as it took scientific effort to reveal the atomic structure of gold, but by displaying their content openly to those who are in a position to make judgements on their basis.

---

issue (with ample references to the primary texts and to relevant secondary literature), see McDowell's 'Criteria, Defeasibility, and Knowledge' (1998*c*, pp. 369–94), where he repudiates the orthodox view that Wittgenstein took criteria, in his special sense, to be defeasible, and my 1995*a*, where I try to defend the orthodox interpretation. I recur to the issue briefly in n. 146 below.

121 *Philosophical Investigations* I, §355 (1958, p. 113). Cf. Ch. VI, §5 below.

I suggest that it is in the context of this point about the right connection between experience and judgement that it makes best sense to locate McDowell's objection against Davidson's transcendental argument that beliefs (or judgements) are, in their nature, veridical, that a system of beliefs must be mostly true. McDowell's objection, it will be recalled, was that Davidson's argument 'comes too late' to secure empirical content. It is tempting to dismiss this objection on the basis that it surely does not matter *when* a constitutive or necessary condition is specified, so long as it is specified: after all, it is not as though one had, absurdly, to earn the right to call something an *X before* one was entitled to go about specifying constitutive or necessary conditions for being an *X*; rather, the entitlement is earned *pari passu* as the specification is given. McDowell's way of putting his objection does give some colour to this dismissal; but I think the point of his criticism of Davidson is really this. We should allow, on McDowell's behalf, that Davidson's transcendental argument does specify a necessary condition on belief or judgement, whether empirical or other: it is indeed in the nature of belief and judgement, in general, to be veridical.[122] But Davidson's argument gives us no assurance that a given belief or judgement is of the right sort to qualify as having *empirical* content. We can have that assurance—so we may, I think, take McDowell to be saying—only if beliefs and judgements are hooked up in the right way to *experiences*: only if they are justified by experiences in virtue of a match in subjectively available content; alternatively expressed, only if the justifying experiences disclose the world not as mere symptoms disclose facts, but as Wittgensteinian criteria do; alternatively again, only if these experiences have their content as a matter of nominal (openly displayed), not real (secret and scientifically discoverable), essence.

It is time to take stock. It seems fair to characterize McDowell's response to our first question as involving a kind of foundationalism

---

[122] *Pace* Schantz 1996, pp. 142–3. The argument, which I do not here rehearse, is found in a number of places in Davidson's writings: there is a good statement of it at 1984, p. 168.

about lookings or, in general, appearings;[123] and, as far as that goes, I am here agreeing with McDowell about that foundationalism. In saying that McDowell's position is foundationalist with respect to appearings, I do not mean to suggest that he takes them to be 'absolute starting points' in the space of reasons:[124] we can join him in concurring with Sellars's insistence that 'if there is a logical dimension in which other empirical propositions rest on observation reports, there is another logical dimension in which the latter rest on the former'.[125] But if observational reports (or, in general, appearings, whether they are reported or not) are not foundational in the absolute sense which Sellars here rejects, it remains the case that we must find a pivotal role for individual experiences—appearings to individuals—in the 'order of justification'. Meeting this requirement indeed commits us to a form of minimal empiricism, as McDowell says, but it does not, as such, commit us to McDowell's version of the doctrine. The empiricism to which we are committed by the need to locate individual experiences in the 'order of justification' is even less substantial than the one McDowell urges on us—we might dub it a 'minimalist' empiricism—because in merely placing individual appearings in the 'order of justification', we undertake no obligation to identify appearings with impressions, understood as (the upshots of) causal transactions, and we undertake no obligation to support any of the doctrines I have examined in this chapter, in connection with the suspicion that McDowell unwittingly commits himself to an interface, rather than a conduit, conception of experience, and which I have rejected, namely: the location of freedom between experience and judgement; the characterization of perception as a mere opportunity to know, as opposed to knowledge itself; and the crediting of the subject of experience with infallibility about how things seem to him or her to be.

---

123 Cf. Gibson 1995, p. 276.
124 That is, that he takes them to be starting points in the sense of the foundationalism which he considers, and rejects, in his essay 'Knowledge by Hearsay' (1998c, pp. 414–43, esp. pp. 430–1 with n. 27); cf. 1995a, p. 284, and other passages cited in Ch. I n. 11.
125 Sellars 1956, §38 (1997, p. 78).

In refusing to identify appearings with impressions, understood as (the upshots of) causal transactions, we concomitantly disembarrass ourselves of any obligation to recognize the existence of a distinctively rational species of causation: we can retain our prejudice, if that is what it is, that causation is nomological, and accordingly belongs exclusively to the realm of law, and that reasons, McDowell's unsupported and unelucidated assertion to the contrary notwithstanding, cannot be causes. But most importantly, in accepting the very modest empiricism imported by the concession that we must find a place for individual appearings in the 'order of justification', we incur no obligation to follow McDowell in putting an individualistic and intellectualistic construction on the individual experiences which thus figure in the 'order of justification'. That implies an answer to the second of our two questions.

For, having agreed that McDowell's response to the first question is correct, we must insist that it does not follow from the acknowledgement that appearings have an epistemologically pivotal role to play in the 'order of justification' that any degree of self-consciousness or verbal articulacy is called for in any given individual who enjoys such justifying experiences. More generally, it does not follow from the fact that an experience that p will serve to justify the observational judgement that p and that, contrariwise, the observational judgement that p is (can only be) justified by an experience that p, that the very same subject who enjoys that experience must make, or even be capable of making, the corresponding judgement, or that the very same subject who makes an observational judgement must enjoy, or even be capable of enjoying, the corresponding experience. In other words, even though, as I have agreed, McDowell is right, as against Davidson, that individual experiences must figure in the 'order of justification', on pain of loss of empirical content, it does not follow that the 'order of justification', so constituted, must be in place, as a whole, *within each individual subject*; in order to secure empirical content for observational judgements, it suffices that the 'order of justification' be instantiated *between individuals*.

The key point is this: from the agreed fact that experience is essentially conceptual in the modest sense—that is, that it has a propositionally structured content expressible in language (that it has a content of the schematic form: *that such and such is the case*)—it does not follow that it is conceptual in the richer sense that its conceptual content (modestly understood) is necessarily available to a critical and reflective faculty possessed by the subject of the experience. Of course a propositionally structured experience by its nature justifies the judgement which expresses the propositional content of the experience: as we have seen, there necessarily is that kind of close, internal relation between them. So we need not repudiate a minimalist empiricism which locates individual experiences within an 'order of justification' established at least interpersonally (intersubjectively). But we have seen no good reason to place the restrictions favoured by McDowell on who must be able to make the judgement warranted by a given experience, or who must have the experience warranting a given judgement; that is, we have seen no good reason to insist that the 'order of justification' must, in every case, be established not merely interpersonally (intersubjectively), but also intrapersonally.[126]

In closing this section, it is worth noting that the excrescences attaching to McDowell's 'minimal' empiricism—the presence of the supernumerary doctrines which my minimalist empiricism extrudes—show how far his position is from being a form of quietism—the patient assembling of truistic reminders for a particular

---

[126] There are structural parallels between my argument here and Byrne's objection to McDowell in his 1995, §1; but Byrne's concerns differ somewhat from mine. Cf. also Schantz 2001, pp. 176–8; 2004, pp. 102–10. Schantz connects his (correct) rejection of McDowell's requirement on subjects of experience that they be capable of self-consciously articulating the content of their experiences with the (incorrect) assertion of the possibility that experience with non-conceptual content in the radical sense (experience which presents the subject with a 'world' which is, in the first instance, an 'ineffable lump, devoid of structure or order': McDowell 1998*b*, p. 178) might rationally ground judgements. I agree with McDowell in rejecting that possibility (the Myth of the Given). How infant and animal experiences can be fully conceptual, in the modest sense (i.e., propositionally structured), despite their subjects' lack of self-consciousness or verbal articulacy, will be the topic of the next chapter.

purpose—as some commentators, and McDowell himself in some moods, would have us believe.[127] In fact even my minimalist version of empiricism could not be described as quietist: it is a substantial, and contestable, claim that individual experiences must figure in the 'order of justification', and that the 'order of justification', so constituted, is a decisive moment in the establishment of empirical content. These central empiricist claims, which are retained in my minimalist version of the doctrine, are very far from being uncontroversial: they have been contested, not only from within the analytic tradition (by Davidson and Brandom, for example), but also, as we noted above, from outside that tradition by thinkers who seek to ground empirical content in our engagement with the world as *agents* rather than as *subjects*. So empiricism, even in my minimalist version (let alone McDowell's more embellished version), is by no means a trite thesis that everyone accepts, and Davidson is quite wrong to imply that giving up what he calls the third dogma of empiricism—the dualism of conceptual scheme and Given—leaves nothing distinctive left to call empiricism.[128]

McDowell likes to think of his philosophy of experience as enjoying pre-theoretical plausibility, as a position which it is natural to adopt in advance of being exposed to traditional philosophy's corrupting influence, and as the default position to which we automatically revert when we have escaped its allurements: he likes to think of his philosophy of experience as achieving the Wittgensteinian ideal of doing no more than reciting truisms.[129] In response to a suggestion made by Paul Davies that he takes a step 'from substantive thesis to truism', McDowell writes that 'there is no substantive thesis in the relevant sense; there is no step'.[130] That is to say: there is just truism. But the pretension to do no more than rehearse truisms is as unpersuasive in McDowell's case as it is in Wittgenstein's. To take

---

[127] See e.g. McDowell 1994, pp. 85–6, 175–8; de Gaynesford 2004, pp. 26–8, 177–9.
[128] 1984, p. 189.
[129] 1994, pp. 27–8. McDowell here refers us to Wittgenstein's *Philosophical Investigations* I, §95; relevant too is §128.
[130] 2000c, p. 342.

one example of many: in Chapter II, §1, I aired the suggestion that the notion of an impression, which plays a key role in McDowell's understanding of the way experience secures empirical content for judgement, is properly a theoretical notion. If that is right, it will not be part of our everyday understanding of the perceptual access to the world which we enjoy that in experience the world *impresses* itself, in any literal sense, on subjects.

It does indeed strike me as quite plausible that the notion of an impression is a theoretical one, and so not available to figure in an avowedly quietistic philosophy of experience: but it must be acknowledged that any substantiation of this point would have to deal with the general difficulty of separating, in a non-question-begging way, what in a position is innocent of theory from what is a product of the influence of traditional philosophy. Of course that difficulty—which is possibly intractable—confronts supporters as well as opponents of the putatively quietistic status of any given claim; indeed one would have thought that, if there is a question of onus here, that onus should be shouldered by the friends rather than the foes of quietism. For we should not lose sight of the obvious point (this in itself is a serious theoretical difficulty for quietists) that the doctrine of quietism, though anti-philosophical in intent, is constitutively a *philosophical doctrine*—those who are innocent of philosophy could hardly be described as *quietists*—just as the myth of Arcadia is not for uncouth swains but for the sophisticated, who scarce themselves know how to hold a sheep-hook, but who have read their Theocritus. These observations strongly suggest, I think, that quietism, as a philosophical position, is close to being self-refuting. (Davies draws an illuminating comparison in this regard between quietism and would-be anti-metaphysical positions such as verificationism.)[131] But even if quietism can, in the abstract, establish its credentials, and even if it could be shown that a given position was determinately quietistic, what follows? Untutored common sense can be, and often has been, wrong; a position does not gain plausibility for itself

---

[131] 2000, p. 314.

merely by establishing its quietistic credentials. After all, in many ages and cultures a belief in the existence of a god or gods, in just the sense in which, as we have seen (Chapter II, §5), McDowell is probably obliged to repudiate it, has had the status of being sheer common sense. But does that fact constitute even a *prima facie* argument for theism? Surely not. If McDowell's minimal empiricism is quietistic, then my minimalist empiricism is even more so; but I do not demand any recognition for it on that account.

III.9. EXTERNALISM AND THE INDIVIDUAL

So far as I can see, McDowell in effect makes two responses to an externalism of the sort I have canvassed in the previous section: but they both fail. The first is a simple appeal to authority:

In the reflective tradition we belong to, there is a time-honoured connection between reason and discourse. We can trace it back at least as far as Plato: if we try to translate 'reason' and 'discourse' into Plato's Greek, we can find only one word, *logos*, for both. (1994, p. 165)[132]

McDowell's objection to an externalism along the lines I have sketched is that such a position 'cannot respect this connection', but 'has to sever the tie between the reasons for which a subject thinks as she does and the reasons she can give for thinking that way' (ibid.). At this point in his text McDowell is responding to a position which allows the individual subject some measure of self-consciousness and verbal articulacy, but does not require that subjects have access to the reasons for their observational judgements. Of course the position I mooted in the last section was more radical than that, for it admitted the possibility that a subject of experience might—like an infant or an animal—enjoy no degree of self-consciousness or verbal articulacy at all; and McDowell's argument here *a fortiori* rejects the more radical along with the less radical

---

132 Cf. 1998*b*, p. 169.

possibility. But what is the argument? Even if we accept the appeal to authority, it goes no distance to controverting the externalism I have put forward. Let us by all means grant, as I readily do, that there is an intimate connection between reason and discourse: for it would certainly be wrong to maintain, as one critic has, in opposition to the claimed connection, that 'we will never be able to make sense of perception and its relation to belief until we abandon the idea that there is a constitutive connection between reason and discourse, however time-honoured it may be'.[133] Still, McDowell does nothing to show that the connection in question is anything other than *general*, to the effect that genuine reasons must be expressible in discourse *by someone* (at some time). He does not show that what counts as a reason for an individual subject must be expressible or open to introspection *by that very subject*.

In the context McDowell's reference to Plato strikes me as bearing somewhat unfortunate associations: it reminds one of Socrates' repeated, and surely misguided, insistence that successful candidates for possessing a virtue must enjoy a significant measure of verbal articulacy and self-consciousness, even to the extent of being able to produce a *definition* of the virtue they purport to possess. Admittedly, as far as the requirements of virtue are concerned, McDowell makes it clear that he would not wish to go as far as Socrates: he allows that a quite modest degree of articulacy can suffice in the virtuous agent.[134] And his contention that a subject of experience need possess only modest verbal and reflective skills indicates that it would be unfair to enrol McDowell in that Socratic branch of our intellectual inheritance which seeks to privilege the kind of reflective activity in which *philosophers* engage, taking that to be the paradigm of thought in general (thought construed as an internalized *elenchus*).[135] Nevertheless, however minimal the requirements of verbal articulacy placed on the virtuous agent and (more to the point in the present context) on the subject of experience, the suspicion remains

---

[133] Heck 2000, p. 520.   [134] 1998*b*, p. 51.
[135] See 1994, p. 165 and the discussion of it in §6 above. Cf. 1998*b*, pp. 45–6.

that McDowell is committed to something like the Platonic image of thought as internal speech,[136] an image which, plausibly, implies that creatures which are incapable of speech (and so incapable of internal speech) are incapable of thought. The suspicion is fuelled by observation of the way the image, under a certain natural application of it, neatly motivates precisely the denial of experience to languageless creatures which, as we shall see in more detail in the next chapter, is McDowell's position. For such creatures, being (as the corollary of the image tells us) incapable of thought, will presumably also be incapable of enjoying experiences which are imbued with thought in the sense that they have representational content matching the content of judgements—judgements which, in view of the match in content, are justified by the corresponding experiences, but which the creatures in question are not themselves capable of making. But that is to say that the creatures in question are incapable of enjoying experiences *tout court*.[137]

McDowell's second response to the brand of externalism I have mooted is slightly more difficult to state because it has to be abstracted from his argumentation against the full Davidsonian position, which extrudes experiences from the 'order of justification'. His objection to this view, which seeks to do without experiences as justifiers of observational judgements, and instead operate with a network of mutually interacting subjects who are able to interpret one another's observational judgements as rational responses to facts, is that the observational judgements putatively *interpreted* as such in the Davidsonian scenario cannot really *be* such if they are not based on experiences.[138] Lacking experience, the putative observer, who is putatively interpreted by another party as rationally responding, in

---

[136] See *Theaetetus* 189e4–190a6; *Sophist* 263e3–6.

[137] There are surely connections to be drawn between the intellectualism I am diagnosing in McDowell's philosophy of experience and a similar strain in his moral philosophy, itself intimately associated with 'the extreme plainness or rigorism' of his interpretation of Aristotelian eudaimonia, as Wiggins nicely puts it (1995, p. 220). But a discussion of McDowell's moral philosophy lies outside the scope of this study.

[138] See here again 1995a, pp. 293–6; 1998a, pp. 408–9.

observational judgements, to observed facts, is in fact 'blind', and his or her so-called judgements in fact empty of content. McDowell now claims that merely multiplying mutual acts of interpretation cannot magic observational content into a scenario whose individual nodes lack it:

> How could multiplying what are, considered in themselves, blind responses, to include blind responses to how the blind responses of one's fellows are related to the circumstances to which they are blind responses, somehow bring it about that the responses are after all not blind? (1998a, pp. 408–9)[139]

The argument is an evident fallacy: for it depends on the false supposition that there cannot be properties which are essentially relational, and which accordingly have no monadic surrogate. Obviously, if the position under consideration is that the content of observational judgements is essentially a relational matter involving a network of mutually interpreting subjects, it is no argument against this position to note—what an adherent of it acknowledges—that the individual nodes in the network do not, taken individually and in abstraction from their place in the network (that is, taken as pure monads), have content. As Brandom rightly objects against McDowell, it simply does not follow, if one analyses perceptual judgement 'as an achievement intelligible only as a feature of *social* practices, practices involving more than one discursive perspective', that one will then be compelled to deny 'that it is an achievement at all—that the perspectives involved are genuine perspectives'.[140]

After all, if one accepted McDowell's line of reasoning one might as well query the conceptual possibility of a market on the ground that it is made up of individuals, none of whom taken as such and in abstraction from his or her role in the market-place is a buyer or a seller: for how, one might ask in the spirit of McDowell's rhetorical

---

[139] Cf. 1997, pp. 160–1; 2002b, p. 188.

[140] 1997a, p. 192. On the Hegelian resonances of the kind of structure in question here, see Brandom 1999, pp. 176–7. McDowell's response to Brandom's 1999 exhibits the same fallacy as I am diagnosing here: 1999b, pp. 192–3.

question, can merely multiplying individuals who are, taken in themselves, not buyers or sellers, yield a market? Surely the mere aggregation of non-buyers and non-sellers cannot turn these individuals into buyers and sellers. Well, it is true that one cannot construct a market out of exclusively monadic bits: but that impossibility plainly does nothing to undermine the intelligibility of a market, understood as an essentially relational phenomenon constructed from individuals standing in the appropriate relations. It is important to be clear that the position which McDowell opposes does *not* claim that individual nodes in the network do *not* enjoy content. Indeed they do: but the point is that their doing so is entirely constituted by their position in the network. Their property of possessing content, like the property of being a buyer, is not monadic, but is essentially relational; it is therefore no embarrassment, but on the contrary exactly what you would expect, that these properties cannot be constructed from exclusively monadic components.

One would be committing the same fallacy if one attacked Hume's account of causation on the basis that merely multiplying individual transactions, in which an event of one kind is prior to and contiguous with an event of another kind, so as to generate a pattern of events of the former sort related in the specified way to events of the latter sort, could do no more than replicate individualistic features of those individual transactions.[141] Hume's account of causation is indeed open to serious objection, as we have seen (Chapter II, §6), but it would not be advisable to mount a case against it on the basis that causal transactions between individual events cannot be constituted as such by locating those events within patterns comprising similar transactions. The idea behind the Humean strategy is that the pattern of constant conjunctions, within which we locate suitably related individual events, constitutes the component

---

[141] I have in mind the first definition of causation Hume gives in the *Treatise*, I.3.14 (1978, p. 170).

individual transactions as, precisely, causal; and it is no objection to this strategy to point out—what is indeed an integral part of the Humean picture—that the relevant component individual transactions are, taken in abstraction from their place in the pattern, not causal.[142]

McDowell's argument against a Davidsonian brand of externalism which simply bypasses individual experiences in setting up its 'order of justification' for observational judgements is, accordingly, uncogent. At least it is uncogent to the extent that it proceeds by way of deploying the fallacious move I have singled out for censure. But I have already conceded that experiences have to figure *somewhere* in the 'order of justification' for observational judgements. Transferred into the context of the kind of externalism I have been urging, which admits that experiences must figure in the 'order of justification' for observational judgements but denies that this 'order of justification' must be established intra- as opposed to interpersonally (or intersubjectively), the fallacious argument McDowell offers against Davidsonian externalism will take the form of claiming that, if the relevant 'order of justification' is established merely interpersonally (intersubjectively), and not intrapersonally, then, since any given individual node in the network, taken monadically

---

[142] Something like the same fallacy (which, at root, is the fallacy that parts must have the same properties as the wholes they compose) seems to be at work in McDowell's argument, against the anti-realist reading of Wittgenstein offered by Wright in his 1980, that an account of rule-following according to which the community is not, taken as a whole, subject to norms cannot make room for normativity at sub-communal level: 1998*b*, pp. 235, 248–9 (cf. pp. 252–3 with n. 49). (This fallacious move must be distinguished from McDowell's rejection, surely correct, of the anti-realist's impoverished conception of what counts as manifesting understanding: see 1998*b*, pp. 249–54, and the essay 'Anti-Realism and the Epistemology of Understanding', 1998*c*, pp. 314–43. The denial of ratification-independence, at the communal level, does not entail the anti-realist's conception of what it is to manifest understanding, according to which behaviour purportedly manifesting understanding must be characterizable in terms which do not presuppose the notions of linguistic meaning and understanding. The entailment is rather in the reverse direction: 1998*b*, pp. 246–7.) Of course in rejecting the fallacy I am not thereby rejecting the point which the fallacious argument is meant to establish, namely that the community as a whole, not just each individual in it, is subject to norms.

and in abstraction from its place in the network, may fail to attain to contentful states, either (conceiving the nodes as individual subjects of experience) because it has an experience which does not serve to justify an observational judgement for the individual who has that experience, or even cannot so serve (perhaps because that individual is an infant or an animal, and cannot make judgements), or alternatively (conceiving the nodes as individual judgers) because it makes an observational judgement but does not enjoy the corresponding experience, or even lacks the capacity to have the corresponding experience, it will follow (here comes the fallacy) that no such contentful states can be conferred on individuals when they are networked in the relevant way. Of course no such conclusion can legitimately be reached on the basis of the premises we have been given; it is for just this reason that McDowell's individualism is unacceptable.

III.10. EXTERNALISM AND THE 'ORDER OF JUSTIFICATION'

There is no need for an externalism of the sort I am urging to deny, as McDowell in his essay 'Knowledge and the Internal' apparently thinks it incumbent on the 'full-blown' externalist to do, that knowledge is 'a certain sort of standing in the space of reasons':[143] on the contrary, my externalist will accept that idea but (unsurprisingly) *externalize* what it is to be located in the space of reasons. The individual nodes of a networked actualization of the 'order of justification' are indeed in the space of reasons, in the sense that those of their mental states which purport to be knowledgeable are up for rational assessment as such: but it is not a requirement on their entitlement to that status that each individual can scrutinize the rational credentials of each—or indeed any—of his or her (or its)

---

[143] 1998*c*, pp. 395, 401; cf. pp. 440–3.

own purportedly knowledgeable mental states. 'Or indeed any': Brandom, in a reply to McDowell's essay, adopts an intermediate position between McDowell's and the one I am here recommending, according to which, while it is not required that individuals be able to justify *each* of their knowledgeable states if they are to count as having knowledge, they must have a *general* capacity to make judgements and assess those judgements' credentials.[144] But if what I said in §8 was along the right lines, there is no warrant for setting the entrance qualification to the space of reasons even so high as that. Now McDowell allows, alongside knowledge strictly so called, an externalized, *ersatz* variety of knowledge, something which on his view is not a standing in the space of reasons, to be achievable by infants and animals.[145] That splits knowledge, taken now as a genus, into two species, one (suitable for mature humans) constituted as a standing in the space of reasons, the other (suitable for infants and animals) constituted as a standing outside the space of reasons. We have already observed (Chapter II, §5) that this kind of move is characteristic of McDowell's thinking. I shall suggest in the next chapter that this approach (which McDowell adopts quite generally) to the apparent commonalities between our mental lives and the mental lives of infants and animals is implausible: here it may just be noted that it is avoidable, for the case of knowledge, if we adopt an externalism about knowledge along the lines I have been canvassing, combined with the claim that knowledge, so construed, *is* a standing in the space of reasons.

In systems where the 'order of justification' can be distributed across nodes, as envisaged by the kind of externalism I am urging, we may have, as I mentioned at the end of §9, two types of node which are disallowed in McDowell's individualistic conception of the 'order of justification' (and also disallowed, we can now add, in Brandom's conception of that order, which still counts, by my lights, as excessively

---

[144] 1995*b*, pp. 897, 904–6. Cf. 1994, pp. 32, 220; 1995*a*, pp. 251, 256–7.
[145] See Ch. I, n. 16 above; cf. Brandom 1995*b*, pp. 899–900 n. 3; McDowell 2002*c*, pp. 103–4, where he tries to limit the damage consequential upon the split between the two species of knowledge.

individualistic): we may have an experiencer who does not, and even cannot, make the corresponding observational judgements, and we may have a maker of observational judgements who does not, and even cannot, enjoy the corresponding experiences. McDowell focuses in his anti-Davidsonian polemic on the alleged incoherence of the latter possibility—naturally enough, since he is seeking to rebut an externalism which finds no role for experiences as justifiers of judgements. But the former possibility is not absent from his considerations. And here we can note that, though he indeed repudiates this possibility, McDowell does nothing to support his repudiation: that is, he fails to give adequate grounds for his rejection of the possibility that the having of an experience and the making of the corresponding observational judgement (the judgement which, by virtue of its matching the content of the experience, is *justified* by that experience) may be distributed between different subjects. Of a putative observer who is not capable of making the corresponding observational judgement, he writes:

Within the putative observer's perspective, ... the fact [sc. observed by the putative observer] is not in view as calling for a rational response. It is not in view as something to be taken into account in building a picture of the world. But that seems indistinguishable from saying that it is not in view as the fact that it is. (1998*a*, p. 408)

But even if we concede the first two sentences, the final sentence does not follow.

Suppose a guide-dog sees (as we might naturally say) that there is a car coming, and stops at the kerb. The fact that there is a car coming is not in view, for the dog, as calling for a rational response in the sense here in question: that is, the dog does not, and cannot, make the observational *judgement*, 'There is a car coming', which is in fact justified by its visual experience. But its blind owner can make that judgement, and so the dog's experience is in view, for the owner, as calling for a rational response. What should we say of the claim that the dog does not take its experience into account in building a picture of the world? Well, we can allow this way of putting things if it is just a variant locution for the dog's inability to make observational judgements. Of course, if it is just a variant locution it is not entirely clear why it needs special mention: the inclusion of the second sentence in the quoted passage perhaps suggests that something more substantial than mere repetition is afoot; and if that is so— and indeed on any natural construal of the words—I would certainly want to reject the claim that a subject lacking in conceptual capacities, such as a dog, is not able to take its experience into account in building a picture of the world. But even if we accept this claim as amounting to no more than a repetition of the uncontroversial point that the dog cannot make observational judgements, the fact remains that the dog's owner can make these judgements, and he or she does so on the basis (in the demanding sense of §8) of the dog's experiences. But there seems no call, merely because the 'order of justification' is articulated in this way (and is necessarily so articulated) between dog and owner, rather than confined within a single subject, to conclude that the relevant fact is not 'in view', for the dog, as the fact it is. It is time to confront the issue of infant and animal mentality directly.[146]

[146] Although it would take us too far afield to discuss the point in detail here, it is worth noting that there is a similarity between McDowell's rejection of externalism in the present context and his rejection of an externalist 'criterial' epistemology (imputed to Wittgenstein by some commentators) in his essay 'Criteria, Defeasibility, and Knowledge' (1998*c*, pp. 369–94), where he endorses the internalist claim that 'one's epistemic standing on some question cannot intelligibly be constituted, even in part, by matters blankly external to how it is with one subjectively' (1998*c*, p. 390; cf. pp. 335–6 n. 50, 362, 370–5). Against this claim, one wants to protest that it is surely obvious that one's epistemic standing is routinely constituted, in part, by such externalities. For example, as a competent ornithologist I know a treecreeper when I see one (in the UK), but I would not count as having that knowledge, even if I correctly identified the bird in front of me as a treecreeper in the usual visual way, at standard viewing range, if unbeknown to me a freak storm had blown into my part of the UK from continental Europe a large number of short-toed treecreepers, which are normally absent from the UK and are visually indistinguishable from ordinary treecreepers at standard viewing range. (There is a useful discussion of cases exhibiting this structure at Brandom 1994, pp. 206–13; cf. Dretske 2000, p. 55.) Whether such an event has occurred or not makes all the difference to my epistemic standing on the point in question, but is external to how matters stand with me subjectively, if anything is. McDowell would no doubt deny this latter claim (cf. 1998*c*, p. 390 n. 37; van Cleve 2004, p. 488), but the expansive conception of the subjective which he favours, and which disallows anything relevant to my epistemic standing to count as exterior to my subjectivity, cannot simply be assumed in a polemic against externalism, as he is inclined to suppose (e.g. at 1998*c*, p. 374): cf. Brewer 1999, pp. 229–30. (Against McDowell's attack on the 'criterial' view of knowledge ascription, see further my 1995*a*, esp. p. 272 n. 22.)

IV

The mental lives of infants and animals

IV.1. TWO SPECIES OF MENTALITY

McDowell's insistence that the 'order of justification' must be in place at the intrapersonal level, and not merely interpersonally (or intersubjectively), has unfortunate consequences for his treatment of infant and animal mentality:[1] this is the third area of his thinking where a suspicion that his empiricism is more than minimal arises.

According to McDowell, infants and animals 'see objects',[2] and have 'perceptual sensitivity to features of the environment';[3] but they do not 'have objects in view'[4] or have 'bits of the world perceptually manifest to them as materials for a world view';[5] they do not live their lives 'in the world', but only 'in an environment';[6] they are not 'in possession of the world' but have 'a mere animal ability to cope with a habitat'.[7] Again, they can feel pain and be in other such 'inner' states, but 'when a dog feels pain, that is not a matter of an object for the dog's consciousness; dogs have no inner world'.[8] What infants

---

[1] Recall that this phrase abbreviates 'human infant mentality and non-human animal mentality'. 'Infant' is here being used in the etymologically strict sense of a child who is not yet able to talk.

[2] 1998a, p. 411.

[3] 1994, p. 69. Cf. 1994, pp. 50, 64, 70, 116–17, 119; 1998a, pp. 367, 409, 411; 1998c, p. 40; 2001, p. 184.

[4] Cf. 1998a, p. 414.

[5] 1998a, p. 413.

[6] 1994, p. 115; cf. 1998b, p. 348.

[7] 1998c, pp. 414–15; cf. p. 433.

[8] 1998b, p. 313 n. 34; cf. p. 311 n. 29. Cf. 1994, pp. 50, 120; 1998a, pp. 367–8, 429–30; 1998c, p. 40.

and animals have, when they engage perceptually with their environments, is not experience in the sense of that word which we invoke when we characterize our mature human cognitive states, for our experience is essentially conceptually structured, but their 'experience' is precisely not conceptually structured: in the absence of a capacity to make judgements, infants and animals cannot have experience strictly so called.[9] As McDowell puts it, 'the very thing that is not conceptual in brutes is conceptual in our lives'.[10] But the conceptuality of our experience is not simply attached externally to a non-conceptual or pre-conceptual core. Rather, as we have noted (Chapter II, §3), the idea is that our animal nature, in evolving from a state of pre-rational awareness to an enjoyment of the kind of awareness that is structured by the space of reasons, undergoes a fundamental *transformation*:

[T]his difference, a difference between perception that is an actualization of conceptual capacities in sensory consciousness and perception that is not, is indeed a difference in perception itself, not just a difference in what a creature can do with some common thing that is what perception, as such, yields to it. (1998*a*, p. 412)

It follows that there are two quite different ways of being perceptually sensitive to an environment, and two ways of being in 'inner' states such as that of pain—our way, which is conceptually structured, and the way of infants and animals, which is not. McDowell makes it clear that he conceives the states of being perceptually sensitive to one's environment, or of being in pain, as genera which admit of subdivision into species—one of conceptually structured such states (states structured by the space of reasons), the other of non-conceptual states (states not so structured).[11]

[9] 2000*c*, p. 335.
[10] 1998*a*, p. 412. Cf. 1998*b*, pp. 23, 39.
[11] 1994, pp. 64, 69; 1998*a*, p. 412; 2001, p. 184; 2002*a*, p. 288. Cf. Brandom 1994, pp. 276–7; Brewer 1999, pp. 177–9.

IV.2. MENTALITY AND THE TRANSCENDENTAL ARGUMENT

What is the point of this division between our mental lives and the mental lives of infants and animals? The division is redolent of McDowell's rationalist rather than his empiricist roots: for it is a familiar rationalist thought that animals are incapable of reason. Descartes opined that the fact that human beings are capable of language whereas animals are not shows 'not merely that the beasts have less reason than men, but that they have no reason at all'.[12] Contrast Hume: 'no truth appears to me more evident, than that beasts are endowed with thought and reason as well as men'.[13] McDowell is keen to disavow any connection with this aspect of his rationalist inheritance: although infants and animals do not have an 'inner world', they are nevertheless said to have 'an analogue to the notion of subjectivity, close enough to ensure that there is no Cartesian automatism in our picture'.[14] In an alternative formulation, they are granted a 'proto-subjectivity'.[15] But, on McDowell's picture, according to which infants and animals are excluded from the space of reasons, an analogue to subjectivity (a proto-subjectivity) appears to be the most they can achieve.[16] One must ask: if they really are excluded from that space, how close an analogue can it be? In what sense is a proto-subjectivity really a *subjectivity*? A fake passport might be said to be in *some* sense a passport; counterfeit money might be said to be in *some* sense money. Is infant and animal mentality in any better shape? If infants and animals have 'intuitions without concepts', why are their intuitions not blind? And if the intuitions of infants and animals are indeed

---

[12] *Discours de la Méthode*, part 5, *Œuvres de Descartes* vi, p. 58. 5–7 (1985, p. 140). Cf. Kant *KrV*, A546–7/B574–5; James 1975, p. 300.

[13] *Treatise* I.3.16 (1978, p. 176).

[14] 1994, p. 116. Cf. 2002*c*, p. 104.

[15] 1994, p. 117. On proto-subjectivity, cf. Putnam 1992, pp. 28–31; 1999, pp. 152–62.

[16] Peacocke 2001, p. 261.

not blind, as McDowell wishes to affirm, how does it come about that the intuitions of evolved and mature language-users would, in the absence of concepts, be blind?

Some of McDowell's formulations concerning infant and animal mentality may be misleading, in suggesting to the reader a more substantial and controversial position than he perhaps intends. For example, we are told that the approved Kantian framework

precludes supposing that sensibility by itself yields content that is less than conceptual but already world-involving. In the absence of spontaneity, no self can be in view, and by the same token, the world cannot be in view either. (1994, p. 114)

Hence the claim with which we started, that infants and animals, whose faculties of sensibility are not structured by a faculty of spontaneity, do not inhabit 'the world' or have 'objects' (including now a self) 'in view'. But how substantial are these claims? They certainly *appear* to be substantial: by which I mean that the reader gains the impression that the self and the other objects which cannot be in view, and the world which cannot be inhabited, in the absence of a faculty of spontaneity are entities of which we have an independent understanding, as though McDowell were offering us (to adopt a phrase of his from another context) a 'mapping of interrelations between concepts that, so far as this exercise goes, can be taken to be already perfectly well understood'.[17] But though that is the impression conveyed by the main text of the lectures in *Mind and World*, the Afterword to that text and subsequent publications show McDowell attempting to neutralize any appearance that the relevant claims are to be taken in a way which is substantial in the above sense.

In these supplementary remarks we are told that the denial of selfhood, experience of objects, and possession of a world to infants and animals is no more than a way of putting the point that they lack spontaneity: 'the point is just that dumb animals do not have Kantian freedom'.[18] And hence, so the argument runs, to that extent

17 1998c, p. 36.   18 1994, p. 182.

the mental life of infants and animals does not help 'dissolve the threat of transcendental mystery' of 'a freely adopted posture with objective purport':[19]

> The point is that it is only in the case of possessors of conceptual capacities that their sensitivity to their environment admits of the transcendentally resonant description, as a propensity to have conceptual capacities actualized in sensory consciousness. ... [I]t is only in the case of possessors of conceptual capacities that perception puts them in touch with the world, as opposed to merely enabling a perceiver to cope with its environment. But that is just language for bringing out the difference between perception whose invocation helps to dissolve the threat of transcendental mystery and perception of which that is not so ... (1998*a*, p. 411)

In other words, the claim is that the transcendental argument which I rehearsed in Chapter III, §1, works only for creatures to whom the interdependence of spontaneity and receptivity applies, and infants and animals are not included in this class. That is all that is meant by saying that they do not experience objects, inhabit a world, or have a self in view.[20] If that is all that is meant, one wants to protest, surely McDowell should have restricted himself to making the point in just those terms: to eschew the literal and humdrum way of putting the point in favour of the rhetorically and philosophically charged language of experiencing objects, inhabiting a world, and having a self in view, is at least to court misunderstanding, and indeed invites the suspicion that the disavowal on McDowell's part of any intention to do more, in invoking such language, than exclude infants and animals from the target area of the transcendental argument may not be quite accurate. I shall return to this point in §6 below.

McDowell does not want to say that infants and animals, enjoying a perceptual sensitivity to their environment unstructured by a faculty of spontaneity, are simply irrelevant to the transcendental argument. On the contrary, it is an implication of the claimed connection between normativity and biology (between second and first nature), which as we have seen (Chapter II, §5) McDowell insists on but fails

---

[19] 1998*a*, pp. 410–11.   [20] 1994, p. 183. Cf. 2000*a*, p. 91.

either to elucidate or to justify, that the kind of perceptual sensitivity to their environment possessed by infants and animals must in some way ground the conceptually structured experience which we enjoy: for it is just their sort of first nature which is (has been) transformed by a process of maturation (evolution) to yield our sort of second nature. The sentence 'Second nature is a transformation of first nature' can be heard with two different emphases. If the stress falls on the word 'transformation' the point is (as in Chapter II, §3) that second nature cannot be *factorized* into a first-natural component plus something extra; if the stress falls on the phrase 'first nature' the point is (as in the present context) that second nature, while not arising out of first nature in the crude aggregative way rejected by the previous point, does indeed, for all that, *evolve* or in some way *emerge* out of first nature—and *must* do so. Here is how McDowell conveys the latter point (in the context of a restatement of the transcendental argument):

To avoid the threat of mystery in the way I recommend, we have to understand the acquisition of conceptual capacities as a matter of acquiring, together, capacities to build world views and capacities to have bits of the world perceptually manifest to one as material for world views. This would be merely another mystery if we could not take the second component of this package to be a transformation, in the presence of the first component, of a prior responsiveness to objective reality. (1998a, p. 412)

This is supposed to capture the respect in which the perceptual sensitivity enjoyed by infants and animals does, after all, have relevance to the transcendental argument.

But, McDowell tells us, the transcendental relevance of a merely animal perceptual sensitivity to the environment is 'only indirect' (ibid.), and the reason for this is supplied by the rejection of the factorizing model. We could not dissolve the mystery if we tried to tack our conceptual capacities (our faculty of spontaneity) onto a perceptual sensitivity to the environment (a faculty of receptivity) conceived as common to creatures without a faculty of spontaneity and creatures with it. There is no such common core. On the contrary, as we have seen, for creatures with a faculty of spontaneity, co-operating in the requisite way with a faculty of receptivity, no such factorization into components one of which is pre-conceptual is feasible. The difference between our perceptual sensitivity to the world and the perceptual sensitivity to their environment had by infants and animals is, as McDowell expresses it in a passage I have already quoted, a 'difference in perception itself'. Apart from the lack of clarity and argumentative underpinning, which I have already censured (Chapter II, §§4 and 5), attaching to McDowell's deployment of the notion of an evolution of second nature out of first nature (or transformation of first nature into second nature) to support his claim that there is some kind of constitutive connection between normativity and biology, there are two further reasons why we should not accept his account of the relation between the perceptual sensitivity enjoyed by infants and animals and our experience.

IV.3. OBJECTIONS TO McDOWELL'S ACCOUNT

In the first place, I have rejected (Chapter III, §2) McDowell's ostensible motivation for his transcendental argument. Recall that it was specifically the location of *freedom* between experience and judgement in the mature adult subject which supposedly gave rise to the threat of a transcendental mystery of 'a freely adopted posture with objective purport'. But I suggested in Chapter III that this mistakes the nature and role of freedom. Freedom is freedom of *action*, and there is no room for manœuvre—no scope for exercising freedom of action—between experience and judgement. Subjects who enjoy experiences, and who are in a position to form the judgements which those experience justify, find themselves forming the relevant judgements *nolens volens*—or would find themselves doing so if circumstances impelled them to arrive at judgements on the contents of their experiences, and presented no hindrance to their doing so. (Of course, as I have indicated, the act of making a judgement public, as distinct from its formation, is different matter: that *would* be a voluntary action.) There are special, and unusual, cases where one experience-based judgement may be defeated by another one; but the existence of such cases does not require us to locate, quite generally, a deliberative distance between experience and judgement—and fortunately so, for to do that would foist on subjects a freedom which they could not, generally, exploit, and which would accordingly plunge them into a crisis of existentialist proportions. Another way of putting the same point is to say that McDowell's transcendental mystery is nothing but an *ignis fatuus*, a will-o'-the-wisp: there is no problem about how to secure objective purport for empirical judgements conceived as freely adopted postures, because empirical judgements are not such postures. Spontaneity, whatever exactly it may be and to whatever extent we may possess it, is at any rate not to be found here; judgement in general, and the involvement of conceptual capacities in particular, are not the *loci* of freedom.

But secondly, even if we granted the terms of McDowell's problem, we would still have to deplore his solution as being unnecessarily extreme,[21] for a reason which has already been anticipated. It simply does not follow from the alleged fact that, to solve the purported mystery, we need to invoke the 'transcendentally resonant description' of experience 'as a propensity to have conceptual capacities actualized in sensory consciousness', that creatures which lack spontaneity are unfit to help solve the mystery (except in the indirect way already acknowledged). Infants and animals, we might say, do indeed have conceptual capacities actualized in their sensory consciousness, and to that extent are in the target area of the transcendental question, if that question is being posed.[22] They do not themselves possess the conceptual capacities which are actualized in their sensory consciousness, but there is another route which they can exploit to achieving the needed actualization of conceptual

21 Cf. Peacocke 1998, p. 384; Putnam 1999, p. 192 n. 16.
22 See here again McDowell 1998a, p. 411.

capacities in their sensory consciousness. For infants and animals can benefit (transcendentally)[23] from the fact that we mature human subjects possess the requisite conceptual capacities: *our* conceptual capacities are actualized in *their* sensory consciousness. Once again,[24] there is simply nothing in the quite general considerations McDowell brings to bear, even supposing they are cogent, to warrant the restrictive interpretation he wishes to put on the conclusion: that the 'propensity to have conceptual capacities actualized in sensory consciousness' must, in order to count as such, be realized at an intrapersonal level. An interpersonal—better: intersubjective—actualization of conceptual capacities in sensory consciousness—an actualization of *A*'s conceptual capacities in *B*'s sensory consciousness—will do perfectly well for the purposes of the transcendental argument, assuming we are required to take that argument seriously.

It is worth noting in passing that a similar kind of fallacy may be observed operating in some of Davidson's writings on animal mentality: for example in his essays 'Rational Animals' and 'The Emergence of Thought'.[25] Davidson concludes, from the fact that an individual belief gets its identity from its place in a large network of beliefs, that a given creature cannot have a single belief without having many. Now it may be independently true that a creature cannot have a single belief without having many; but it does not follow, from the fact that a belief is *essentially constituted* by its place in a network of related beliefs, that in order to *have* that belief a given creature has to *have* other beliefs in the network. Similarly, returning to our current topic of concern, from the fact that a subject's mental state *constitutively involves* the actualization of conceptual capacities in that subject's sensory consciousness, it does not follow that the subject in question must *itself have* those conceptual capacities.

---

[23] I shall return to this qualification in the next section.

[24] Cf. Ch. III, §8.

[25] 2001, pp. 95–105, 123–34. Cf. 1984, p. 170. The fallacy is also present in e.g. Evans 1985, pp. 335–9. (But Evans's thinking on this point subsequently underwent a change: see Ch. II, n. 131 above.)

IV.4. CONCEPTUAL CONSCIOUSNESS AND THE PRIVATE LANGUAGE ARGUMENT

McDowell misses this point.[26] Invoking Wittgenstein's Private Language Argument, he suggests that to allow that a dog, say, has an 'inner world'—that when it is in pain, that is 'a matter of an object for the dog's consciousness'[27]—is to succumb to the myth of a private object:

> [T]he idea that for a creature to feel pain is for some state of affairs to obtain within its consciousness, from which it may or may not go on to an actualization of a conceptual capacity, is just the supposed conception of the private object, which is conclusively exposed as hopeless by Wittgenstein. There is an insurmountable problem about the supposed going on from a state of affairs within one's consciousness, conceived independently of one's conceptual powers, to an actualization of a conceptual capacity. Even if we contrive to conceive what one supposedly goes on to as otherwise than private, the going on would have to be private. (1998*a*, p. 429)[28]

McDowell here conceives of a purported object in the animal's consciousness as something non-conceptual in the radical sense, a 'bare presence' devoid of linguistically expressible structure or con-

---

[26] As does Collins (1998). Collins suggests that if we see *B*, a dog, growling and chasing a cat around the house, we are forced to ascribe perceptual experience to *B*, but not experience with conceptual content: 'We can use *our* concepts for describing *B*'s perception without imputing any conceptualized experience to *B*' (1998, p. 378). This would be correct if by 'conceptualized experience' Collins meant 'experience conceptualized by *B*'; but it is precisely wrong if by 'conceptualized experience' he means 'experience in conceptual form', in the modest sense of 'conceptual' (i.e., propositionally structured and hence expressible in language): for in using our concepts to describe *B*'s experience we inevitably ascribe experience in conceptual form (in the modest sense) to *B*, for instance, the experience *that the cat is running away*. Taking this point on board, and insisting (against Collins: see n. 73 below) that animal as well as human experiences are propositional in form, as this example indeed illustrates, we can accept Collins's claim that the difference between a human subject, *S*, and *B* is that 'a description that fits something that both *S* and *B* can perceive *can* [sc. only] *be given* by *S*. In itself, this is not a difference in perception' (1998, p. 380).

[27] 1998*b*, p. 313 n. 34.

[28] Cf. 1998*b*, p. 294; 2002*a*, p. 288.

tent: that is guaranteed by his assimilation of it to the target of Wittgenstein's Private Language Argument, together with his understanding of that, as we have construed it.[29] He asks, in effect, how the *animal itself* can 'go on' to actualize the conceptual capacities needed to bring the object under the right concept (say, that of a pain). Well, obviously it cannot: *no* subject could achieve that remarkable feat. But it is confused to suppose that this point tells against our right to think of canine pain, say, as objectually present to a dog's consciousness. When a dog feels a pain—construing this as a state in which an object is present in the dog's consciousness—we do not have to do with a bit of structureless and contentless Given, the conceptualization of which, by the dog itself or indeed by any subject, it is then impossible to set in train, for familiar Wittgensteinian reasons. Rather, the object which is there in the dog's consciousness is already fully conceptual—it is, as we agreed at the outset, a *pain*—but its status as such does not depend on an implausible actualization of a purported conceptual capacity on the *dog's* part. It depends on *our* actualizing *our* conceptual capacities; but—to stress the point again— we do not exercise them on a piece of (radically) non-conceptual input, in this case any more than in any other case.

We find in the passage I quoted in the last paragraph the same crossing of wires over the idea of non-conceptual content which we analysed in Chapter II, §6. McDowell in effect supposes that *because* the pain supposedly present as an object in an animal's consciousness is there independently of *the animal's* conceptual powers (for the animal has no such powers), it follows that the pain, if construed as an object present to the animal's consciousness, must be taken to be a private object. The reasoning is explicit in his essay 'Intentionality and Interiority in Wittgenstein', where at one point McDowell tells us that 'objects for consciousness' which are 'independent of the conceptual resources *of their subjects*' (my emphasis) are 'private objects' in the objectionable Wittgensteinian sense.[30] In other words, because the content of the relevant

---

[29] Cf. Ch. II, §6.　　[30] 1998*b*, pp. 312–13, with n. 34.

experience (or 'experience', scare-quoting to indicate that mere perceptual sensitivity may be in question) is non-conceptual in the sense that it is not available to the subject's critical and reflective faculty (for in this case the subject has no such faculty), it must be non-conceptual in the much more radical sense that it is a piece of the Given, a 'bare presence' devoid of any feature on which language might get a grip. But the supposed entailment fails.

The content of the experience in question is indeed non-conceptual in the sense that it is not available to a critical and reflective faculty possessed by *the subject of the experience*: but it is available to *us*, and *we* can see that the experience is *of a pain*—that it is an awareness of just that sort of object—present in the animal's consciousness. It simply does not follow that the content of the experience is non-conceptual in the more radical sense, that it is a 'bare presence'.[31]

Recall that a 'bare presence' is a non-thing in the most funda-mental possible sense (Chapter II, §6): it cannot be correctly characterized in any way at all; language cannot 'embrace' it. It is not even correctly characterized as a 'presence', since that charac-terization seeks to bring it under a concept, whereas a 'bare pres-ence' is supposed to be an utterly noumenal object, about which we cannot even say the minimal things Kant would like us to say about it.[32] Even to call it a 'noumenal object'—even to speak of 'it'—is to go beyond what is permissible. (Even the attempt to specify what it is that we are not allowed to say is to court paradox, as the foregoing sentences demonstrate.) Such a 'thing' could not possibly provide material for a rationally motivated move in a

---

[31] A passage where the fallacious slide from the one form of non-conceptual content to the other is particularly clear is the following: 'The idea [to be repudiated] is that mere animals already enjoy perceptual experience in which the world strikes them as being a certain way, and the only difference our understanding makes for us is that we can impose conceptual form on the already world-representing but less than conceptual content [i.e., non-conceptual content in the sense exploited in the third lecture of *Mind and World*: cf. Ch. II, §6] that, like them, we receive in experience. ... So the picture is that mere animals only receive the Given [i.e., non-conceptual content in the first-lecture sense], whereas we not only receive it but are also able to put it into conceptual shape' (1994, pp. 122–3).

[32] As Kant himself reminds us: *non entis nulla sunt praedicata* (*KrV*, A793/B821).

language-game, even in such an apparently (though not actually)[33] autonomous language-game as that of naming: that, on McDowell's conception of the point of the Private Language Argument, is Wittgenstein's purpose in repudiating the idea of a private object. But McDowell is wrong to suppose that if we construe an animal's pain as an object present in its consciousness we thereby incur the charge of assimilating it to a private object in this objectionable sense. For in being available to us—creatures who possess the requisite conceptual powers to characterize in language the object of the animal's awareness—as a possible object of cognition, the sensation in question is revealed as being (or having as its content) an object of a certain sort—precisely, a pain—available to figure in an animal experience with a certain determinate conceptual content, and, as such, present in that animal's consciousness.[34]

That is why there is a sense in which, as I put it above (§3), infants and animals benefit from our presence on the scene. I described the benefit as 'transcendental', for there is no empirical sense in which an infant or an animal needs us or any other extraneous subject to effect the constitution of an object in its consciousness as being, for example, a pain. Or, putting it another way, the claim that infants and animals so benefit from our presence on the scene is one whose truth can at best be shown, but not said.[35] The same applies to McDowell's comment that 'what we might call "conceptual consciousness" is not a datum but an achievement, won by acquiring mastery of language'.[36] For it is only in a transcendental sense that 'conceptual consciousness' depends on the acquisition of the mastery of language. That is, 'conceptual consciousness' depends on the

---

[33] Wittgenstein *Philosophical Investigations* I, §49, quoted in Ch. VI, §2 below.

[34] I distinguish here between experiencing a pain and cognizing it: only the subject can *experience* his or her (or its) pain (that is a trivial logical truth, and has no implications for privacy in any objectionable sense), but other subjects may *cognize* a given subject's pain, by seeing the pain in that subject's behaviour (broadly construed), whether that subject be a mature human, an infant, or a non-linguistic animal.

[35] Cf. McDowell's remarks on Wright's anti-realistic interpretation of Wittgenstein (1998*b*, p. 256), and on Dummettian anti-realism more generally (1998*c*, p. 342).

[36] 1998*c*, p. 106.

possibility of the expression, in language, of the contents of that consciousness, and hence indirectly on the possibility of the acquisition of language by someone or something; it does not depend on the existence of any *actual* mastery of language, either by the creature whose 'conceptual consciousness' is in question or by any other subject. A dog's entitlement to feel pains (or be in any other experiential state with conceptual content) depends on the possibility of formulating in language correct characterizations of its mental states. Since dogs do not themselves possess the requisite conceptual powers to formulate these characterizations, they in effect depend for their entitlement to mentality on the possible existence of other creatures, who do possess those powers. But that dependence is only on the possibility of such existence, not its actuality: that is what is meant by saying that the dependence is merely transcendental. Dogs could feel pains, taking this as a fully conceptual state in which an object is present in a canine consciousness, even if there did not actually exist any humans or other subjects with the requisite conceptual powers to classify objects of canine experience in language.[37]

---

[37] The point I am making is close to one that Wright tries to make in a couple of places (1998*a*, pp. 399–402; 2002*a*, pp. 149–50, 171–3), but unfortunately Wright spoils his polemic by using some formulations which suggest that he conceives objects for an infant's or for an animal's consciousness in just the way McDowell is right to repudiate, that is, as being, in themselves, bits of non-conceptual Given. For sometimes Wright implies that he conceives experience as intrinsically 'shapeless' or 'unarticulated', and merely such as to *permit* the subject to *give* it shape or articulation, and indeed such as to permit various shapings or articulations (1998*a*, pp. 401–2; 2002*a*, pp. 149–50; note also the description of experience, at 2002*a*, p. 171, as consisting in the subject's 'standing in a certain mental relation to a chunk of material reality', which latter phrase is suggestive of the Kantian thing-in-itself). My conception of experience, on the other hand (of all experience, including infant and animal experience), is that it is fully conceptual, and not such as to require the subject to *give* it shape, but such as to enable the subject to *register* its shape, nor such as permit *various* articulations, but such as to admit just *one* articulation (the one it actually has). At one point Wright initially seems to give expression to the conception of experience I recommend: he says that when I judge that *p* on the basis of a (veridical) experience that *p*, the experienced fact that *p* ' "sustains" and "commands" that particular conceptual articulation—that is just a fancy way of saying that I recognize it for what it is' (2002*a*, p. 172). But the appearance is compromised by Wright's subsequent admission that his conception of 'experience as material for recognition is just scheme/content dualism of the kind which Davidson famously rejects' (2002*a*, p. 172; cf. 1998*a*,

We can assent to the position which Sellars calls 'psychological nominalism' according to which '*all* awareness of *sorts, resemblances, facts*, etc., in short, all awareness of abstract entities—indeed, all awareness even of particulars—is a linguistic affair'.[38] McDowell can assent to it too, so long as we gloss 'awareness' as 'experience'. But whereas McDowell reads Sellars's claim, so construed, empirically, I read it transcendentally. Actually, 'psychological nominalism' is a bad name for the characterized position, as Brandom points out,[39] and in closing this section it is worth saying briefly why this is so. The reason is this. The realization that all awareness is a linguistic affair in fact tells *against* the doctrine of nominalism, as traditionally conceived: for nominalists take themselves to be entitled to criticize some parts of our apparently referential grammar (for example, our apparent ability to refer to universals and to abstract objects such as numbers) on the basis of a suppositious *pre-linguistic* insight into the layout of the world, the putative insight putatively revealing that there are no such objects as universals or numbers, so that our apparent references to them must be differently construed, or 'analysed out'. But it is an illusion to imagine that one can step outside

p. 402), which takes us back to a conception of experience's content as being the thing-in-itself. Note that the debate between Wright and McDowell on this matter is partly vitiated by a lack of clarity in the use of the verb 'conceptualize', which in the present context is crucially ambiguous. It can either mean 'take a piece of non-conceptual Given as input and deliver something in conceptual form as output' (this is the sense in which McDowell usually uses the word), or it can mean 'actively recognize something already conceptual in form for what it is' (this sense is not entirely absent from McDowell: there is a relevant use near the foot of 1994, p. 118). The same ambiguity applies, *mutatis mutandis*, to cognate forms of this word: so when Wright says that the experience that *p* 'could obtain unconceptualized in just the same way as the fact that *p* itself' (2002*a*, p. 171), which sense of 'conceptualize' underlies his use of 'unconceptualized'? He ought, in my view, to have the second sense of 'conceptualize' I have identified in mind, and some of his formulations do indeed support that reading, but unfortunately others support the alternative reading that he has the first sense in mind, and that permits McDowell to respond unsympathetically to Wright's proposal (1998*a*, pp. 429–31; 2002*a*, pp. 288–9); had Wright clearly embraced the position I favour that unsympathetic response would not have been available to McDowell.

[38] Sellars 1956, §29; 1997, p. 63.
[39] 1997*b*, p. 150.

language in this way, and assess from an extra-linguistic standpoint the adequacy of our grammatical practices.[40]

IV.5. 'NOT A SOMETHING, BUT NOT A NOTHING EITHER'

McDowell's characterization of infant and animal sensation ineluctably invites comparison with Wittgenstein's notorious description of the (object of) sensation in general as 'not a something, but not a nothing either'.[41] McDowell rightly repudiates this conception of ordinary sensations.[42] It would indeed appear that, in producing this description, Wittgenstein has mistakenly allowed elements of his polemic against private sensations to contaminate the way he thinks about our ordinary, non-private sensations—sensations which we can describe in public language.[43] The result is a monster of a description which fits nothing. The objects of ordinary sensations, describable in public language, are somethings in as good a sense as anything at all is a something: they are not even partly, or in some sense, nothings. The objects of purportedly private sensations, on the other hand, are not even partly, or in some sense, somethings, but are just nothings: there are no objects which can only be talked about in a private language, a language logically inaccessible to anyone other than the subject of the sensations in question,[44] for there is no such language.

---

[40] See on this point my 1996. I shall return to the doctrine of nominalism, which has a central role to play in my criticism of McDowell's philosophy of language, in the next chapter.

[41] *Philosophical Investigations* I, §304 (1958, p. 102).

[42] In his essay 'One Strand in the Private Language Argument', 1998*b*, pp. 279–96, esp. pp. 283–7.

[43] As he does at the end of the 'beetle in the box' passage (*Philosophical Investigations* I, §293; 1958, p. 100), where he remarks, quite generally, that 'if we construe the grammar of the expression of sensation on the model of "object and designation", the object drops out of consideration as irrelevant'. Instead of 'sensation' Wittgenstein should have said 'private sensation'.

[44] Cf. *Philosophical Investigations* I, §243.

Now McDowell's reading of why Wittgenstein reaches his wrong characterization exploits the suggestion that sensations represent

a *limiting case* of the model of object and designation—a limiting case of the idea of an object that we can designate and classify. The idea of encountering a particular is in place here *only because* the experience involves a concept (*pain*, say, or *toothache*): the particular has no status except as what is experienced as instantiating the concept. (1998*b*, p. 284)

This passage seems to lodge the claim that particular (objects of) sensations exist only if they are experienced, and that interpretation can be supported from elsewhere in McDowell's writings.[45] The claim is of course a controversial one, and its presence in McDowell's thinking may help account for his erroneous tendency to grant subjects infallibility about how things seem to them to be, which we examined in Chapter III (§4), mediated by the thought that objects of sensations sit closer to the experiencing subject than 'outer' objects in the sense that, in the case of 'inner' objects, no distinction between 'seems right' and 'is right' opens up from the subject's point of view. Now I have rejected both the doctrine of infallibility, in respect of the subject's thinking about how things seem to him or her to be, and the suggestion that no distinction opens up with respect to the obtaining of 'inner' states of affairs, from the subject's point of view, between 'seems right' and 'is right'. McDowell appears to suppose that if we reject the controversial claim, we are committed to construing sensations as private in the objectionable Wittgensteinian sense.[46] But that by no means follows. I suspect that he is mixing up two things: allowing that 'inner' objects (such as pains) may exist without being experienced (and so without being 'experienced as instantiating the concept'), and—what does not follow from this admission—supposing that such objects do not, taken in themselves, instantiate the relevant concept at all (for example, are

---

[45] See the wider context from which the quoted passage is drawn, 1998*b*, pp. 283–7, together with 1994, pp. 21, 36–8, 119–20, and 1998*b*, pp. 310–11.

[46] 1998*b*, p. 311.

not, in themselves, pains), but are featureless Kantian things-in-themselves.

The point I wish to focus on here, however, is McDowell's characterization of a sensation in the above passage as 'a limiting case of the idea of an object that *we* can designate and classify' (my emphasis). For here again there is a suggestion of the same crossing of wires as the one to which I have already drawn attention. Who are 'we'? Must subjects of sensations—as it might be, infants and animals—*themselves* be able to 'designate and classify' an object as a sensation if they are to count as having sensations, or is it enough if those sensations are classifiable as such by others, say by members of the adult linguistic community?[47] I have argued, against McDowell, that infant and animal sensations (and, in general, experience) can be transcendentally constituted as such by powers of designation and classification which infants and animals do not themselves possess, but which we do. That means that infants and animals can 'have objects in view' and have 'bits of the world perceptually manifest to them as materials for a world view'; that they can live their lives 'in a world', and not merely 'in an environment'; that when a dog feels pain or is in another such 'inner' state, the pain or other sensation is indeed 'a matter of an object for the dog's consciousness'. In the sense in which we have an 'inner world'—a world of felt sensations—dogs have such a world too. Now although McDowell does not of course confuse public and private objects in the way Wittgenstein appears to do, it nevertheless seems fair to appropriate Wittgenstein's notorious description of sensation to characterize McDowell's way of thinking about infant and animal sensation. For, in stating that 'when a dog feels pain, that is not a matter of an object for the

---

[47] Or by *other* members of that community, this proviso allowing for the possibility that some mature adults may have experiences whose content they cannot—perhaps cannot in any way at all (not even in the minimal way required by McDowell)—articulate. In general what I say about the transcendental constitution of the conceptuality of infant and animal experience (in the sense of its having essentially propositional content) applies also to members of the adult human community whose level of articulacy is naturally (or has by accident or disease been reduced to) a lower level than the norm. But for ease of exposition I concentrate here on the case of infants and animals.

dog's consciousness; dogs have no inner world',[48] McDowell seems to banish canine pain to a kind of Hades of the senses—a twilight realm hovering between existence and non-existence, a realm of objects that are not somethings, but not nothings either.

IV.6. FEELING PAIN AND FEELING A PAIN

It is striking that in the passage I have just cited McDowell concedes not that a dog feels *a pain*, but that it feels *pain*. The point applies to other texts where he is acknowledging the fact of animal mentality.[49] In the following passage, McDowell seems to go out of his way to avoid conceding that cats feel *pains*:

The opponent's inclination is to say, focusing on a felt pain, 'You are saying that cats do not have *this*'. The right response is to say: 'If by "this" you mean something that is there in your consciousness only as falling under a concept, then certainly the claim is that cats have no such thing; but this is fully consistent with agreeing that cats can really suffer.' (1998*b*, p. 295)

I take it that the repeated avoidance of an explicitly objectual formulation, with its unwelcome suggestion that there might be objects for an infant's or animal's 'inner' world after all, in favour of a formulation which, while not explicitly adverbial, at any rate does not overtly invite the reader to think in terms of a possible existential generalization, is a conscious or unconscious stratagem to block the generalizing move. But if that is the purpose behind the more cautious style of formulation, it fails, for two reasons.

First, there is no more justification in the case of infant or animal pain than there is in the case of mature human pain for the attempt to arrest the natural entailment from the idea of *feeling pain* to that of *feeling a pain*; or to try to stop the latter idea from in turn insinuating an existential generalization so as to yield an object—in as good a

[48] 1998*b*, p. 313 n. 34.
[49] See e.g. 1994, p. 120.

sense as anything at all is an object—onto which the subject, whether mature human, infant, or brute animal, may direct his, her, or its attention. And there is no gap in ordinary discourse between saying that a subject (any subject) *feels* a pain and saying that that subject is *conscious* of that pain, and hence that the pain is an object for the subject's consciousness: or are we guilty of a solecism when we say that a dog can lose and regain consciousness? So there is no stopping point on the road from feeling pain to having an inner world in the relevant sense.

Secondly, even if we agree to accept the formulation according to which a dog feels not *a pain*, but simply *pain*, where this ascription is construed, in a nominalistic spirit, adverbially (equivalent to: the dog feels painfully), there is again no more reason to insist on the adverbial analysis in the case of infants and animals than there is in the case of mature humans. And the ontological parsimony which the nominalistic formulation strives for is, in any case, an illusion, for the attempt to reconstruct objects which are suspect to nominalists as modes is both futile and self-defeating:[50] it is futile because every penny saved on objects has to be spent on modes, so that what might be called the level of our overall ontological commitment remains constant; and it is self-defeating because modes are in any case themselves objects.[51]

Of course, McDowell might respond to both these objections by reaffirming that his denial that a dog's feeling pain involves 'an object for the dog's consciousness', or entails a canine 'inner world', is simply 'language for bringing out the difference between [sensation] whose invocation helps to dissolve the threat of transcendental mystery and [sensation] of which that is not so',[52] the transcendental mystery being of 'a freely adopted posture with objective purport'.[53] Now I have rejected the suggestion that there is a relevant contrast

---

[50] Quite apart from the reservations expressed at the end of §4 above concerning the putative extra-linguistic standpoint which the nominalist seeks to adopt.

[51] See further on this point (with reference to Ockham's nominalism) Spade 1990 and my 2001*a*.

[52] 1998*a*, p. 411.   [53] 1998*a*, p. 410.

between ourselves on the one hand and infants and animals on the other in point of possession or otherwise of Kantian freedom: we do not possess Kantian freedom in the place where McDowell locates it, so that infants and animals are no worse off than ourselves in this respect. And, further, even supposing that I am wrong about this, and that something like McDowell's transcendental argument is required to remove a threat of mystery attaching to our possession of a faculty of spontaneity, I have urged that nothing in the transcendental argument requires the restrictive interpretation McDowell places on its conclusion, by virtue of which infant and animal experience is excluded from the target area of the transcendental reflection.

But, apart from these points, there may now be a qualm about accepting any such response as I envisaged McDowell making at the beginning of the last paragraph. For it is natural to object that the involvement of an appeal to Wittgenstein's Private Language Argument in McDowell's polemic against 'the idea that for a creature to feel pain is for some state of affairs to obtain within its consciousness' indicates that the claim that pains (for example) are not objects present in an animal's consciousness is a substantial one in the sense I specified earlier (§2). That is, it is natural to object that McDowell's polemic against objects of animal consciousness cannot, in view of the involvement of the Wittgensteinian considerations, be merely shorthand for the claim that animal sensation does not help dissolve the transcendental mystery. McDowell's response to this objection would presumably be that the involvement of the Wittgensteinian considerations is actually a way of bringing out the point that animal mentality cannot serve to dissolve the transcendental mystery: for any object in an animal's consciousness would, given the animal's lack of conceptual capacities, have to be a private object in the objectionable sense. So I think the qualm to which what I have called the natural objection gives voice can be met; but in meeting it we see what the real sticking point in McDowell's treatment of infant and animal mentality is. It is the point I have already stressed (§§3–4), namely that, if we start with the non-conceptuality of infant and animal experience in the sense that their experience is not available, *intrasubjectively*, to a faculty of spontaneity possessed by the creature in question, there is then no entailment, if we suppose additionally that objects of experience are present to infant and animal consciousness, to the non-conceptuality of infant and animal experience in the much more radical sense that their experience furnishes them with (purported) access to nothing more than 'bare presences', private objects in the objectionable, Wittgensteinian sense. The entailment is blocked by the availability of an *intersubjective* transcendental constitution, by means of *our* conceptual capacities, of objects of certain sorts in *their* (infant and animal) sensory consciousness.

IV.7. MENTALITY AND CONCEPTUAL SOPHISTICATION

Taking the line I have recommended enables us to offer a solution to an old puzzle about infant and animal mentality. In ascribing mental states to these creatures we necessarily employ our conceptual apparatus: we say, for instance, that the dog fears that its master will beat it, or is looking for a buried bone. But how can any such characterizations be accurate? For the dog, lacking the conceptual capacities which command of a language brings, surely has no understanding either of the concept *master*, which would require knowledge of human social conventions which a dog simply lacks, or of the concept *bone*, which would require a grasp of anatomy which, again, cannot plausibly be ascribed to a dog.[54] Is not any ascription of propositional attitudes to languageless creatures going to suffer from a similar problem, that of crediting the creatures concerned with access to concepts of a sophistication and complexity far exceeding anything the creatures in question could be supposed to cognize? But if anything we try to say about an infant's or animal's mental state is bound to miss its target in this

---

[54] For this familiar point, see e.g. Wittgenstein, *Philosophical Investigations* I, §650; B. Williams 1973, esp. p. 139; Stich 1979, esp. pp. 18–19; Davidson 1984, p. 163; Dennett 1987, pp. 107–8; Putnam 1992, pp. 28–31.

way, how *should* we characterize a dog's mental state in a situation where we find it natural to say—what the above line of thought would disallow our saying—that the dog fears that its master will beat it or is looking for a bone?

The correct response to this traditional difficulty is that it only arises on a particular, non-compulsory conception of what it is for an infant or an animal to have cognitive access to a concept. According to this conception, infants and animals have their own powers of designation and classification—in effect their own conceptual apparatus. Then, since this apparatus is not isomorphic to ours—for its method of classification is much more primitive than ours—the problem is that we have no way of capturing its deliverances in our terms. We then have no choice but to employ our own apparatus which, no matter how hard we seek to avoid this consequence, always forces us to impute an unrealistic level of sophistication to the mental lives of the creatures we are trying to describe. But if we drop that problematic conception, and allow infants and animals to benefit transcendentally from our powers of designation and classification in the way I have suggested, rather than crediting them with their own peculiar such powers—ones which necessarily escape the net of our language—the purported problem no longer arises. In saying that a dog fears that its master will beat it or is looking for a bone, we are not trying, and inevitably failing, to reproduce in human language what the dog would say if, *per impossibile*, it could speak a canine language purportedly embodying its own peculiarly canine system of designation and classification.[55] Rather, we are characterizing, in the only way it is possible to characterize, the dog's mental state, and we are doing so with complete accuracy: at least, our characterizations will be completely accurate if the ascriptions are true. And if they are false they will be false in the ordinary way: that is, they will be false in just the way ascriptions of mental states to mature humans are normally false, when they are

---

[55] The misconception I am criticizing is poignantly captured in Wittgenstein's notorious remark that 'if a lion could speak, we could not understand him': *Philosophical Investigations* II. xi (1977, p. 358). On this passage see the remarks in my 2001c, at p. 211.

(the subject could be, but as it happens is not, in the relevant mental state), and not for some deeper reason such as the metaphysical inadequacy of our language to its subject matter. (Still less are our characterizations condemned, by any such purported inadequacy, to be nonsense.) The problem only seems to arise, we might say, because of a misconception of the transcendental constitution of infant and animal mentality. It is not that we have to earn the right to speak of (say) canine mental life, conceived as constituted independently of our powers of designation and classification (and then, since our tools are wrong for the job, we perforce produce descriptions that fail); rather, anything which aspires to have a mental life earns its entitlement to be minded only by virtue of the possibility that its mental states can be characterized in our language.[56]

IV.8. TWO SPECIES OF MENTALITY REVISITED

On the approach to the mentality of infants and animals which I recommend, these subjects can have experiences which, though non-conceptual in the sense that they are not intrasubjectively available to a critical and reflective mental faculty (the subjects in question having no such faculty to employ), nevertheless, by virtue of their intersubjective availability to the scrutiny of those (namely mature humans) who do possess such a faculty, are fully conceptual in the sense of being both propositionally structured and contentful in a way which is adequately capturable in language. The possibility of *our* expressing the content of *their* experiences transcendentally constitutes infants' and animals' experiences as conceptually structured in the relevant sense. It follows that those experiences can enjoy not only causal relations (if we want to include these in our analysis

---

[56] The equation, which I here presuppose, between what makes sense *to us* and what makes sense *simpliciter*, was famously advocated by Davidson in his essay 'On the Very Idea of a Conceptual Scheme' (1984, pp. 183–198), and is clearly endorsed by McDowell: 1998*b*, p. 337; 2002*b*, pp. 175–80. Cf. Putnam 1981, pp. 113–19.

of the genesis of empirical content) but more importantly just the right kind of normative relations with the world on the one hand, and with (our) judgements on the other, to entitle them to figure as appropriate relata in the complex model of empirical content which I outlined in Chapter I. Hence, to the extent that, with that complex model in place, we are entitled to move to a simple model of empirical content in which experience is conceived no longer as a *relatum* but as a normatively operative *relation* between the world and empirical judgement, there is no bar to conceiving infant and animal experience in just these terms. Infant and animal experience may take its place in the 'order of justification', intersubjectively construed.

The transcendental constitution of infant and animal mentality as conceptual, in the sense of being propositionally structured, entitles us now to say that infant and animal mental states, in general, are at least in the *same genus* as those mature human such states to which they are similar in the sense of matching them in structure and intentional content. Are they also in the *same species*? McDowell, it will be recalled (§1), answers this question in the negative. The correct answer, it seems to me, is likely to depend on contextual factors. (The genus–species distinction is in any case context-relative.) But I am willing to agree that there may well be contexts in which we shall want to distinguish, within a common genus of propositionally structured experiential states, between states which are available, *intra*subjectively, to a critical and reflective faculty, on the one hand, and states which are at best *inter*subjectively so available, on the other; and I can see no general reason why this distinction should not be registered in terms of the language of specific differences. For certain purposes it might be helpful to label the distinction in this way. But even if we adopted, in full generality (dispensing with the suggested relativization to contextual factors), a position according to which infant and animal mental states counted as generically the same as, but specifically different from, mature human such states of corresponding structure and intentional content, there would still remain a crucial divergence between the resulting position and the one which McDowell puts forward, despite a superficial similarity of overall shape.

On the position I advance, and regardless of how we adjudicate the issue of specific difference, the thesis that infants and animals enjoy experiential states which share a common genus with mature human such states is not just a piece of unmotivated sentimentality: rather, its presence is justified in the way I have indicated, namely by adverting to the manner in which the deployment of our critical and reflective capacities transcendentally constitutes infant and animal mental states as having just the intentional contents they do have. In McDowell's position, by contrast, the presence of the 'same genus' thesis is an unjustified dangler. To see this, consider by way of example the mental state of being in pain.

McDowell's view, as we have said (§1), is that mature human pain on the one hand and infant and animal pain on the other are distinct species—the one conceptually structured, the other not—of a common genus. But not only does he fail to motivate this position; his elaboration of it actually works against his entitlement to group the two varieties of pain together under a single genus. For his stress on the fact that, in mature human experience, 'receptivity does not make an even notionally separable contribution to the co-operation [sc. with spontaneity]'[57] renders it hard to see how something conceptually structured (as mature human pain is conceived to be), in the sense of being essentially permeated by the operations of a faculty of spontaneity, could be in the same genus as something not conceptually structured (as infant and animal pain is conceived to be), in the sense of being a chunk of brute receptivity.[58] (Of course, if we move to a sufficiently high level of generality we can always find a common 'genus' for any two things. But, just as the tradition of Aristotelian category theory rejected the introduction of catch-all categories like Being and One,[59] so we should avoid trivializing the notion of a genus in this way.)

---

[57] 1994, p. 9. Cf. 2000c, p. 343 n. 14.   [58] Cf. Wright 2002a, p. 164.
[59] Cf. Aristotle *Metaphysics*, 998b14–28; Porphyry *Isagoge*, 6.6–9.

Suppose we ask: what does my feeling pain have in common with a dog's feeling pain? Just that, answers McDowell—the fact that they are both cases of feeling pain.[60] Of course they *are* both cases of feeling pain—that much is uncontroversial—but the difficulty is to see how *McDowell* is entitled to give this reply, given the chasm he places between the two species of the supposed common genus. It is all very well for him to assure us that he wants 'no truck with' a Cartesian denial that an animal's 'awareness' of its prey is a case of genuine awareness.[61] That simply invites the riposte that one does not automatically disembarrass oneself of an unpalatable doctrine by expressly disavowing it: that will depend on the implications of the rest of one's philosophical position. If a doctrine is substantially rooted in central parts of a philosopher's thinking, the mere act of publicly disclaiming the doctrine will not be effective; or at best it will generate inconsistency.

In McDowell's case the question is how, given the alleged specific difference between human awareness and animal 'awareness'— merely 'alleged', because we await enlightenment on the nature of the supposed common genus—he can be entitled to rebut the charge of adhering to an unacceptable Cartesianism in respect of infant and animal mentality. For since on McDowell's view dogs have no 'inner world', the fact that their perception is non-conceptual, in the sense that it does not draw on critical and reflective capacities possessed by the subject of the perception, means that if we insist, as I have done (§6), that there is no conceptual gap between a dog's feeling pain and its feeling a pain, or between its feeling a pain and its being conscious of that pain, or between its being conscious of that pain and the pain's being an object for its consciousness, it will follow, according to McDowell, who contraposes the three interlocking conditionals implied in what I have just said, that the object in question is a

---

[60] 1998*a*, p. 409; 2002*a*, p. 288. Cf. 1998*b*, p. 282, where McDowell wants to be entitled to say that 'attributing pain to pre-linguistic infants is not a courtesy, an exercise of fancy, but an acknowledgement of plain fact'.

[61] 2002*c*, p. 104.

private object in the philosophically objectionable sense—an object which is non-conceptual in the radical sense of being a piece of the Given, a 'bare presence' on which language cannot get a grip. Why is this? The three interlocking conditionals which McDowell contraposes are: if *S* feels pain then *S* feels a pain; if *S* feels a pain then *S* is conscious of that pain; if *S* is conscious of that pain then it is an object for *S*'s consciousness. Since he rejects the consequent of the third of these conditionals in respect of infants and animals—that is, if *S* is an infant or animal, and so a creature lacking a critical and reflective faculty, a pain cannot, in his view, be an object for *S*'s consciousness—McDowell is also obliged, I claim, to reject the antecedent of the first of them. But given that he concedes that infants and animals do have some sort of awareness—both 'inner' and 'outer' awareness—it follows that the awareness they are allowed to have cannot be of objects of certain classifiable sorts, such as pains, but must be of 'bare presences' or Kantian things-in-themselves. That, then, inevitably invites the question: how could something which is non-conceptual in the radical sense of possessing no structure or content be in the same genus as something which is conceptually structured, such as a pain felt by an adult human? A 'bare presence' is not in any genus at all.

Let us go through this argument again, picking up the reasoning from a slightly earlier point in the dialectic. McDowell's idea was that infant and animal perception is non-conceptual in the sense that it does not draw on critical and reflective capacities possessed by the subject of the perception (the subjects in question having no such capacities), and he evidently thinks that the non-conceptuality of infant and animal perception in this sense can (and should) be embraced without a commitment to the non-conceptuality of the perceived objects in the more radical sense which envisages the subject as accessing pieces of the Given. He in effect thinks that we can accept the first commitment without being lumbered with the second so long as we do not conceive of the objects of infant and animal perceptual sensitivities as objects which are present in their consciousness. But the difficulty is to see how he can avoid this latter commitment, given the inevitability (as I have contended) of the move from the idea of a subject's feeling pain to its feeling a pain—in general: to its perceiving an object of a certain sort, whether 'inner' or 'outer'—and from there to the idea that the perceived object is an object present in that subject's consciousness: for that entailment ensures that in denying that perceived objects can be present in an infant or animal consciousness, McDowell is saddled with denying that infants and animals perceive ordinary objects of certain sorts (whether 'inner' or 'outer'), at all, and hence saddled with a construal of the perceptual sensitivity which infants and animals undeniably have as a sensitivity not to ordinary objects (of certain sorts), but to things-in-themselves. That is what makes it impossible for him to justify his 'same genus' thesis: for a thing-in-itself is not in a genus, and so *a fortiori* not in the same genus as anything else. Merely stressing, as McDowell does in many places, that infants and animals enjoy perceptual sensitivity to their environments, and that this means, for example, that they 'see objects' and 'can really suffer', goes no distance at all towards repairing the deficit; it does not begin to show *how* the alleged common genus of perceptual sensitivity can contain such diverse species as, on his account, it apparently must. I shall return to this point in the next chapter. In the remainder of this chapter I want to focus on one way in which McDowell sometimes tries to register a *difference* between the two species he identifies of the genus of perception.

IV.9. MENTALITY AND PROPOSITIONAL CONTENT

The difference I have in mind is arrived at by deploying a distinction between mental states that involve the subject's merely being acquainted with an object and states which are, additionally, propositionally structured. In one place McDowell contends that, though animals can *see objects*, they do not, in a strict sense, *see that such and such is the case*.[62] And it is noticeable how careful McDowell is, both in *Mind and World* and in subsequent publications in which he responds to critics of that work, to avoid ascribing to infants and animals any abilities that would imply that they are not only perceptually acquainted with objects, but also enjoy perceptual mental states which are propositionally structured.

In writings unconnected with *Mind and World* and the reactions it has provoked, however, he is not so careful. In a discussion of communication among birds in his essay 'Meaning, Communication, and Knowledge', McDowell allows that a 'no doubt rudimentary' notion of content—and the context makes clear that propositional content is what is in question—'seems undeniably applicable'.[63] In his essay 'The Content of Perceptual Experience', he is quite happy to say that a frog is not merely aware of objects, but is also aware that such and such is the case, for example that it 'becomes informed ... that there is a bug-like object at such and such a position';[64] or, in a grammatically equivalent locution, it is allowed that a frog 'becomes informed of ... the presence of a bug-like object at a certain place'.[65] Frogs are permitted, in language that is reminiscent of the *Mind and World* story, to have 'modes of sensitivity or openness to features of the environment',[66] but here, unlike there, they and other non-human animals are granted 'involvement with content'.[67] It is accepted that non-human animals are (in Daniel Dennett's memorable phrase) semantic and not merely syntactic engines.[68]

Now in the context of this latter essay McDowell is trying to counter the suggestion that the ascription of content-involving states to systems of a creature which operate below the level of conscious-

---

[62] 1998c, pp. 432–3. In this passage the capacities of infants and animals are held to be, strictly, 'pre-factive', phraseology which recalls the 'proto-subjectivity' granted to them in *Mind and World* (1994, p. 117).

[63] 1998c, p. 45; cf. p. 40.

[64] 1998b, p. 351.

[65] 1998b, p. 349.

[66] 1998b, p. 350; cf. pp. 348, 354.

[67] 1998b, p. 347; cf. pp. 349, 351, 356.

[68] 1998b, p. 351; Dennett 1987, pp. 141–2.

ness ('sub-personal' states, this phrase being scare-quoted to allow it to be applied to non-persons such as frogs)[69] is literal. We can, if we wish, talk about 'what the frog's eye tells the frog's brain', but this is just a metaphorical way of referring to informational transactions between one part of the frog and another part.[70] McDowell indeed concedes (not only here but also in *Mind and World*) that it may be theoretically indispensable to talk *as if* 'sub-personal' states were contentful; but he suggests that this theoretical imperative should not blind us to the fact that such states are not *literally* contentful.[71] By contrast, when we say that a frog (the whole organism, not one of its parts) becomes informed or aware *that* such and such is the case, McDowell assures us that 'the involvement of content … is literal'.[72]

On the face of it, there seems to be a straight antinomy in McDowell's thinking on the question whether the ascription to an organism like a frog of content-involving states, such as the awareness that there is a bug-like object in front of it, is literal or not: in one context it is affirmed that the ascription is literal, whereas in another context just this is denied. As far as I can see, the best that can be done, on McDowell's behalf, to resolve this tension without jettisoning either of the claims which generate it, is to relativize the issue of the literalness of the ascription of content in the following way: relative to the ascription of content to mature humans, we might say, the ascription of content-involving states to organisms like frogs counts as non-literal; but relative to the ascription of content to a frog's 'sub-personal' states, ascription of content to the frog itself is allowed to count as literal. If that strategy does indeed represent the best way of reconciling McDowell's various pronouncements in this area, we have the upshot that, on his amended view, ascription of content to 'sub-personal' states of an animal such as a frog is at two removes from the strict ascription of content. In the first place, while we naturally *say* that a frog is aware that there is a

---

[69] 1998*b*, p. 347.   [70] 1998*b*, pp. 346–50.
[71] 1998*b*, pp. 350–4; 1994, pp. 55, 121.   [72] 1998*b*, p. 349.

bug-like object in front of it, the ascription of content to the frog, though *relatively* literal in the sense explained, is not *absolutely* literal, or strict: in the strict sense of the locution, it is not the case that a frog sees *that* (schematically) such and such is the case. Secondly, any content we wish to attribute to the frog's 'sub-personal' states, those underlying its seeing that such and such is the case, is at a yet further remove from the absolutely literal or strict ascription of content, however theoretically unavoidable such language may be for us. But if McDowell's position can be rendered consistent in this way, it nevertheless has to be rejected. There are two reasons why this is so.

The first of these reasons is that it is simply not acceptable to suggest that there is a level at which, or a sense in which, a creature perceives objects, but does not perceive *that* (schematically) such and such is the case.[73] To perceive an object is to pick it out from its environment in some way, however primitive; and to do that is to register, in however rudimentary a way, *that* the object in question is at least *not the same as* other objects in its vicinity. Other abilities will also be involved in the perception of an object, and some of these further abilities will also require us to ascribe propositional attitudes to the relevant creature; but this very basic ability to distinguish one object from its neighbours will serve quite well enough to make the necessary point, which is that if a creature strictly perceives objects, it strictly perceives *that* (schematically) such and such is the case. So where we have every reason to affirm the antecedent of this conditional, we should also affirm the consequent. Richard Schantz has suggested that 'not all perceiving is perceiving *as* or perceiving *that*', on the basis that 'we can see a crocodile, even though we do not recognize it as such, and even though we do not possess the concept

---

[73] *Pace* Collins, who argues that experiences as such should not be taken to have propositional content (1998, p. 379): his line is rejected—at least for subjects who possess a faculty of spontaneity—by McDowell (1998a, p. 413; cf. Willaschek 2003, pp. 269–72). I am suggesting that McDowell is wrong to restrict the scope of his rejection to subjects in possession of a faculty of spontaneity.

of a crocodile'.[74] Schantz is right in the second part of his claim, but that does not support the first part: of course any subject of experience can fail to recognize a perceived object for what it is, but it does not follow that that subject does not see that object *as* a thing of a certain sort (perhaps merely bringing it under a very general classification, or perhaps misclassifying it), and it does not follow that the subject in question does not see *that* the object is distinct from other things in its vicinity.

The second difficulty with McDowell's position is this: it is not acceptable to concede that it is theoretically indispensable to talk *as if* a creature enjoys—whether at a 'personal' or at a 'sub-personal' level—content-involving states, but deny that these ascriptions need be taken literally or strictly. If the ascriptions are indispensable, that means that they *must* be taken strictly; for otherwise they would *not* be indispensable—there would be a better characterization of what was going on, one that was strictly true, and the ascription of content could be relinquished in favour of this more accurate mode of discourse. There is a *tu quoque* point to be made against McDowell here. He himself, in a polemic against Simon Blackburn's projectivism in his essay 'Projection and Truth in Ethics', raises the sound objection that if there is no alternative way of identifying a purported projective response, other than in terms of the predicates which we apply to the world *after* the purported activity of projection has occurred (something that Blackburn concedes), then 'there is no way of saying what has happened, in detail, in terms of the image of projection';[75] but if projectivism were true there *ought* to be some such way, so that Blackburn's concession (which seems independently correct) can hardly be allowed to be consistent with projectivism.[76] A precisely parallel point applies against McDowell's attempted combination of the theoretical indispensability of content-ascription in certain contexts with the non-literal status in such contexts of the relevant ascriptions.

[74] 2004, p. 105.
[75] 1998*b*, pp. 158–9 n. 15.
[76] Cf. 1998*b*, pp. 122–6, 143–4.

For McDowell, ascription of content to 'sub-personal' states of an animal is theoretically indispensable in a 'causal or enabling', not a 'constitutive', sense.[77] The ascription is indispensable because it 'makes it possible to understand' how content, strictly or literally so called (perhaps only relatively literally, on the amended interpretation of his position), arises causally;[78] but precisely because the understanding yielded is not of constitutive connections, the ascription of content to 'sub-personal' states cannot be strict or literal. There is a partial similarity of dialectical shape here with McDowell's claim, in the context of his treatment in *Mind and World* of normativity, that we engage with reasons as a matter of our biological constitution,[79] but with one crucial difference. In the case of the alleged connection between biology and normativity, the idea is that there is a connection, not (or not merely) of a causal and enabling kind, between our biological nature and our capacity to engage with normativity, but of a constitutive kind.

In both cases there is a lacuna where we expect explanation and elucidation. I have already complained about this deficit in the case of the alleged connection between biology and normativity; and a related complaint applies in the present context. For one is bound to ask *why* 'sub-personal' states, treated as if they have content, play the enabling role assigned to them, given their constitutive isolation from the contentful states they supposedly enable. It is hard to see that there is room here for the sort of middle position McDowell wants to occupy: surely, if the connections in question are *not* constitutive, there can be no theoretical *requirement* to explain the provenance of contentful 'personal' mental states by reference to literally non-contentful 'sub-personal' states; on the other hand, if indeed there is, as McDowell claims, no *other* way to understand how the superior contentful states have emerged except by tracing

---

[77] 1998*b*, pp. 352–6.   [78] 1998*b*, p. 353. Cf. 1995*a*, p. 289.

[79] Cf. Ch. II, §5. Recall 1994, p. 103: 'the idea of a subjectively continuous series of "representations" could no more stand alone, independent of the idea of a living thing in whose life these events occur, than could the idea of a series of digestive events with its appropriate kind of continuity'.

their origin to inferior 'sub-personal' states, treated as if they have content, how could the connection between them *not* be constitutive? We are owed some explanation of the availability of the supposed intermediate position, not the mere assertion of faith that it exists.

V

Diagnosis and treatment

V.1. THE AILMENT: KANTIAN TRANSCENDENTAL IDEALISM

A question which McDowell never raises, but which ought to seem pressing for anyone who adopts his approach to the question of infant and animal mentality, is this: given that subjects whose sensibility is structured by a faculty of spontaneity (subjects who are in the 'target area' of the transcendental argument)[1] experience objects as falling under concepts—experience objects *by virtue of* the fact that their experience is conceptually structured—how is it that infants and animals, whose sensibility is *not* structured by a faculty of spontaneity—whose 'experience' of (mere sensibility to) their environment is in that sense non-conceptual[2]—manage to latch on cognitively to many of the same objects? We adult humans isolate in cognition certain objects as things of certain sorts, by dint of bringing to bear our faculty of spontaneity—from its co-operation with which, so we are assured by McDowell, our faculty of receptivity is not even notionally separable—and yet we find that, remarkably, infants and animals, lacking the benefit of a conceptualizing apparatus and with only a faculty of receptivity to aid them, are nevertheless able to cognize many of the same objects. This ought to seem like the most extraordinary coincidence—indeed really an inexplicable one, given the terms in which it has to be described by an approach such as

---

[1] Cf. 1998a, p. 411.   [2] 1998a, p. 412.

McDowell's: our conceptually structured sensibility is a transformation, so we are told (cf. Chapter II, §§3–5), of a more primitive sensibility which is not so structured, but if the unstructured sensibility is able to cognize many of the same objects as the structured one, it seems either that the transformation was (at least for the purpose of cognizing the common objects) unnecessary, or that it must in fact have occurred before we are told that it occurred. The problem is a version of one I have already mentioned (Chapter IV, §8), namely the problem how conceptual and non-conceptual perceptual routes to the world can be species of an interesting common genus. But focusing on the problem in the terms I have just introduced—that is, focusing on the claim that there can be both conceptual and non-conceptual perceptual routes to the very same objects—can, I suggest, be illuminating in pointing to an initial characterization of McDowell's metaphysical economy, and ultimately to a diagnosis of what has misled him into making some of the mistakes which I have been concerned in this study to expose, and in particular the mistake of downgrading the metaphysics of infant and animal experience.

The initial characterization of McDowell's metaphysical position I have in mind is this: he is in effect committed to transcendental idealism in its objectionable Kantian form, that is, to a world lying not only beyond the reach of human experience, but utterly beyond the conceptual (in the sense of what is propositionally structured, and hence expressible in language), a world of bare things-in-themselves. Kant is committed to such a world: for although officially he claims that the notion of the noumenal is negative and regulatory, a mere *Grenzbegriff*[3] in practice his characterizations of the noumenal go well beyond what that official doctrine would lead us to expect. In particular, his willingness in many passages to assign a causal and explanatory role to noumena (cf. Chapter II, §6) commits him to a

---

[3] See esp. the section of *KrV* entitled 'Phaenomena und Noumena', A235–60/B294–315.

positive, transcendent conception of them.[4] A similar failure to hold the line against the noumenal and the transcendent occurs in McDowell's thinking. For though officially hostile to Kantian things-in-themselves, which as we have noted he identifies with the target of Wittgenstein's Private Language Argument, the position he adopts on the question of infant and animal mentality opens the door to just such 'things'. How does this come about?

As we have seen, McDowell thinks that, as well as a conceptual route to objects, a non-conceptual route to the same objects (or to some of them) is available. In itself, this is not a thesis that we need contest, so long as 'non-conceptual' is glossed along the lines of 'not available to a critical and reflective faculty possessed by the subject in question' (the sense of 'non-conceptual' introduced in the third lecture of *Mind and World*). In the previous chapter (Chapter IV, §4) I tried to show how we can accommodate infant and animal experience, in the fullest sense, despite the fact that infants and animals lack any such critical and reflective faculty, by allowing them to exploit, transcendentally, our critical and reflective faculty. I suggest that it is only by taking such a line that we can assuage the sense of puzzlement I expressed at the beginning of this section, the sense of surprise we naturally feel that there can be both conceptual and non-conceptual routes to the very same objects. McDowell, by contrast, has no way of allaying this sense of puzzlement, for he has no transcendental story about the constitution of infant and animal conceptual consciousness: for him it is just a brute, and extraordinary, fact that there can be two such routes to the same objects. Now I also suggested, in my discussion in Chapter IV, that there is no coherent way of granting infants and animals perceptual sensitivity to objects, as McDowell is obliged to do, without also conceding that such objects—whether 'outer' or 'inner'—figure as such (as the

---

[4] See the passages cited above in Ch. II, n. 113. I am not sympathetic to recent attempts to query the traditional 'two worlds' interpretation of Kant, which strike me as misguided: see on this issue Bird 1996, pp. 227–9; Allison 1997, pp. 44–6; Sedgwick 2000; along with McDowell 1998*d*, p. 469 n. 23; 2000*c*, pp. 330–2. But my interpretation of McDowell obviously does not depend upon this point.

objects they are) in infant and animal states of consciousness, something that McDowell seeks to deny. For McDowell, the concession that when a dog feels pain that is 'a matter of an object for the dog's consciousness' or of 'a state of affairs [obtaining] within its consciousness'[5] would be tantamount to the positing of private objects of infant and animal consciousness in the sense condemned by Wittgenstein.

Given, now, that the concession is simply unavoidable, McDowell is saddled with the undesired and undesirable upshot that the objects which can be accessed in the two very different ways he permits—conceptually and non-conceptually, in the sense explained—must, in themselves, be noumenal with respect to the conceptual. That is, these objects must be things-in-themselves: they must be non-conceptual in the radical sense (introduced in the first lecture of *Mind and World*) of being 'bare presences' which fail to fall under any concepts at all, and on which therefore language can get no grip. For, on McDowell's own showing, an object that is present to an infant or an animal consciousness—and I have suggested that, if we allow infants and animals to be perceptually sensitive to objects at all, we cannot but recognize the existence of such objects—is a private object in the offending sense; that is, it is an 'object' about which nothing can be said, because language is incompetent to embrace it.

V.2. SENSE, REFERENCE, AND CONCEPTS

If we put the point in terms of the distinction between sense and reference, as these notions figure in the familiar Fregean semantic hierarchy, what we in effect have on McDowell's approach is a picture according to which the conceptual—in the sense of what is conceptually structured—is located not in the realm of reference, but in the realm of sense; objects, which exist in the realm of reference, are not intrinsically conceptually structured but are, taken as entities

---

5 1998*b*, p. 313 n. 34; 1998*a*, p. 429.

in the realm of reference, Kantian things-in-themselves. These objects (or some of them) may be accessed by perceptual modes of presentation (senses), and these modes of presentation fall into two species, the conceptual and the non-conceptual: for subjects such as ourselves, whose faculty of receptivity is essentially structured by a faculty of spontaneity, the perceptual modes of access to objects are conceptual; for subjects who possess only a faculty of receptivity they are non-conceptual. The realm of reference, so conceived, is in effect what McDowell calls the 'environment': it is what we share with infants and animals, and to which both we and they are perceptually sensitive. The environment is not the world: that latter title is reserved for what is experienced by subjects whose faculty of receptivity is structured by a faculty of spontaneity. The world, so conceived, and the conceptual in general, belong to the realm of sense. That, I submit, is the story to which McDowell is committed.

Of course the claim that the environment which we share with infants and animals is noumenal with respect to the conceptual is not one which McDowell would wish to acknowledge as part of his metaphysical picture: he makes amply clear his hostility to the idea of a Kantian noumenal realm.[6] I have been suggesting that he is, nevertheless, and despite his overt opposition to it, committed to exactly that claim. In contradistinction—and oddly—the correlative thesis that the world, and the conceptual, belong to the realm of Fregean sense, is one that he enthusiastically embraces. We are told that 'if we want to identify the conceptual realm with the realm of thought, the right gloss on "conceptual" is ... "belonging to the realm of Fregean sense" '.[7] And further:

Given the identity between what one thinks (when one's thought is true) and what is the case, to conceive the world as everything that is the case (as in *Tractatus Logico-Philosophicus*, §1)[8] is to incorporate the world into what

---

[6] 1994, pp. 41–5; cf. 2004, pp. 395–7.　　[7] 1994, p. 107.

[8] A conception which McDowell endorses: 1994, p. 27; 1998*b*, pp. 178, 306; 1998*c*, p. 288 n. 19.

figures in Frege as the realm of sense. The realm of sense (*Sinn*) contains thoughts in the sense of what can be thought (thinkables) as opposed to acts or episodes of thinking. The identity displays facts, things that are the case, as thoughts in that sense—the thinkables that are the case. (1994, p. 179)

This passage both affirms what is known as the identity theory of truth,[9] and locates the world at the level of sense. Shortly afterwards, McDowell cites with approval 'the Fregean view, that thought and reality meet in the realm of sense',[10] which he takes to convey the point of Wittgenstein's aphorism that 'when we say, and *mean*, that such and such is the case, we—and our meaning—do not stop anywhere short of the fact; but we mean: *this—is—so*'.[11] In McDowell's view these moves secure the result that 'reality . . . is not to be pictured as outside an outer boundary that encloses the conceptual sphere'.[12] Evidently they do secure that result: whatever lies beyond the conceptual sphere (the level of Fregean sense), it certainly cannot, on McDowell's approach, be *reality*.

McDowell is aware that his position is apt to elicit an accusation of idealism, but unfortunately he does not correctly identify where the real danger for him of a lapse into idealism lies.[13] He envisages, in effect, three forms of the charge of idealism, to which he offers three responses: first, as we saw in the quoted passage he draws a distinction between thought-episodes and 'thinkables' (that is, thinkable contents), and elsewhere he makes it clear that he identifies the world only with true thinkables;[14] secondly, he avers that the fact that 'there is a permanent possibility of having to decide we were wrong' protects the doctrine that the world consists of the totality of

---

[9] *Pace* de Gaynesford, who claims that McDowell never explicitly espouses the identity theory: 2004, pp. 125–6. But the cited passage is surely as clear a commitment as one could wish for: cf. also 1995*a*, p. 284; 2000*a*, pp. 93–5. De Gaynesford concomitantly denies, mistakenly in my view, that McDowell is in the business of 'constructing the world out of Fregean senses' (2004, p. 130).

[10] 1994, p. 180.

[11] 1994, p. 27; *Philosophical Investigations* I, §95 (1958, p. 44).

[12] 1994, p. 26. Cf. Brandom 1994, pp. 614–23. Brandom too makes clear that he identifies the conceptual with the realm of Fregean sense: 1994, p. 712 n. 9.

[13] Cf. Dodd 1995, p. 163.

[14] 1994, pp. 27–8; 2000*a*, p. 96; 2000*c*, p. 339.

true thoughts (that is, true thinkables) from being idealistic;[15] and thirdly, he thinks that provided we conceive of (at least some) senses as *de re*, not specificatory, we will secure for cognition the kind of direct bearing on objects that suits a realist posture in semantics and the philosophy of mind.[16] In other words, the senses in question are to be conceived as essentially presenting their respective *res*—the notion of *de re* sense being governed by the principle: no object, no sense—not externally connected to them in such a way that the objects are merely contingent satisfiers of a blueprint or description. We are assured that these non-specificatory relations between thinkers and objects 'need not be conceived as carrying thought outside an outer boundary of the conceptual realm',[17] and that 'for an object to figure in a thought, a thinkable, is for it to be the *Bedeutung* associated with a *Sinn* that is a constituent of the thinkable'.[18] These manoeuvres perhaps block charges of idealism when such charges are motivated in the ways McDowell anticipates. (There is room for doubt on this score;[19] and recall the argument

---

[15] 1995*a*, pp. 284–5. Cf. 1994, p. 40.

[16] 1994, pp. 179–80. Cf. 1998*c*, pp. 171–98, 214–27; 2000*c*, p. 339. This is the response I focus on when I discuss the threat of idealism to McDowell's position in my 2001*b*, pp. 3–4. There I interpret McDowell's talk of incorporating the *world* into the realm of sense as expressive of the impulse to incorporate the *realm of reference* into the realm of sense: it is this position which I aim to refute at pp. 14–16. This interpretation is also, in effect, presupposed by one of Lyne's criticisms of McDowell in his 2000, p. 308 (the 'sense–reference problem'); but I am no longer sure whether it represents the most accurate reading of McDowell's texts. Here, accordingly, I focus on a simpler interpretation of the passage I have cited from 1994, p. 179, one which construes McDowell's words more literally: on this understanding of McDowell's position it is indeed the *world* that is incorporated into the realm of sense, leaving the realm of reference intact. Note that, immediately after the passage cited from 1994, p. 179, McDowell agrees that 'objects belong in the realm of reference (*Bedeutung*), not the realm of sense', a remark which discourages Lyne's and my previous interpretation of his position. The purely technical considerations which I adduced in my earlier discussion, in order to rebut the suggestion that we can incorporate the realm of reference into the realm of sense, are therefore not germane in the present context: here my charge against McDowell is rather that the objects which he locates in the realm of reference—acknowledged to be distinct from the realm of sense—are, given his identification of the world with the level of sense, rendered noumenal with respect to the world.

[17] 1994, p. 107.

[18] 2000*a*, pp. 94–5.

[19] See here Willaschek 2000.

of Chapter III, §7, that his individualism renders McDowell liable to a devastating scepticism.) But they are not the directions from which the real threat to his position in the present context comes: if he has (here at least) escaped the Circean enchantments of Berkeley, he has done so only to be lured to destruction by the siren voice of Kant.

McDowell unavoidably attracts a charge of embracing an unacceptable Kantian transcendental idealism, because in locating concepts in the realm of sense, not of reference, he renders the objects which inhabit the realm of reference noumenal with respect to the conceptual. It is no comfort to be assured that at least some modes of presentation of those objects are conceptual: the point is that, in the absence of concepts housed at the level of reference, and structuring objects at that level (this is an important proviso to which I shall return in the next chapter), the objects so presented, however they may be conceived, are not *intrinsically* (that is, taken as realm-of-reference entities) structured by concepts. Hence relations between thinkers and objects, whether *de re* or specificatory, must, contrary to his claim, be conceived by McDowell as carrying thought outside the conceptual sphere: for thought is carried to objects, and these, being entities at the level of reference and being, for McDowell, unstructured by concepts at that level, *are*, in themselves, outside a boundary enclosing the conceptual sphere. The sheer fact, if it is one, that objects are *Bedeutungen* of conceptual *Sinne* cannot save McDowell from this consequence. Moreover (as the reservation I inserted at the beginning of the previous sentence hints), there must be a serious question whether it makes sense to suppose that conceptual modes of presentation are capable of carrying thought to objects which, in themselves, are not conceptually structured and so lie outside the conceptual sphere. If objects are, in themselves, noumenal with respect to the conceptual, how can we have cognitive access to them? And why should we want such access? Why should we wish to transcend our world? If our world lies within the conceptual sphere, then objects, by being cast out from the conceptual sphere, fall away past this world's verge. How could such objects be anything to us?[20]

Now given that McDowell apparently embraces an idealism of this highly unsatisfactory variety in his treatment of the distinction between sense and reference, it should come as no surprise that his handling of the thesis—in itself innocent, provided it is correctly interpreted—that the very same objects (or some of them) which we access conceptually (in this sense: by deploying our faculty for critical and reflective thought) may also be accessed non-conceptually (in the corresponding sense) by infants and animals, commits him, despite his intention, to the noumenal status of the 'objects' and 'environment' inhabited by creatures lacking a faculty of spontaneity. There is a symbiosis, hitherto unnoticed either by McDowell himself or, so far as I know, by any of his critics, between a construal of infant and animal experience to which he is unintentionally committed and a thesis in the philosophy of language which he willingly espouses.

Of course in one sense McDowell is happy to be called an idealist: if 'idealism' imports the essential conceptuality (in both senses of that vexed word which have played a role in this study) of experience, together with the thesis of the unboundedness of the conceptual, then he is willing to be enlisted amongst the idealists, so understood.[21] The form of idealism he wishes to circumnavigate is Davidsonian coherentism, with its unhappy commitment to regarding our operations of spontaneity as mere 'frictionless spinning in a void'.[22] Davidson of course contends that his transcendental argument that belief is largely veridical, together with an insistence on the obtaining of causal relations between world and mind, secure him against charges of adhering to an unwarrantable idealism. We have already noted that McDowell thinks that Davidson's transcendental argument 'comes too late' to secure empirical content for mental entities (Chapter III, §8), and hence that the charge that he embraces an

---

[20] Cf. Suhm, Wagemann, and Wessels 2000, p. 32. Thornton mentions a similar difficulty (2004, p. 243), but fails to appreciate either its source (the absence of the conceptual from McDowell's level of reference) or its gravity.

[21] 1994, pp. 44–5.   [22] 1994, p. 11.

unacceptable idealism is inevitable. As far as the causal considerations go, it is clear that, for Davidson, the causal relations in
question would be realm-of-law transactions. McDowell responds
to an accusation that he is offering a similar picture by insisting that
the causal relations connecting mind and world in his account are
space-of-reasons transactions, not realm-of-law ones,[23] and I have
already suggested (Chapter II, §§2–3) that his best strategy for
avoiding an unpalatable Anomalous Monism would indeed be to
insist that the receiving of impressions in experience is a transaction
wholly within the space of reasons. But although that is his 'best
position', we can now, in the light of the considerations I have
brought to bear in this chapter, see that this line is problematic for
McDowell. This is not simply because he tells us so little about what
space-of-reasons causation is. More seriously, the problem is that
given, as I have suggested, that the objects which inhabit McDowell's
realm of reference are Kantian things-in-themselves, it follows that
they cannot participate in *any* causal transactions, either space-of-
reasons or realm-of-law ones.[24] The failure to locate concepts at the
level of reference destroys any possibility of our enjoying causal
relations with objects housed at that level. Such objects are, conceptually and causally, utterly beyond our reach.

McDowell is aware that Frege himself located concepts not at the
level of sense but at the level of reference.[25] But he chooses not to
follow Frege on this point: it is quite clear, not only from the passages
I have already cited, but from much of the language McDowell
adduces to talk about our grasp of concepts, that, for him (and
here he follows a more traditional understanding of concepts than

[23] 2002*b*, §II.

[24] Recall the discussion of Ch. II, §6.

[25] McDowell 1998*c*, pp. 87, 218–19; Frege 1892*a*, p. 193. Frege's location of
concepts at the level of reference is, in one sense, pointless in the context of the rest of
his semantics: for he fails to link up objects and concepts in propositionally structured
combinations at the level of reference. Propositions exist, for Frege, exclusively at the
level of sense, so that in one way McDowell is right to attribute to Frege the view that
reality (the world) is a sense-level phenomenon. But Frege's failure to locate propositionally structured entities at the level of reference is not a feature of his semantics to be
applauded, but one to be corrected. This will be the topic of Ch. VI.

Frege's), concepts reside not at the level of reference, but at the level of sense. In the very first sentence of *Mind and World* McDowell tells us that his topic is 'the way concepts mediate the relation between minds and the world',[26] a way of talking which already points to the location of concepts at the level of sense. He regularly talks of *exercising, using, deploying* and *exploiting* concepts,[27] language which is inappropriate to a Fregean understanding of what concepts are: for concepts at the level of reference cannot be *exercised* or *deployed*, but merely *grasped*.[28] He frequently speaks in one breath of 'concepts and conceptions', as if there were no significant ontological differences between them.[29] He talks of our standing obligation to 'refashion concepts and conceptions':[30] but concepts at the level of reference cannot be refashioned; they are simply there, like Fregean objects, for subjects to grasp or not. (A purported refashioning of a Fregean concept would change the concept.)

In his essay 'One Strand in the Private Language Argument', McDowell remarks, in connection with his claim (which we have encountered before: Chapter IV, §5) that 'external' objects, unlike objects of sensation, are 'there for one's thinking anyway, independently of what one thinks about them', that one can misconstrue this claim as encouraging

the idea that reference is a point where a remarkable contact between Thought (conceptually structured) and World (brutely external to anything conceptual) is effected. What is wrong with this, to put it telegraphically, is

---

[26] 1994, p. 3. Cf. 2002*b*, p. 191 n. 18.

[27] 1994, pp. 5, 6, 11, 37, 50, 57. Cf. 1998*b*, p. 221; 1998*c*, p. 289 n. 22.

[28] In another type of locution, McDowell talks of 'exercising conceptual capacities': e.g. 1994, pp. 7, 9, 10, 11, 28, 39 etc. (in the last of these—the passage, cited above in Ch. I, §5, on which Larmore takes McDowell to task—the 'conceptual contents' which are 'passively received in experience' are said to bear on, or be about, the world). In a yet further locution, McDowell sometimes speaks of 'operations of conceptual capacities' *vel sim.*: e.g. 1994, pp. 12, 13, 36, 37, 49, 52, 120 (and cf. 1998*a*, p. 426). Neither of these phrases attracts the censure I direct against talk of exercising or deploying concepts: they are not incompatible with the location of concepts at the level of reference.

[29] 1994, pp. 13, 40, 47, 81, 82, 136. But contrast 1998*b*, p. 46; 2000*c*, p. 333. On the distinction between concepts and conceptions, see Putnam 1981, pp. 116–19.

[30] 1994, pp. 12–13; cf. pp. 33–4, 46–7, 81.

that it involves forgetting or denying a point of Frege's that we can put like this: even if an object is there for one's thinking independently of what one predicates of it in thought, it nevertheless figures in one's thought *as something*—'under a mode of presentation'. (1998*b*, p. 287)

But to say that an object figures in one's thought *as something* ought to mean that it figures in one's thought *as instantiating some property*, that is, as exemplifying a universal which inhabits the same ontological level as the object itself, namely the level of reference. Hence if we want to put the point in Fregean terms, we must say that the object in question has to be thought of as falling under a concept, where the latter kind of entity is to be conceived, as Frege did conceive it, as a denizen of the level of reference and not of the level of sense. McDowell's gloss on thinking of an object 'as something' as thinking of it 'under a mode of presentation' is accordingly incorrect as an interpretation of Frege: for Frege, thinking of an object (or for that matter a concept) under a mode of presentation would be thinking of it not *as something* but *in some particular way*. But the key point for us about his gloss is what it reveals not about McDowell's understanding of Frege but about his own metaphysical economy. In seeking to utilize Fregean sense to effect the needed connection between thought and world—that is, in seeking to exploit the fact that objects of thought are necessarily thought about in some way, in order to ensure that object-directed thinking is conceptually structured—McDowell confines the conceptual to the level of sense, leaving objects, taken as entities at the level of reference, out in the cold as Kantian things-in-themselves.[31]

In this connection it is worth observing that, in passages where McDowell discusses the sense–reference distinction in detail, as for example in his essays 'On the Sense and Reference of a Proper

---

[31] For McDowell's location of concepts at the level of sense, see further his essay 'Wittgenstein on Following a Rule' (1998*b*, pp. 221–62) *passim*, e.g. at p. 248, where the 'normative status' of concepts is under discussion: the question of normative status (the dictating of patterns of use etc.) cannot intelligibly be raised in respect of concepts at the level of *reference* (or of anything else at that level), but only in respect of concept-*words* (or other words) and their *senses*: only the latter kinds of item can *dictate* patterns of use; concepts at the level of reference *are* patterns of use. Note also 1998*c*, pp. 287, 408–9.

Name', 'Truth-Value Gaps', and '*De Re* Senses', he focuses on the case of proper names, almost entirely ignoring concept-words or, in general, the predicative component of sentences.[32] Brandom states that in '*De Re* Senses', McDowell 'indicates some reasons why' Frege's location of concepts at the level of reference 'is not a harmless or philosophically neutral choice of terminology'.[33] But this is an egregious misinterpretation of that essay, in which McDowell simply *assumes* that concepts and the conceptual have to do with the level of Fregean sense. He indeed notes that this disposition is non-Fregean,[34] but nowhere does he *argue* against Frege. McDowell's target in that essay—what he regards as philosophically offensive—is rather the widespread resistance to the idea that some Fregean senses might be *de re*, i.e., object-dependent. He does not discuss the possibility that, equally, there might be kinds of Fregean sense (namely senses of concept-expressions) that are concept- or property-dependent, where concepts and properties are construed as reference-level entities.[35] It is significant that in one of the few passages in the essays in question where properties are so much as mentioned—a critical discussion in the essay 'Truth-Value Gaps' of Russell's 'ordered pair' conception of the contents of propositions and singular thoughts,[36] according to which objects and properties figure as literal constituents of propositions and singular thoughts—only objects are selected for attention. McDowell's point is that Russell's treatment of the relation between proper names and objects ought to be corrected so as to accommodate Fregean sense, and accordingly needs to be articulated into a tripartite structure comprising proper names, their senses, and their referents (bearers). But it is striking that no corresponding point is

[32] See 1998c, pp. 171–227; Cf. too pp. 123, 233–6, 268–9.

[33] 1994, p. 694 n. 10.

[34] 1998c, p. 218.

[35] A similar remark applies to the discussion of object-dependency in the essays 'Singular Thought and the Extent of Inner Space' (1998c, pp. 232–6; cf. pp. 247–9, 252–9) and 'Intentionality *De Re*' (1998c, pp. 260–74). In both cases the omission is to be explained by adverting to McDowell's exclusive focus on the way objects figure in *perception*. The concept- or property-dependence of thought, by contrast, pervades all thinking in which there is a general component.

[36] 1998c, pp. 204–9.

made concerning the relation between predicates and properties (or concept-expressions and concepts), and, so far as anything McDowell says goes, properties (concepts) might already, in his view, *be* sense-level entities. That is, in insisting that objects can figure in thought in such a way as to permit more than one *way* in which a given object so figures[37]—they figure sufficiently intimately to render the thoughts in question *object-dependent*, but not so intimately that objects become literal *constituents* of thoughts, as it were blocking all but a single mode of presentation of them[38]—McDowell makes no parallel stipulation for properties (concepts), which suggests (or at any rate is compatible with the supposition) that he regards properties (concepts) as being in any case sense-level entities, figuring as literal constituents of thoughts.[39]

There is also a suggestive comment in his essay 'Putnam on Mind and Meaning'. In considering the question 'how does thinking hook on to the world?', McDowell remarks:

Such a question looks like a pressing one if we saddle ourselves with a conception of what thinking is, considered in itself, that deprives thinking of its characteristic bearing on the world—its being about this or that object in the world, and its being to the effect that this or that state of affairs obtains in the world. (1998c, p. 288)

Notice the two candidates for things in the world on which thinking can bear: objects and states of affairs. We might wonder whether states of affairs are being conceived, in a Tractarian manner, as combinations of objects: for there is no mention here of anything

---

[37] Cf. 1998c, p. 209.

[38] In fact, of course, the idea of an object which admits only one mode of presentation of it is incoherent: in the case of such an object (assuming, *per impossibile*, that there could be one), the notion of sense would have no application.

[39] Note also his revealing concession at 1998c, p. 268, that a descriptivist treatment of singular terms which deploys the apparatus of Russell's Theory of Descriptions does at least (whatever its other drawbacks) provide us with the fineness of grain which it was the purpose of the introduction of Fregean sense to secure. But the Russellian apparatus is powerless to model fineness of grain in respect of *concept-expressions*: nothing short of Fregean sense will equip us to distinguish the meanings of complex expressions which differ only in point of their employment of distinct, but co-referential, concept-words (e.g., 'woodchuck'/'groundhog', 'Rotrückenwürger'/'Neuntöter').

like concepts or properties construed as inhabiting the realm of reference and structuring objects at that level. Of course, in itself the omission in this passage of any suggestion that concepts might be found at the level of reference is no doubt unremarkable, but in the context of the other points I have adduced it acquires some significance: the omission points to a housing of concepts at the level of sense.

In his recent study of McDowell's thought, Maximilian de Gaynesford suggests that McDowell locates not only objects and states of affairs but also properties at the level of reference:[40] but the texts which he cites in support of his claim contain nothing about properties to justify any such confidence,[41] and indeed (as I have already observed in respect of some of the essays to which de Gaynesford refers) these texts hardly mention properties at all. (The essay 'Truth-Value Gaps' is an exception in this regard, but we have seen how disappointingly recessive the role which McDowell there assigns to properties is.) More generally, apart from the Kantian transcendental idealism to which, as I have argued, McDowell's views on infant and animal mentality commit him, the fact that he locates the world at the level of sense tells against his having an intention to recognize anything like properties existing at the level of reference. It is one thing to banish *objects* to an extramundane level of reference: for that disposition, though incoherent, can at least boast a distinguished precedent in Kantian thought. It would be quite another thing to banish *objects and properties* to a level of reference conceived as lying beyond the world. That would betoken a quite extraordinary insouciance.[42]

---

[40] 2004, p. 132.

[41] He cites McDowell 1990; the essays collected at 1998c, pp. 171–291; and 1998g.

[42] Admittedly, this is, in one sense, Frege's position, as I have observed (n. 25 above). But there is an obvious mitigating circumstance which one can plead in Frege's defence. For although I have conceded (ibid.) that, in view of his location of propositionally structured entities not at the level of reference but at the level of sense, it is in one way fair to *gloss* Frege's position as anticipating McDowell's, it is important to stress that it is a gloss: so far as I know, Frege nowhere expressly asserts that, as McDowell would have it, the world is to be identified with the level of sense. Frege's insouciance, we might say, is merely implicit.

V.3. PROPOSITIONS AND STATES OF AFFAIRS

McDowell evidently equates (at least officially) propositions with Fregean Thoughts, which exist at the level of sense: he is unhappy with the early Russell's doctrine of propositions as worldly entities composed of the referents of the corresponding sentences' significant words.[43] But in the last section I speculated whether McDowell conceives of states of affairs as Tractarian combinations of objects at the level of reference. If we assumed that both this speculation and my understanding of his official position on propositions were correct, and if, further, we identified (as it is quite natural to do) states of affairs with propositions, we would arrive at a reading of McDowell's position which in effect coincided with one offered by Julian Dodd.[44] Dodd's view is that McDowell commits himself incoherently to two incompatible conceptions of the location of propositions: on the one hand, in agreement with my diagnosis of his official view, McDowell is said to locate propositions at the level of sense; but on the other hand Dodd treats McDowell's endorsement of the Tractarian claim that the world is everything that is the case as evidencing an impulse to locate propositions at the level of reference, given that the early Wittgenstein seems not to have recognized a level of Fregean sense.

[43] 1998*c*, pp. 160 with n. 8, 233 (cf. pp. 147 with n. 16, 215 n. 6, 225 n. 35); 2000*a*, p. 94. At 1998*c*, p. 233 'content' is clearly taken (at least in one of its occurrences, where it glosses 'thoughts') to be a sense-level phenomenon; cf. 1998*c*, pp. 218–19. At 1998*c*, p. 225 n. 35 it is remarkable that McDowell refers to a passage in Russell's 'The Philosophy of Logical Atomism' (written in 1918) as raising difficulties for Russell's earlier (1903) conception of propositions as reference-level entities with objects and properties as constituents. For the text to which McDowell alludes (1956, pp. 224–7) is not only a patent nest of confusion, insufficiently coherent to raise difficulties for any position, but is in any case primarily directed not against Russell's 1903 theory, but against his 1910–13 multiple relation theory of judgement: see here my 1997*c*, pp. 142–5.

[44] In his 1995. There are discussions of Dodd's interpretation by Thornton (2004, pp. 233–44) and by Suhm, Wagemann, and Wessels (2000).

At least as far as his position in *Mind and World* is concerned, it strikes me as a misinterpretation of McDowell to read his appeal to the Wittgensteinian claim (that the world is everything that is the case) as *eo ipso* committing him to locating propositions at the level of reference. For McDowell could respond, I think reasonably, that his endorsement of that claim was not intended to imply a commitment to Tractarian metaphysics quite generally; and indeed, as we have seen, what he explicitly says about the Tractarian claim in *Mind and World* is that 'to conceive the world as everything that is the case … is to incorporate the world into what figures in Frege as the realm of sense', which gives the claim a pointedly *non*-Tractarian application.[45] Hence I think it is preferable, as far as our understanding of *Mind and World* is concerned, to grant McDowell a consistent position according to which propositions are located along with concepts exclusively at the level of sense: the difficulty for him on my interpretation is then that objects, being located at the level of reference and so banished from the precincts of the conceptual (which inhabits the level of sense), stand exposed as Kantian things-in-themselves.

But when we take into account a wider range of McDowell's texts than just *Mind and World*, and in particular when we take note of the passage I have cited from the essay 'Putnam on Mind and Meaning', we do find a problem in the matter of McDowell's location, not specifically of *propositions*, taken on their own, but of *propositions and states of affairs*. For propositions are located at the level of sense, and states of affairs at the level of reference. Why is this problematic for McDowell? Even if we do not identify states of affairs with propositions, and regardless of whether or not we accept the speculation according to which states of affairs, conceived as denizens of the realm of reference (and not now identified with propositions), are taken to be sheer combinations of objects, this disposition is incoherent. The incoherence does not now consist in a

---

[45] In effect this is McDowell's response to Dodd (given in his discussion of Suhm et al.): 2000*a*, pp. 93–4. Cf. 1998*c*, p. 288 n. 19.

commitment on McDowell's part to housing the very same entities (i.e., propositions, and indeed the very same propositions)[46] both at the level of sense and at the level of reference, as on Dodd's interpretation, but rather in a commitment to drawing a distinction between, on the one hand, entities at the level of sense (propositions) which are both conceptual and propositionally structured, and, on the other, entities at the level of reference (states of affairs) which are non-conceptual (in the radical sense propounded in the first lecture of *Mind and World*), but are nevertheless undeniably propositionally structured. But this will simply not do. How can two kinds of entity which are, even if not identical, at least structurally isomorphic be assigned to opposite sides of a division between the conceptual and the non-conceptual? States of affairs are, even if not identical with propositions, at any rate structured just like propositions—we refer to them in exactly the same way as we refer to propositions (by means of noun clauses of the form *that such and such is the case*)—and so surely cannot fall outside a boundary enclosing the conceptual if propositions are to be placed inside it.

Corresponding to the dislocation between propositions and states of affairs in McDowell's metaphysical economy, we have an antinomy on the question: where, in McDowell's semantical hierarchy, should we locate the world? In the passage I have quoted from 'Putnam on Mind and Meaning', it seems clear that the world is where objects and states of affairs are, namely at the level of reference.

---

[46] It must be stressed that the antinomy which Dodd purports to find in McDowell resides in the attempt to locate *the very same propositional entities* both at the level of sense and at the level of reference. Unlike Dodd, I see no objection to locating *some* propositionally structured entities and the level of sense and *other* such entities at the level of reference. I locate propositions strictly so called, composed of objects and (Fregean) concepts, at the level of reference (see my 2001*b* and further below), but I also locate propositionally structured entities, namely senses of the corresponding sentences (Fregean Thoughts), at the level of sense. On this model, although there are propositionally structured entities both at the level of sense and at the level of reference, the Fregean Thoughts which are housed at the level of sense are *modes of presentation* of the worldly propositions located at the level of reference: there is no question of an *identity* between entities of these two sorts (i.e., an identity of any entity at the level of reference with any entity at the level of sense), and so the antinomy which, on Dodd's interpretation, bedevils McDowell's semantics is avoided.

For one would naturally suppose that if at least objects and states of affairs are being housed at the level of reference, the level of reference must be identified with the world. But McDowell's *Mind and World* position is, as we have seen, that the world is located at the level of sense, inside a boundary enclosing the conceptual (which is identified with the level of sense), and beyond which objects are left to fend for themselves in a featureless, unstructured realm of 'reference' (I scare-quote because the label no longer makes sense). These two answers to our question, concerning where we should locate the world in the semantical hierarchy, are plainly incompatible.

V.4. CONCEPTS AND NOMINALISM

I have already indicated how McDowell's treatment of infant and animal mentality fits the metaphysical picture I am imputing to him. But his location of the conceptual in the realm of Fregean sense, and his identification (at least sometimes) of that realm with the world, gives us an explanation for two further prominent features of McDowell's thinking that have exercised us in this study.

First, it explains the apparent antinomy which I have noted (in Chapter I) concerning the 'order of justification'. Why does McDowell sometimes speak of *the world* as 'ultimate in the order of justification', and sometimes of *experience*? Earlier, I tried to provide an interpretation of McDowell which neutralized the appearance of conflict: I suggested that the position he is aiming to take up is that it is not the world, as such, nor experience, as such, which is ultimate in the 'order of justification', but rather *the experienced world*, the world as accessed in that particular way. But I did not try to account for the presence of the antinomy (or the appearance of its presence) in McDowell's texts in the first place. Why does he write in such a way as at least to give the impression that he is not clear in his own mind whether it is the world or experience which is ultimate in the 'order of justification'? The answer is that McDowell does not sufficiently distinguish these two things: more accurately, he does not locate them at different levels in the semantic hierarchy, in the following sense. The experience of creatures such as ourselves whose faculty of receptivity is structured by a faculty of spontaneity is essentially conceptual, and the conceptual is located by McDowell at the level of Fregean sense in the semantic hierarchy. His further identification (at least in *Mind and World*) of the level of sense with the world then precipitates a semantic concertinaing of experience and the world, which in turn yields a wavering, in his texts, on the question which of them is ultimate in the 'order of justification'.

Secondly, we also have an explanation why, in spite of his official hostility to an interface conception of experience, some of his views seem to commit him to just that conception (Chapter III). For if the conceptual is being located at the level of sense, and if, what seems to be a corollary of this, objects in the realm of reference are intrinsically noumenal with respect to the conceptual, and given that experience is essentially a conceptually structured phenomenon, there will be a clear sense in which experience does not function as a conduit to objects—at least, not to objects as they intrinsically are—but as a means of processing whatever input we may (incoherently, of course) conceive as emanating from objects, which taken in themselves are no more than 'bare presences', to yield a conceptualized output. When objects are conceived as noumenal in this sense, experience cannot but be conceived as an interface between minds and objects, for there is no such thing as confronting noumenal objects directly. As Kant half-recognized,[47] a veil descends unstoppably between us and the objects themselves.

I have been suggesting that we can explain much of what is unsatisfactory in McDowell's metaphysical economy if we focus on the fact that he locates concepts at the level of sense, rather than at the level of reference. That commits him to a nominalistic construal of the conceptual as essentially mental, in the sense in which Fregean sense is mental (of course this need not be, and for Frege was not, a

---

[47] See the extraordinary *KrV*, A779–80/B807–8.

psychologistic sense),[48] dislocated from real objects which, in view of the dislocation, retreat to a penumbra where, taken in themselves and construed as entities in the realm of reference, they exist as mere Kantian things-in-themselves. Nominalism has some claim to be a dogma of empiricism: in fact the third dogma on the traditional numeration, namely the dualism of conceptual scheme and uninterpreted content.[49] Or perhaps we should say that nominalism is a *consequence* of this dualism. However such issues of nomenclature are to be settled, I take it as given that any such nominalism is to be spurned.[50]

To make a start on disentangling ourselves from this unacceptable nominalism (it is no more than a start, as we shall see in due course), we need to follow Frege in locating concepts in the realm of reference. The realm of sense will then contain not concepts but senses of concept-expressions. Lest this point strike the unwary as amounting to no more than a piece of terminological legislation, it must be clearly emphasized that what is in question here is a substantial and not a merely verbal constraint. The crucial requirement, for the avoidance of an unacceptable Kantian transcendental idealism, is that objects at the level of reference should be held to be structured by universal entities, however these are styled, at that level. Of course I have no objection to employing the label 'concepts' for the entities which Frege introduces as the senses of concept-expressions. One is perfectly at liberty to follow ancient tradition, rather than Frege, in confining the entities which one calls concepts to the level of sense, *so long as* one recognizes that entities of the right universal kind,

---

[48] McDowell discusses and rejects psychologism in his essay 'Anti-Realism and the Epistemology of Understanding': 1998*c*, pp. 314–43; cf. pp. 177–81.

[49] The scheme/content dualism is thus styled by Davidson (1984, pp. 183–98), capping Quine's 1953, ch. 2.

[50] The species of nominalism in question is sometimes called (for obvious reasons) 'conceptualism' (see Boehner's studies of Ockham in his 1958). There is a fine (and insufficiently appreciated) refutation of both conceptualism and nominalism narrowly so called (the former represented by Locke's *Essay,* the latter by Horne Tooke's *Diversions of Purley*) in Hazlitt's *Lectures on English Philosophy* (1967, pp. 195–6, 279–80). Cf. Park 1971, pp. 95–9.

whatever one chooses to call them, both exist at the level of reference—as referents of the sense-level items, whatever one calls them, playing the role of Frege's senses of concept-expressions—and structure objects at that level. (One might, for example, take concepts to be sense-level modes of presentation of reference-level properties.)[51] But that is not McDowell's strategy, and that is why his confinement of concepts to the level of sense cannot simply be nodded through as a mere matter of terminological preference. For if one respects what I presented above as the crucial requirement for the avoidance of an unacceptable Kantian transcendental idealism, it will not be an option to imply, as we have seen McDowell implying (§2), that when an object figures in one's thought *as something*, that is merely tantamount to its figuring *under a mode of presentation*; and, more substantially, it will not be an option to follow McDowell's *Mind and World* strategy of identifying the world (or reality) with the conceptual realm, when this latter is understood in the traditional, non-Fregean way as coinciding with the level of sense.

I shall return to these points in my final chapter. But first we must ask *why* McDowell makes what, when it is spelt out, represents such an unappealing metaphysical disposition, especially in view of the fact that he so forcefully repudiates the third dogma of empiricism, the dualism of scheme and Given, in his attack on the Myth of the Given. Why, having resisted the dualism of scheme and Given when this is construed as a dualism purportedly obtaining exclusively at the level of sense, does he then succumb to it when it is construed as a dualism articulated between the levels of sense (the purported home of scheme) and reference (the purported home of the Given)? What, in McDowell's view, is wrong with locating concepts—universal entities available to structure objects—at the level of reference? There are several passages in McDowell's discussions of the Wittgensteinian rule-following considerations which suggest an answer to this question.

---

[51] This would be roughly the position of a medieval realist such as Walter Burleigh.

V.5. WITTGENSTEIN AND ULTRA-REALISM

In analysing the position of Wittgenstein's platonist opponent—the position which in *Mind and World* is characterized as *rampant platonism*—McDowell identifies a cluster of ultra-realist (as I shall call them) ideas and images against which Wittgenstein polemicizes.

(i) First, if we suppose that following a rule is a matter of having an interpretation (that is, of substituting one expression of the rule for another), we find ourselves launched on a regress of interpretations.[52] In the particular case of linguistic understanding, it would be viciously regressive to construe understanding a given expression as mentally putting another expression in its place: for understanding the substituted expression would require a repeat of the exercise, the process would never terminate, and so a state of understanding would never be attained. It would be no use trying to halt the regress which arises in this way by identifying the meaning of a linguistic expression with the *last* interpretation, for there is no last interpretation: once we are embarked on the regress there is no stopping point.[53] So understanding does not consist in having an interpretation (in the defined sense): any interpretation just 'stands there like a sign-post' alongside the original sign-post, so to speak, and cannot give it life.[54]

(ii) Secondly, we should reject the idea that the normativity embedded in our rule-following practices can be certified as such from a perspective *outside* those practices themselves—from what McDowell calls a 'sideways-on' perspective—as if those practices magically engaged with normative rails which were there anyway, utterly independently of the practices themselves. (The image of a

---

[52] Wittgenstein *Philosophical Investigations* I, §§198–201; McDowell 1998*b*, pp. 264–6.

[53] Wittgenstein *Blue Book*, p. 34; *Zettel*, §231; McDowell 1998*b*, pp. 272–5.

[54] Wittgenstein *Philosophical Investigations* I, §§85, 432. This point is the Ariadne's thread of Thornton's reading of McDowell's philosophy in his 2004.

'sideways-on' perspective is McDowell's own, but he means it to capture a central Wittgensteinian idea.)[55]

(iii) Thirdly, there are several passages in which Wittgenstein rejects (sc. realm-of-law) *causal processes* (and in particular mechanical ones) as offering a way of reconstructing the normativity of rule-following: for if we supposed that rule-following were a matter of mimicking the operations of a machine, the machine in question would have to be a *supermachine*, a machine protected as a matter of logic—like the rule itself—from malfunctioning, a machine whose outputs were logically guaranteed to be correct applications of the rule. But there is no such machine: any actual machine is an empirical object which obeys causal laws, however these may turn out to be (they are not prescribed by us), and accordingly its operations may always, as we say, misfire or malfunction, by which we mean that, when the machine malfunctions, though it has behaved in accordance with the laws of nature—it *is* protected as a matter of logic from departing from *them*, for they are just a compendious description of things' (including its) actual behaviour—it has not done what the rule requires. (It has not done what its designer intended it to do.) There can be no guarantee in logic that *causal* process will follow a *rule*.[56]

In presenting these three arguments against ultra-realism, McDowell tends to conflate them, as if they were different aspects of the same basic argument. In particular, he plainly regards (i) and (ii) as functioning for Wittgenstein as mere variants of (iii).[57] That seems to me a mistake. Consider first (i) and (iii). There is surely nothing in the idea of a last interpretation, just as such, which requires us to represent it as driven by a supermechanism; and the converse point

---

[55] 1994, pp. 34–5, 82–3, 168; 1998*b*, pp. 203, 207–8, 211–12. Cf. 1994, pp. 152–3; 1998*d*, p. 490; 2000*b*, *passim*.

[56] Wittgenstein *Philosophical Investigations* I, §§191–5; *Remarks on the Foundations of Mathematics* I, §§118–28; *Zettel*, §296; McDowell 1998*b*, pp. 273, 315, 320; Brandom 1994, pp. 13–15.

[57] Conflation of (i) and (iii): 1998*b*, pp. 230–2, 237, 244, 272–3, 309, 320. Conflation of (ii) and (iii): 1998*b*, pp. 61–2, 203–4, 208–9, 215, 256.

applies as well. McDowell seems to make the connection between these two arguments via the following Wittgensteinian text:

> A wish seems already to know what will or would satisfy it; a proposition, a thought, what makes it true—even when that thing is not there at all! Whence this *determining* of what is not yet there? This despotic demand? ('The hardness of the logical "must".') (*Philosophical Investigations* I, §437; 1958, p. 129; trans. adapted)[58]

Here it is plausible that Wittgenstein means to connect the idea of a supermechanism ('the hardness of the logical "must" ' in a pejorative, ultra-realist sense) with that of a 'determining of what is not yet there' by a 'despotic demand' or by what McDowell calls 'a superlatively unyielding authority',[59] and McDowell's thought is evidently that the idea of a last interpretation is relevantly similar to that of a despot who tries to impose an end on the regress of interpretations by sheer fiat.[60] But the idea of a last interpretation, one which purportedly halts the regress of interpretations, is not obviously, just as such, the idea of a despotic or superlatively unyielding *authority*, and certainly not the idea of an authority which forces its interpretation on us *causally*. The point about the 'last' interpretation is not that it forces the cessation of the regress as a matter of (super)causation, but that it purports to be more than just another sign: it purports to be the very meaning itself. (Of course in actual fact it is nothing but another sign; that is why there is no last interpretation.) Conversely, there is nothing in the idea of a supermechanism, just as such, which purports to stop a regress of interpretations. For the idea of supermechanism is the idea of a normativity that is supposedly constructed out of purely *causal*

---

[58] Cf. I, §223 (1958, p. 86): 'One does not feel that one has always got to wait upon the nod (the whisper) of the rule. On the contrary, we are not on tenterhooks about what it will tell us next, but it always tells us the same, and we do what it tells us'.

[59] 1998*b*, p. 309: the idea of a last interpretation 'is the germ of the platonist idea ... that meaning's "normativity" is a matter of a superlatively unyielding authority'.

[60] Cf. 1998*b*, p. 244, where he speaks of the idea of a super-rigid machine as being the 'natural accompaniment' of the assimilation of understanding to having an interpretation (and so, by extension, the natural accompaniment of the fantasy of a last interpretation).

materials, and there is nothing in the idea of a causal connection, just as such, which points to the notion of an *interpretation*.

It is true, as McDowell points out, that Wittgenstein's polemic against the idea of supermechanism is part of a more general attack which he mounts on what we might call the idea of a superconnection, the idea of a purported construction of internal relations out of external-relations materials.[61] A superconnection, so understood, may be, but does not have to be, constructed out of specifically *causal* connections. A case where the more general but not the more specific polemic applies is provided by the relation between a mental image and its object. Wittgenstein attacks the temptation to suppose that a mental image is 'more like its object than any picture': that is not how a mental image earns its entitlement to be *of* its object. Yielding to the temptation leads to a conception of the image as being a 'superdepiction' (*Über-Bildnis*) of its object,[62] in the sense of its being, on the one hand, a picture of its object, and so something with an intrinsic character (as a physical picture, for example, might consist of a particular arrangement of brush strokes on canvas) and, as such, merely externally related to its object, but, on the other hand, so similar to its object that the external relation between image and object becomes alchemically transmuted into an internal relation. Of course, a physical picture *taken as a cultural artefact* is not merely externally related to its object (if it has one), because in identifying it as such we have incorporated the artist's intentions, to which the picture's object is internally related, into the identity of the picture itself: but the point is that this internal relation cannot be constructed out of the external-relations materials to which we would be confined if we started with the idea of a picture characterized in purely intrinsic—say, material—terms, and then tried to secure the desired internal relation to the intended

---

[61] 1998*b*, pp. 290–3, 301–2; cf. 1998*g*, pp. 50–7. A superconnection would be what McDowell at one point (1998*b*, p. 315) calls a 'super-factual linkage' (echoing the 'superlative fact' of *Philosophical Investigations* I, §192.

[62] *Philosophical Investigations* I, §389; *Lectures and Conversations on Aesthetics, Psychology and Religious Belief*, 1966, p. 67.

object by subliming the relation of similarity—by idealizing it as a relation of supersimilarity—and thereby purportedly guaranteeing, as a matter of logic, the unique routing of that relation from the picture to what is in fact the picture's intended object.[63] The incoherence which results from such an attempted strategy obviously generalizes the incoherence we found above in the idea of a supermechanism. Now this quite general attack on the idea of a superconnection is certainly present in Wittgenstein's writings: but, contrary to McDowell's suggestion,[64] the general idea of a superconnection does not of itself import the notion of a *last interpretation*, purportedly halting a regress of interpretations, any more than the more limited idea of supermechanism (or supercausation) imports that notion; and again the converse point holds as well.

Nor, to turn to the case of (ii) and (iii), is there anything in the idea of a sideways-on perspective on our practices which requires us to represent such a perspective as discerning supermechanism in those practices (though in this case the converse claim has more plausibility). The wrong idea of rules-as-rails figures as part of Wittgenstein's polemic against the spurious causal reconstruction of rule-following (rule-following as involving supercausation), and not as part of an attack on a 'sideways-on' perspective on our

---

[63] So-called mental images do not, like physical pictures, have an intrinsic character, whose external relations with an object one might seek (of course hopelessly) to transmute into internal relations. They have nothing but their intentionality, so that the idea of a superconnection purportedly mimicking the intentionality relation has even less plausibility, if that is possible, in their case than it has in the case of pictures strictly so called. On the point that mental images have no intrinsic nature, see McDowell's response to Wright's suggestion that 'in the sense in which an image or mental picture can come before the mind, its intentionality cannot' (1998*b*, p. 31). McDowell's reply is: 'This strikes me as back to front. The truth is more like this: the *only* thing that comes before the mind, when (as we say) an image does, is its intentionality—the image's content, what it is that is pictured. It is *my wife's face* that comes before my mind when I imagine my wife's face. Nothing else does, at least nothing that is relevant to the fact that I am imagining my wife's face; certainly not some inner analogue of, say, a photograph, with properties describable independently of any [sc. intentional] content it can be seen as carrying' (1998*g*, p. 56). This is surely exactly right. Cf. 1998*c*, pp. 286–7, for the parallel point about thoughts.

[64] 1998*b*, p. 320.

practices.[65] Giving a causally reductive account of our rule-following practices might be one way—but need not be the only way—of giving (or rather purporting to give) a 'sideways-on' account of those practices.[66] So I am not convinced by McDowell's conflation of (i), (ii), and (iii): I do not think it aids our understanding of Wittgenstein to merge what are in fact separate argumentative strands.

V.6. ULTRA-REALISM AND UNIVERSALS

But the issue of the propriety of these conflations, important though the matter be for the correct exegesis of Wittgenstein, is not my principal concern here. What is of interest here is the fact that, in treating ultra-realism of the second and third varieties as different facets of the same basic position, McDowell also associates that position with realism in the old sense, namely realism about universals. In the following passage from his essay 'Non-Cognitivism and Rule-Following', for instance, McDowell is considering a version of ultra-realism about rule-following which attempts to deal with cases where there is allegedly no non-trivial formulation of the rule:

> Sometimes ... a practice of concept-application resists codification otherwise than trivially (as in 'It is correct to call all and only red things "red" '), and in such cases we tend [sc. if we are attracted by ultra-realism] to ... appeal to grasp of a universal, conceiving this as a mechanism of an analogous sort [sc. to the case where the rule is non-trivially codifiable]: one that, like knowledge of an explicitly stateable rule, constitutes a capacity to run along a rail that is independently there. (1998*b*, p. 204)[67]

This passage is drafted in such a way that it seems to leave open the possibility that there could be an innocuous conception of 'grasp of a

---

[65] See here *Philosophical Investigations* I, §§218–20. Cf. McDowell 1998*b*, pp. 231–2.

[66] Cf. McDowell 1994, pp. 152–3.

[67] In fact it is a mistake to suppose that the sample codification offered in this passage is trivial: I return to this point below in this section.

universal', one which did not construe this grasp in terms of the mythology of supermechanism. But unfortunately, if it was indeed McDowell's intention to leave open this possibility, he did not make it sufficiently clear, and a later passage in the same essay speaks quite generally of 'grasp of the universal',[68] without qualification, as though there could not be a realism about universals which escaped the second and third ultra-realist commitments. In adopting this position McDowell seems to have been influenced by a famous description given by Stanley Cavell of Wittgenstein's vision of our 'form of life': in this description Cavell rejects, on Wittgenstein's behalf, the 'grasping of universals' as a means of ensuring that our 'whirl of organism' is sufficiently coherent to enable us to follow common rules.[69] There is no suggestion, in Cavell's characterization of Wittgenstein's position, that the grasping of universals deserves to be rejected as a candidate for what sustains our rule-following practices only on a particular, ultra-realist conception of what it is to grasp universals.

In the same essay McDowell makes use of an interesting and revealing variant of the locution 'grasping a universal': concerning an ultra-realist conception of disputes about the application of concepts which give rise to 'hard cases', he writes that where the application of the concept 'is not codifiable (except trivially), ... one's problem is to use words as hints and pointers, in order to get one's opponent to divine the right universal'.[70] The suggestion that the act of grasping a universal—which ought to be an innocuous matter of understanding an appropriate linguistic expression (centrally, a common noun)—is in point of fact to be construed as a feat of divination, an act of setting up a quasi-magical connection between mind and world (ultra-realistically conceived), is another sign of McDowell's readiness to make a present of realism

---

[68] 1998*b*, p. 211.

[69] 1969, p. 52, cited by McDowell in his essay 'Virtue and Reason', at 1998*b*, p. 60, and again in 'Non-Cognitivism and Rule-Following' at 1998*b*, pp. 206–7. Note too Rorty's disparaging remarks on grasping universals: 1979, pp. 38–45; cf. 1982, p. 24.

[70] 1998*b*, p. 210.

about universals to the ultra-realist. As a further instance of this regrettable tendency we may cite a passage in his essay 'Wittgenstein on Following a Rule', where McDowell remarks that the 'occult' idea of a 'wholly autonomous meaning (one is tempted to say "out there")'—which again he identifies with the idea of supermechanism, and which he contrasts with the good notion of 'acting within a communal custom'—is 'reminiscent of realism as the term is used in the old debate about universals'.[71]

In this latter case the picture is complicated by McDowell's characterization of ultra-realism as representing a possible fact 'as an unconceptualized configuration of things in themselves',[72] a characterization which, as I tentatively speculated above (§2), might be thought to fit McDowell's own position. But, setting that speculation aside, the point here is that the realist *about universals* can hardly be saddled with a conception of facts as 'unconceptualized configurations of things in themselves', at least not just by virtue of being a realist: this realist locates universals in the world—at the level of reference—in as objective a sense as anything at all is in the world, and provided he or she does not make the mistake of isolating universals from the entities which may instantiate them, it follows that configurations of worldly things will be, at the most fundamental level, configurations of things of certain (universal) sorts.[73] And nor, as I have observed (Chapter II, §6), can 'unconceptualized things in themselves' be supposed to interact causally—and so *a fortiori* not supercausally either—given that (to put it in the terms

---

[71] 1998*b*, p. 255.

[72] Ibid. Cf. 1998*c*, p. 364 n. 41, where 'language-independent "aspects of reality" ' seem to discharge the same role in the realist's—here clearly the ultra-realist's—inventory as do unconceptualized things-in-themselves in Kantian transcendental idealism. See also 1998*c*, p. 92 with Christensen 2000, p. 906.

[73] The things so configured will themselves include universals (for universals themselves fall under universals). If the realism in question is strongly derivative of Plato, it may take its class of basic worldly things to be composed exclusively of universals; but a less austere realism will allow both individuals and universals to be comprised in our fundamental ontology. I will return in my final chapter to the important point that objects and concepts at the level of reference (to put it in Fregean terms) must not be held apart from one another (as Frege arguably did hold them apart).

of Plato's creation myth) the demiurge's allocation of causal dispositions to things was coeval with (and necessarily accompanied) his
dividing them into sorts. So it is not entirely clear what McDowell
thinks 'unconceptualized things in themselves' are doing in the ultra-
realist's inventory, unless we are meant to think of them as universals-
in-themselves—but it is utterly unclear what they might be—or
perhaps as meanings-in-themselves, their characterization as 'unconceptualized' then alluding to the fact that, for the ultra-realist—who
now steps forward in the full regalia of the rampant platonist—they
are supposed to be constituted in 'splendid isolation' from human
rule-following practices, in the sense that 'meanings take care of
themselves, needing, as it were, no help from us',[74] a metaphor
which is, in turn, presumably to be cashed in the terms I set out in
Chapter II (§5) when I discussed the definition of rampant platonism: namely, as the claim that it is not essential to them (the
unconceptualized meanings-in-themselves), and not essential to us
(human rule-followers), that we engage with them.

However this may be, my diagnosis of McDowell's hostility
towards locating concepts or universals at the level of reference is
that he thinks that, if we locate them there, there is at least a risk
(putting it cautiously) that we will be seduced into adopting an ultra-
realist posture towards meaning, conceiving concepts or universals at
the level of reference as somehow escaping the 'whirl of organism', as
somehow constituted in splendid isolation from our rule-following
practices. (I will return in the next chapter to comment on the
collocation 'concepts or universals'.) There may indeed be such a
risk, but it is one which need not be realized; for someone who
locates concepts or universals at the level of reference is not *eo ipso*
committed to denying either that it is essential to those concepts, or
that it is essential to us, that we grasp them. So if McDowell's
naturalized platonism is indeed the right metaphysical position,
and if I have interpreted it correctly, it need not conflict with a
sane realism about concepts and universals. And the price of refusing

---

[74] 1998*b*, p. 254.

to locate concepts or universals at the level of reference is too high to leave us the option of following McDowell in locating them exclusively at the level of sense.

After all, McDowell himself concedes that Plato, who was clearly some sort of realist about universals, was not a (rampant) platonist in his sense.[75] So it may be conjectured that McDowell would agree that it is possible to be a sane realist about universals—that it is possible to locate concepts at the level of reference—without succumbing to rampant platonism. There must indeed be conceptual room for a sane realism in the sense here in question: it cannot be the case that *any* notion of 'grasp of a universal' is tainted with ultra-realism. For, quite apart from other considerations, it seems obvious that a correct explication of the notion of following a rule will appeal to the grasping of a universal. To take the example McDowell mentions in a passage cited above, following the rule for 'red' involves knowing that this word applies to all and only red things, a piece of—evidently non-trivial[76]—knowledge that, in turn, requires one to know what all and only red things have in common, which in turn entails the possession of a practical capacity to identify, under favourable viewing conditions, red objects as such, and to be able to distinguish them from objects which are not red; but having that capacity just *is* grasping the universal *red*. So when Cavell writes, in a passage which elicits McDowell's approval,[77] that 'the grasping of universals' does not *ensure* the correct following of a rule, the sane realist will hear him as making a category mistake: the correct following of a rule *is* a matter of grasping the (right) universal.[78]

---

[75] 1994, p. 110; 1998*b*, p. 177 n. 19. Cf. 1998*b*, pp. 216 n. 25, 273.

[76] *Contra* McDowell's claim in his essay 'Non-Cognitivism and Rule-Following' (1998*b*, pp. 204, 210; cf. pp. 240–1). Actually, he had recognized the non-triviality of the knowledge in question in Evans and McDowell 1976, pp. x–xi. Did McDowell lose grip of his earlier insight under the influence of Rorty 1979, p. 260? If so, it seems that further reflection on Rorty may have enabled him to regain it: with 1998*b*, p. 240–1 compare 2000*b*, pp. 117–18 (see also 1998*h*, pp. 38–43).

[77] See n. 69 above.

[78] Cf. n. 31 above. At the end of 'Virtue and Reason', McDowell enters a reservation about Cavell's treatment of 'the grasping of universals': 'though Plato's forms are a myth,

It follows from these considerations that there must be an innocuous form of realism about universals: and in that case McDowell should have adhered to realism in this sense. But his aversion to worldly universal entities, and his consequential locating of concepts at the level of sense rather than at the level of reference, stand in the way of his recognizing the real danger to his position, namely the threat of a lapse into an unacceptable Kantian transcendental idealism. It is ultimately that feature of his metaphysical economy which ensures that, despite its official characterization as 'minimal', his empiricism is in fact a good deal more substantial and contentious than its billing suggests.

they are not a consolation, a mere avoidance of vertigo [i.e., a mere refusal to acknowledge that rule-following rests on nothing more than shared forms of life]; vision of them is portrayed as too difficult an attainment for that to be so' (1998*b*, p. 73; cf. 2000*b*, pp. 113–14). McDowell has ethical forms in mind, and particularly the Form of the Good, but Plato's doctrine of forms extends (at least sometimes) more widely than that: in the tenth book of the *Republic* they exist wherever a common name is applied (596a6–7); that is, they are genuine universals. McDowell's reservation is not of the right shape to deal with the general case.

VI

The world's own language

VI.1. COMBINING OBJECTS AND CONCEPTS AT THE LEVEL OF REFERENCE

Had he been more hospitable to locating concepts as well as objects at the level of reference, McDowell might have seen his way to locating propositions there too. In fact, as we have noted, alongside what may be called his official doctrine, according to which the world exists at the level of sense, with the realm of reference containing only (individual) objects, McDowell maintains a kind of 'minority doctrine', according to which, in effect, the realm of reference, and not merely the realm of sense, must contain propositionally structured entities: that is an implication of a passage I cited in the previous chapter (§2) in which states of affairs were mentioned as worldly entities.[1] It is also implied by several other texts, including a passage in *Mind and World*, where McDowell appears to speak of the worldly truth-makers of the sentences 'I am *this* tall' and 'It looks to me as if something is of *that* shade'.[2] Compare too a remark from his early essay 'Falsehood and Not-being in Plato's *Sophist*':

The notion of a state of affairs is the notion of something with a complexity of a different kind from that of a mere composite thing; it is the notion of a chunk of reality with a structure such as to mirror that of the proposition or statement it would render true. (1982, p. 131)

---

[1] 1998*c*, p. 288. [2] 1994, p. 57.

Presumably the truth-makers which McDowell mentions in these texts (and truth-makers of sentences in general) are being construed as realm-of-reference entities, for McDowell can hardly be taking such truth-makers to be thinkable contents housed at the level of sense.

Further, in his essay 'Mathematical Platonism and Dummettian Anti-Realism', McDowell suggests that mathematical platonism—which here figures in a rampant rather than a naturalized manifest-ation—is committed to the existence of propositionally structured entities at the level of reference, namely possible configurations in arithmetical reality, which may obtain or fail to obtain.[3] But there is no suggestion that it is this commitment as such, as opposed to a (rampantly) platonistic construal of it, which is what is objectionable in the doctrine of (rampant) platonism; indeed the tenor of the essay allows that we may continue to think of the mathematical domain as constituting a (sc. propositionally structured) reality, provided we are clear that mathematical reality, so construed, 'has no properties beyond those it can be proved to have'.[4] So, in spite of his official location of the world at the level of Fregean sense, there is at least an undercurrent in McDowell's thinking which envisages the placing, not only of objects, but also of propositionally structured entities such as possible states of affairs, at the level of reference.

Now in order to achieve the locating of propositions, or of propositionally structured entities such as possible states of affairs, at the level of reference, it is not sufficient to follow Frege in locating concepts, as well as objects, at that level. To see this it is necessary to look no further than Frege's own semantics. As is familiar, Frege located propositions, which he called Thoughts, exclusively at the level of sense, and he held that corresponding to Thoughts in the realm of reference were not propositions or possible states of affairs, but truth-values.[5] Frege's argument for making truth-values the

---

[3] 1998*c*, p. 345.   [4] 1998*c*, pp. 360–1; cf. pp. 347–8.

[5] For a convenient sketch of Frege's conception of the semantics of the simple categorical sentence and its components, see his letter to Husserl of 24th May 1891 (1976, pp. 94–8), with Wiggins 1984, p. 126, and my 2001*b*, p. 7.

referents of declarative sentences was simply that under intersubstitution of co-referential parts of a declarative sentence, while the Thought introduced by the sentence might change, its truth-value would not.[6] But, of course, taken as an argument for the location of truth-values *as opposed to propositions* (or propositionally structured entities such as possible states of affairs) at the level of reference, this is hopeless: for any such propositions (or propositionally structured entities), being extensional in nature, will by definition remain unchanged under intersubstitution of co-referential parts of the corresponding declarative sentence.[7] So Frege's argument is inconclusive; and in fact his candidate for the referent of a declarative sentence should be dismissed in favour of one of its propositionally structured rivals: there are decisive reasons why we *must* house propositionally structured extensional items, comprising suitable combinations of objects and concepts, at the level of reference. One of these reasons constitutes a metaphysical argument in favour of locating propositionally structured entities, whether propositions or possible states of affairs (if these are distinct), at the level of reference.

We can approach this argument by revisiting the criticism of McDowell which I offered in the last chapter. McDowell, as we have seen, locates objects but not concepts at the level of reference. The cost of that strategy was an unacceptable Kantian transcendental idealism in which the level of reference was conceived to be populated by unstructured and characterless things-in-themselves. Now Frege in effect improves on McDowell's position (if I may reverse the chronology) by recognizing the existence not merely of objects but also of concepts at the level of reference. That is certainly a step in the right direction. But if we simply leave it at that, if we simply add concepts to the inventory of entities at the level of reference, we will not yet have done anything to avoid the transcendental idealism which accrues to McDowell's disposition of entities. We will have

---

[6] See e.g. his letter to Russell of 28th Dec. 1902 (1976, pp. 234–7). Cf. Dummett 1981*a*, p. 182.

[7] Cf. Schantz 1996, p. 160.

done nothing to bring the objects and concepts which are now both housed at the level of reference together in appropriate combinations: Frege is still, in effect, obliged to locate *the world* at the level of *sense*, just as McDowell says he does, since it will only be at that level, and not below it in the semantical hierarchy, that facts (which Frege identifies with propositions or Thoughts that are true)[8] come into view. At the level of reference, on Frege's picture, we will have, as well as objects-in-themselves, what we might call concepts-in-themselves, but these distinct types of entity—objects-in-themselves and concepts-in-themselves—will stand disastrously aloof from one another.[9] In effect we will simply have two kinds of thing-in-itself instead of one kind. (That is incoherent, of course, but then the basic idea of a thing-in-itself is incoherent anyway: it is no more incoherent to suppose that the level of reference houses two 'kinds' of thing-in-itself than to suppose that it houses just one 'kind'.) Frege's 'advance' on McDowell is certainly to be welcomed, because the location of concepts at the level of reference is a necessary condition of overcoming an unacceptable Kantian transcendental idealism; but it is not a sufficient condition. Unless the concepts located at the level of reference structure and characterize the objects located at the same level, there will be no prospect of overcoming of an intolerable idealism. To overcome that idealism we need first to identify the world with the level of reference and not, as on McDowell's Fregean approach, with the level of sense, and secondly we need to populate the level of reference with the right kind of entity—propositionally structured combinations of objects and concepts or properties (including of course relational concepts or properties).

The argument we have just rehearsed for the location of propositionally structured entities at the level of reference has to do with the nature of objects and concepts, rather than with the semantics of sentences: what it in effect says is that if the location of objects and concepts at the level of reference is to be *effective*, that is, if their location there is genuinely to overcome the threat of an unacceptable

<hr />

[8] 1918–19, p. 74.   [9] Cf. Frege 1892*a*, p. 205.

Kantian transcendental idealism, then they must be united in appropriate propositionally structured combinations. But notice that the argument does not compel us to locate *propositions,* as opposed to *propositionally structured entities such as possible states of affairs,* at the level of reference, if these are distinct. Are they distinct? It would only make sense to distinguish them, I suggest, if the case for locating propositionally structured entities at the level of reference could not be improved into a case for locating propositions there. In that eventuality there might be an argument for casting possible states of affairs, say, as reference-level truth-makers for propositions existing at the level of sense. (That is, those possible states of affairs which *obtained* would render corresponding propositions true.) But if we can show not merely that items which have a propositional structure but specifically that *propositions*—the meanings of declarative sentences—must be located at the level of reference, there will then be no point in drawing a distinction between propositions and possible states of affairs. For the suggestion that obtaining states of affairs, located at the level of reference, might *still* function as truth-makers for true propositions, now also located at the level of reference, would amount to no more than a futile attempt to prise true propositions apart from themselves and then announce a spurious match between the resultant halves.[10] I think we can indeed show, on the basis of considerations having to do with the semantics of declarative sentences, that propositions should be located at the level of reference as their referents.

VI.2. LOCATING PROPOSITIONS AT THE LEVEL OF REFERENCE

The reason why we must locate propositions—as opposed to entities, such as possible states of affairs, which have a propositional

---

[10] It is fruitful in this connection to compare McDowell's criticism of Mackie's theory of truth at 1998*b*, p. 137 with n. 21.

structure but which might be conceived to fall short of full propositional status—at the level of reference as the referents of declarative sentences has to do with the nature of propositions themselves and the role we require them to discharge in our semantic theory. To see this we need first to remind ourselves what reference, semantically speaking, is.[11] Reference is an essentially theoretical notion required by a semanticist who is in the business of constructing a finitely axiomatized theory of meaning for a natural language. This semanticist ultimately aims to produce a theory which entails meaning specifications for whole sentences (perhaps by way of specifying truth-conditions, as Frege and Wittgenstein intimated,[12] and as Davidson has elaborated; but we do not need to commit ourselves here to any particular strategy for effecting the needed specifications). For, as theorists, we need to have at our disposal interpretations of whole sentences—the sentence being the smallest unit of significance with which one can 'make a move in the language-game'[13]—if we are to understand our subjects, and it is at the level of the whole sentence that a semantic theory will be tested for adequacy against the evidence provided by the speech behaviour of its subjects.

---

[11] The inspiration for the view of reference I am about to expound comes, as the reader will recognize, from work in the Frege–Tarski tradition of formal semantics, the primary application of which was originally to formal languages: but here I shall be concerned only with the application of the theoretical notion of reference to natural languages. (A useful introductory text to formal semantics in this tradition is Heim and Kratzer 1998.) In outline I follow Davidson, though I diverge from him on some points of detail (in particular, as I shall explain, on the nature of the reference relation as applied to concept-expressions): see his 1984, *passim*, and on the theoretical status of the reference relation, see esp. pp. 74, 133–7, 193, 208–10, 219–25 (at p. 221 the reader should consult the original printing of the essay for two paragraphs omitted by oversight in the 1984 reprint: Davidson 1980, p. 136; cf. Schantz 1996, p. 178 n. 1), 235–6; 2001, pp. 131–4. Since McDowell also adopts the same general approach to reference (see 1998c, pp. 144–9, 196–8; cf. 1997, pp. 158–9 with n. 1; 1998b, pp. 40–1), I will allow myself to be fairly concise. See here also Wallace 1977; Brandom 1994, ch. 6, esp. pp. 360–7, 414. On the topics of this section and the next two sections see in general my 2001b, from which some of the material presented here is drawn.

[12] Frege 1962, §32; cf. Wittgenstein 1922, §4.024. On the significance of these texts in the history of semantics, see Wiggins 1997.

[13] See Brandom 1994, pp. 338, 399. Cf. Plato, *Sophist* 262d2–6.

But in order to devise a theory with the requisite deductive power—in order to model what is often called creative language use, that is, the ability of speakers to form, and understand, an indefinite number of novel sentences on the basis of a finite training—the semanticist must discern *structure* in the object-language sentences: he or she must assign relevant semantic properties not only to sentences *as wholes*, but also to *parts* of sentences.[14] Those assignments of semantic properties to parts of sentences, in concert with appropriate combinatorial axioms, will then permit the derivation of meaning-specifications for a potentially unlimited number of well-formed sentences of the language to be interpreted, enabling the theorist to model the capacity of speakers of that language to understand an indefinite number of novel sentences on the basis of a finite training. (The single infinitary axiom schema ' "φ" means that φ' will not suffice to model that capacity,[15] since it does not enable us to predict—and so cannot encapsulate speakers' ability to tell, on the

---

[14] See here Frege 1923–6; Evans 1982, pp. 100–5; 1985, ch. 11; Davidson 1984, pp. 8–9, 127–8, 141; Brandom 1994, p. 365. Many, if not most, of the sentences we produce and understand *are* novel: Brandom 1979, p. 193. Evans rejects the suggestion that creative language use is essentially connected with the unboundedness of natural languages, arguing that even finite languages may impose on the semanticist a requirement to discern in them significant structure: 1985, pp. 326–35; cf. Fricker 1982–3, p. 55. But this contention seems to me incorrect. It depends on Evans's view that the semanticist's project of modelling linguistic competence is ultimately the same as, or at least continuous with, the neurophysiologist's project of uncovering causal structures underlying that competence (1985, p. 331). On that view, empirical evidence concerning the precise way in which speakers acquire (and lose) linguistic capacities will impose constraints on the correct way to model their understanding in a formal theory, and these constraints are likely to be such, so Evans, that the theorist is required to discern semantic structure even in a finite language. But, by the same token, Evans cannot rule out in advance the possibility that the operation of the same constraints may actually prohibit the theorist from discerning structure, even in an infinitistic language, let alone a finite one (cf. Sainsbury 1979–80, pp. 131–2). That indicates that something has gone wrong, for we know that natural languages *are* structured. Evans's view wrongly conflates two quite distinct projects (cf. Campbell 1982, pp. 24–5), and if we insist on keeping them apart the infinitistic nature of natural languages, which is an artefact of their recursiveness, will be seen to be crucial in generating a requirement on the theorist to discern structure in them. (Note that the project is to *model* linguistic understanding, not to *explain* it.)

[15] Cf. Campbell 1982, p. 23.

basis of their previous training—which novel strings of words constitute sentences and which do not.) Reference, now, is just the semantic relation which the theorist posits to model the semantic properties of sentences and their parts. Since the theory works by deducing meaning-specifications for whole sentences, from a finite number of axioms, and since meaning is correlative with understanding, it follows that the referent of a linguistic expression is just what such a theory of meaning, assuming it is correct, specifies as what understanders need to think of (in Russellian terms: be acquainted with), and what it suffices for them to think of (be acquainted with)—so long as they think of the relevant object *as* the meaning of the relevant linguistic expression[16]—in order to count as understanding the expression in question.

It follows from these considerations that the referent of an expression need not be an object, in Frege's sense, but may be (as in the case of concept-expressions) a (simple or complex) concept or (as in the case of sentential connectives) a function from sets of propositions to propositions.[17] The case of concept-expressions is worth dwelling on for a moment. We have seen (§1) that Frege was right to locate concepts at the level of reference. What the considerations I have just rehearsed show is that Frege was also right to introduce concepts, located at the level of reference, as *the referents of concept-expressions*. There is a widespread tendency, of which Davidson may serve as an exemplar—but Davidson is only a familiar and recent exponent of a very old tradition extending back at least to medieval supposition theory in some of its manifestations—to identify the referent of a concept-expression with the object or objects, if any, which satisfy

---

[16] Cf. Heck 1995, pp. 6–7.

[17] Here I assume that, as I shall argue below, propositions are the referents of declarative sentences. Indexical expressions introduce complications in this connection, since they have not merely sense and reference but also what Kaplan has called their 'character' (1989, pp. 505–6), that is, an aspect of their meaning which does not vary from context of use to context of use, as their sense and reference do, but is constant across all contexts of use; but these complications are not such as to upset the claim in the text. (Brandom offers a sophisticated treatment of these complications, in line with his general approach to semantics, at 1994, pp. 559–67.)

that expression.[18] But any such strategy founders on the elementary point that acquaintance with the object(s) satisfying a concept-expression, assuming that there are some, is neither necessary nor sufficient for understanding that expression, for there can be no question either of requiring such acquaintance of a thinker who purports to understand the expression in question, or of allowing it to suffice for the understanding of that expression: hence acquaintance with any such objects cannot be equated with the understanding of a concept-expression.

There is a standing temptation to resist the theoretical status of the reference relation: there is an inclination to suppose that in our understanding of reference we need to bring pre-theoretical intuitions to bear about how the relation works in the particular case of proper names and their bearers.[19] But yielding to the temptation is in effect illicitly to restrict the scope of the Context Principle: it is to ignore the fact that that principle, which states that it is only in the context of a sentence that a word has meaning,[20] applies to *all* subsentential linguistic expressions, proper names included. As for names, one can hardly improve on Wittgenstein's lapidary formulation:

Naming is so far not a move in the language-game—any more than putting a piece in its place on the board is a move in chess. We may say: *nothing* has so far been done, when a thing has been named. It has not even *got* a name except in the language-game. This was what Frege meant too, when he said that a word had meaning only as part of a sentence. (*Philosophical Investigations* I, §49; 1958, p. 24)

The point is also well made by McDowell,[21] who is plainly not disposed to exempt the name–bearer relation from the purview of

---

[18] Davidson 1984, pp. 216–17, 223, 229; on the medieval background see my 1997*b*, pp. 87–8 and 2001*b*, pp. 10–14.

[19] This tendency is exemplified in many places by Dummett: see his 1981*a*, *passim*, e.g. pp. 199–203, 210, 223–6, 406; 1981*b*, p. 243. For the right approach, see Tugendhat 1976, unsuccessfully attacked by Dummett at 1981*a*, pp. 199–203.

[20] Frege 1884, p. x, §§46, 60, 62; cf. Brandom 1994, p. 363.

[21] 1998*c*, p. 197. Cf. Brandom 1994, chs. 6–7, esp. p. 403.

Frege's principle. To fail to accord full scope to the Context Principle, by supposing that we have some prior, pre-theoretical grasp of the name–bearer relationship, is, in effect, to commit the same error as Frege himself surprisingly did in the *Grundgesetze der Arithmetik* when he argued against the mathematical formalists. It is worth expanding briefly on this point.

According to Frege, formalism is the doctrine that arithmetic is just a game with words, played according to certain rules, but without content, that is, without application to a *world*.[22] Frege's criticism of this doctrine was, in essence, that the formalist obscures the difference between arithmetic and, say, chess. For while the formalist's position does indeed apply to chess—chess is just a game with pieces, and the pieces have no objective reference (they do not designate anything in the world)—to go on to apply the position to arithmetic is to miss the fact, so Frege, that number words *do* have an objective reference.[23] As it stands, this argument is simply question-begging: for that a number word has an objective reference is just what the formalist denies. A deeper statement of the difference between number words and chess pieces is that number words can be combined with other words to form *sentences*, whereas chess pieces cannot (or perhaps simply: are not). And (declarative) sentences are characterized by their ability to express something *true* or *false*, as Aristotle taught us,[24] whereas no combination of chess pieces will result in anything that can intelligibly be thought of as having a truth-value. It is precisely their ability to combine with other words to yield complexes which say something true or false that empowers number words to bear on a world.

Of course Frege is right to say that the difference between number words and chess pieces is that the former do, while the latter do not, have objective reference. That is indeed the difference, and the formalist is wrong to deny it. But saying just that much is not a philosophically satisfactory account of the matter, because it starts

---

[22] 1962, §88.   [23] 1962, §90.
[24] *De Interpretatione*, 17a2–3.

the account at the end (the conclusion), not at the beginning. That number words—any words, indeed—have a reference is not the prior fact. The prior fact is that words can be formed into sentences with a truth-value: that is where the connection between language and world—where the fact (on which Frege insists)[25] that arithmetical equations do, whereas chess configurations do not, have *application* to the world—is *originally* set up. That words have reference is then a theoretical *consequence* of this prior fact. For to recognize this consequence by building it into the formalism of any adequate theory of meaning for a natural language is nothing other than to discern compositionality in the sentences of the language in question; and to discern that compositionality is, as we have seen, a *sine qua non* of our capacity to model linguistic understanding. The referent of an expression will be, as we have said, just what an adequate theory of meaning specifies as the entity acquaintance with which is necessary and sufficient for understanding the linguistic expression in question.

Given this framework, it will simply not be an option to follow Frege in selecting truth-values to be the referents of declarative sentences. The objection to making truth-values the referents of declarative sentences is not that it would be regressive to do so, as Brandom suggests: the regress which is thereby generated is innocent.[26] Rather, the problem with the strategy is (once more) that it is in general neither necessary nor sufficient for the understanding of a

---

[25] 1962, §91.
[26] 1983, p. 638. The supposed problem is that Frege is committed to construing the assertion of, say, the sentence 'Snow is white' as the issuing of an identity statement of the form 'Snow is white = the True', the assertion of which will generate a further identity statement, and so on. But why is the regress thought to be vicious? There is, of course, another (and rather more fundamental) problem with the sentence 'Snow is white = the True': it is not well formed. And it is often suggested that a Fregean (or any other) account of sentential reference is undermined by the fact that purportedly co-referential items may not intersubstitutable *salva veritate*—or even *salva congruitate*—in transparent contexts. But though the fact must be acknowledged, the interpretation put upon it is misguided: for it is not the business of a theory of reference to duplicate the work done by a theory of semantic categories, for which intersubstitutability is the governing notion (see here Tarski 1956, pp. 215–16). See further my 2001*b*, pp. 9–10.

sentence that one know its truth-value. That it is not necessary is surely obvious. The reason why it is not sufficient has to do with the Principle of Compositionality: we must conceive of the object of the understander's acquaintance at the level of reference, corresponding to the sentence at the level of spoken and written language, as being *composed of* other entities at the level of reference (in the simplest case, of an object and a monadic concept), corresponding to the semantically significant parts of the sentence; otherwise we fail to provide a sufficiently fine-grained account of linguistic understanding. Frege's preferred candidate for what a sentence refers to is too crude to do justice to this important principle, for sentences with the same truth-value may express propositions composed of distinct objects and concepts, and it is possible to know the truth-value of a sentence (perhaps by being reliably informed of it) without being acquainted with the proposition it expresses, and so, in an intuitive sense, without understanding it. The entities we descry at the level of reference corresponding to the declarative sentence at the level of spoken and written language (and to the Fregean Thought at the level of sense) must therefore be exactly as finely individuated as the Principle of Compositionality requires: only entities which are composed, in some suitable way, of the entities at the level of reference corresponding to all the semantically significant parts of the sentence can meet this requirement.[27]

---

[27] It is worth noting in this connection that it is often supposed, wrongly, that the case for sentential reference is undermined by the so-called 'slingshot' argument, an argument to the effect that, if sentences had reference, all true sentences would refer to the same thing, an upshot which would not unduly upset Frege, of course, but which would be devastating for an approach, such as mine, which favours propositional referents for sentences. But the argument is fallacious: it depends in some versions (e.g. Davidson's: see his 1984, pp. 19, 42; 1990, p. 303) on an egregious *petitio principii* (the assumption that logically equivalent sentences are co-referential, which obviously begs the question against an approach such as mine), and in all versions on an implausible semantics for definite descriptions—implausible by virtue of assimilating their semantics to the semantics of (genuine) proper names. Given that, as we have observed, the referent of a concept-expression will not be the object or objects, if any, which satisfy it, but a concept, it follows that the referent of a definite description, which is constructed out of one or more concept-expressions, will be a complex conceptual entity functionally dependent on its component concept(s), and not the object or objects, if any, which satisfy it. Hence

Now it is not sufficient—to counter an obvious line of objection in the spirit of Frege—to discern the requisite degree of fineness of grain merely at the level of sense and not also at the level of reference.[28] That is because appeal to the notion of sense only models *how* understanders think of what they must be acquainted with in order to count as understanding a linguistic expression, not *what* they must be acquainted with if they are to have that understanding. Of course it was undeniably a signal achievement on Frege's part to insist that in some contexts we need to appeal to an expression's *sense*—its mode of presentation of the referent—as well as to the *referent* itself, if we are to give an adequate model of understanding. The notion of sense is governed (and the metaphor of mode of presentation is cashed), for Frege, by a principle which Evans calls the Intuitive Criterion of Difference, the principle that two sentences differ in sense (express distinct Thoughts) provided it is possible for some thinker, while understanding both sentences, coherently to take different attitudes to them at a given time, accepting (rejecting) one while rejecting (accepting), or being agnostic about, the other.[29] But, despite the great significance of this contribution, it remains the case that the notion of sense is of essentially secondary importance to semantics: reference—*what* an understander needs to think of in order to count as having understanding—remains the key theoretical notion. As Evans puts it, 'what is primary, for purposes of communication, is the referent'.[30]

Admittedly, the fact that sense is mode of presentation (of a referent) does not in itself show that complexity at the level of sense must be matched by complexity at the level of reference:

the meaningfulness of a definite description is, in general, indifferent to the existence or otherwise of satisfying objects. The reference of a definite description will diverge in this respect from that of a (genuine) proper name, for given that the referent of such a name is that name's bearer, absence of an appropriate bearer destroys the corresponding name's meaningfulness. (On the fallaciousness of traditional slingshot arguments, see the useful discussions of Neale 1995 and Schantz 1996, pp. 147–56.)

[28] Cf. Frege 1891, pp. 13–14.
[29] 1982, pp. 18–19. Frege commits himself to this principle in many places, e.g. at 1892*b*, p. 32. See Evans ibid. for further references.
[30] 1982, p. 315; cf. pp. 333–7.

someone who endorsed Frege's semantics for sentences (as Evans seems to have done)[31] might hold that the coarseness of grain at the level of reference—the claim that all true (false) sentences refer to the same thing—is compensated for in Frege's picture by complexity at the level of sense, enabling thinkers entertaining sentences which share a truth-value but differ in meaning to think of the common referent (one of the truth-values) in distinct ways which encode the relevant semantical differences between the sentences. But the point which tells decisively against this approach is that there will be many contexts in which the particular senses—as individuated by the Intuitive Criterion of Difference—which an understander exploits in thinking of a referent are irrelevant to successful communication and to criteria of fair reportage: in these contexts communication is achieved, despite differences of sense attaching to key words employed in the act of communication, on the basis of shared reference.[32] A semantics which hampers itself by refusing to locate propositionally structured entities at the level of

---

[31] See 1982, p. 17 with n. 17, where Evans tells us that despite the obstacles he has 'felt able to grasp the nettle—to suppose that in understanding a sentence one *would*, in one way, be thinking of its truth-value'. But it is plausible that Evans only thinks himself obliged to espouse the pure Fregean position because he sees it as the sole alternative to a Dummettian verificationism, which he (rightly) considers unattractive both in itself and as an interpretation of Frege. He overlooks the possibility of adopting the kind of position I am canvassing, which combines realism about reference with housing propositionally structured entities at the level of reference, rather than unstructured truth-values, to serve as the referents of sentences.

[32] Evans states (1982, p. 21) that the Intuitive Criterion of Difference cannot, as it stands, be deployed when more than one thinking subject is involved, or when we have to do with a single subject entertaining thoughts at different times. In fact this claim is not quite accurate. The truth is, rather, that the Criterion *may* not as it stands be able to deal with these cases *if* they involve the use of, respectively, distinct *personal pronouns* or distinct *temporal indexicals*. There is no difficulty in applying the principle, just as it stands, to a case where one thinker entertains a thought he would express by '*a* is *F*', and another thinker entertains a thought she would express by '*b* is *F*', where '*a*' and '*b*' are, say, distinct proper names. These thoughts can differ in sense according to the Criterion, even though they are entertained by distinct thinkers, on the basis that if they *were* entertained by a single thinker at a time, he or she *could*, while understanding both corresponding sentences, coherently take different cognitive attitudes to the thoughts they express. In other words, the Criterion can be applied to the cases Evans mentions, so long as there is, so to speak, no logistical difficulty about supposing the relevant senses to be taken up into the cognition of a single thinker at a given time. See further n. 36 below.

reference, mirroring in structure and complexity the sentences corresponding to them at the level of spoken and written language (and the Thoughts at the level of sense), will simply be unable to do justice to this fact.

The possibility that successful communication may proceed on the basis of shared reference alone is frequently exemplified by acts of communication involving ordinary proper names. Proper names are indeed best thought of as devices for circumventing the requirement imposed by many 'one-off' referring devices, such as demonstrative and other indexical expressions, that the hearer think of the referent in a quite particular way, whether (as for instance in the case of the indexicals 'here' and 'now') in the *same* way as the speaker thinks of it, or (as in the case of the indexicals 'I' and 'you') in a *different* (but systematically related) way.[33] In contradistinction to 'one-off' devices, proper names are useful as tools of communication precisely because speaker and hearer may employ them to home in on the same referent no matter how—and no matter how differently—they severally think of it.[34] It follows that one superficially attractive model of communication, according to which speaker and hearer must grasp the same Thought, is not in general valid.[35] Of course, if we move to a sufficiently high level of generality, it will no doubt be possible to frame descriptions of 'ways of thinking' about referents which, in a given act of communication, have to be common to participants in that act. But the point is that it will be the commonality of the referent which is shaping this higher-level conception of shared sense, and not *vice versa*: that conception will simply be an artefact of our way of describing the situation, gerrymandered in order to get round the difficulty that at lower levels of description the

---

[33] Evans 1982, p. 316. Cf. McDowell 1998*c*, p. 222.

[34] See here again Evans 1982, p. 400: 'The single main requirement for understanding a use of a proper name is that one think of the referent' (cf. pp. 40, 379–80). The same applies to concept-expressions, and indeed to all non-indexical linguistic expressions.

[35] This is Frege's model in his late essay 'Der Gedanke' (1918–19): see Evans 1982, p. 16, and my 1997*a*, p. 131. There are useful discussions of the point at issue here in Evans 1982, app. to ch. 6, §1 (pp. 192–6) and app. to ch. 9, §2 (pp. 341–2).

senses involved in acts of communication frequently differ from speaker to hearer.[36] If necessary, the artificially constructed common sense, for a given referent x, can be something along the lines of 'any way of thinking which homes in on x' (and for some uses of proper names in acts of communication, not much better than this, by way of specifying a sense which communicators *have* to entertain, will be available), in which the constitutive role of the referent in securing the right specification of the common sense is manifest, and any requirement that senses be shared between speaker and hearer in any more detailed or interesting respect is plainly forgone.

These considerations do not show that Frege was wrong to think of linguistic understanding as, in general, grasp of an expression's sense. But since sense is just an epistemically direct route to the

---

[36] See n. 32 above, where it was noted that the Intuitive Criterion of Difference is not guaranteed to be able to deal with cases involving personal or temporal indexicals such as 'I' and 'you' or 'now' and 'then'. A different approach may be required, in such cases, in order to establish if and when thoughts involving distinct indexicals are the same. In the case of the indexicals 'I' and 'you' it seems to me that familiar thought-experiments establish that 'I am F' entertained by me, say, and 'You are F', entertained by another thinker in respect of me, will normally *differ* in sense: for there are at least some situations in which I might, while entertaining 'I am F', simultaneously entertain 'You are F', in respect of myself, but without realizing that I am thinking of myself (perhaps because of the use of trick mirrors etc.), and coherently take different cognitive attitudes to the thoughts expressed by these sentences in these uses. So at least in these cases an analogue of the Intuitive Criterion can be applied—only an analogue, because it is hard to see how, at least normally, exactly the same sense as another thinker attaches to 'you', entertained in respect of me, could be taken up into my cognition, in respect of myself. In the case of 'now' and 'then', it seems that a parallel point will hold. That is, one can allow an analogue of the Intuitive Criterion to apply, dropping the requirement that a thinker entertain the relevant thoughts simultaneously. So, for example, it is plausible that the thoughts expressed by 'Today is F', on a given day, and 'Yesterday was F', entertained a day later, will be certified as distinct by the extended Intuitive Criterion, since a thinker may (perhaps because of a faulty memory) take different attitudes to these thoughts. It is true that an account of the functioning of temporal indexicals will have to incorporate a story about their cognitive dynamics along the lines of Evans 1982, pp. 192–6, and that that will block any radically atomistic approach to temporal thought. But it is perfectly possible to accommodate such a story without having to conflate the senses of temporally indexed sentences which are truth-value-linked in the manner of the above example: a thinker can be forgetful without 'losing track of time', and so can think temporal thoughts certified as distinct by the extended Intuitive Criterion (though they are in fact truth-value-linked) without forfeiting the right to entertain temporal thoughts at all. See on this point Dennett 1987, pp. 128–9.

referent—this point holds of all semantically significant expressions, not merely of those ordinary proper names and demonstrative expressions which are the focus of the so-called neo-Fregean programme in semantics that has been spearheaded by Evans and McDowell—all that grasp of sense can come to is the possession of cognitive access to (acquaintance with) the right entity—the referent of the relevant linguistic expression, whether object, concept, or proposition—mediated in some particular way. An entity at the level of reference cannot be cognitively accessed in *no* way, of course,[37] but the particular, detailed way in which one thinks of it does not play a semantic role in all communicative contexts. Hence whatever complexity of structure the semanticist needs to postulate in order to model the understanding of sentential and subsentential expressions must, in general, be in place at the level of reference, and not merely at the level of sense. It follows from the considerations of this section that we must admit propositions to the level of reference, as the referents of declarative sentences.

VI.3. THE PROBLEM OF FALSITY

If McDowell had admitted propositions to the realm of reference, he might have been less ready to claim that 'thought can be distanced from the world by being false',[38] or that 'when experience misleads us there is a sense in which it intervenes between us and the world'.[39] He might not have felt the need to ask, rhetorically: 'What complex item, containing Scott as a constituent, could be what I assert if I say "Scott wrote *Bleak House*"?'.[40] For if the world contains not merely objects but also concepts, and combinations of these in propositions, it will contain false propositions as well as true ones: mistakes will then distance us from the *facts* (true propositions) but not from the

---

[37] Cf. Evans 1982, p. 16.
[38] 1994, p. 27.
[39] 1994, p. 143.
[40] 1998*c*, p. 160 n. 8. Cf. 1982, pp. 127–34.

world as such. For if the realm of reference, with which we are identifying the world (recall that the metaphysical argument of §1 required us to make this identification), contains objects, concepts, and propositionally structured combinations of these, it must contain not merely combinations which, as we say, 'hold' or 'obtain' (true propositions) but also combinations which do not 'hold' or 'obtain' (false propositions): after all, there are significant false sentences, as well as true ones, to which the full panoply of the tripartite semantical hierarchy, consisting of written and spoken sentences and their semantically significant parts, the senses of those sentences and their (semantically significant) parts, and the referents of the same, must be taken to apply. Hence the answer to McDowell's rhetorical question is that the complex item, containing Scott as a constituent, which is what I assert when I say 'Scott wrote *Bleak House*' is a real (i.e., worldly) proposition, containing Scott (the man himself),[41] the novel *Bleak House*, the relation of authoring, a tensing component corresponding to the past-tense operator, and some appropriate unifying element (to which I shall return briefly below)—all of which adds up to the proposition that Scott wrote *Bleak House*. As it happens this is a false proposition, but that does not derogate from its status as a worldly entity, appropriately housed, as the entity which any aspiring understander of the sentence 'Scott wrote *Bleak House*' needs to be acquainted with, at the level of reference.

Brandom, like McDowell, objects to talking of propositions as worldly entities, and he gives as his reason that

that way of talking is liable to be misunderstood as involving the identification of propositions with the facts or states of affairs successfully represented by true claims ... rather than with the claims or purported representations expressed by sentences. (1994, p. 72)

---

[41] For the purposes of this example I assume that 'Scott' is a genuine proper name, and not a descriptive name (in the sense of Evans 1982, ch. 2) or an abbreviated definite description. In fact it is highly unlikely that 'Scott' is a genuine proper name for us now, who are mere 'consumers' of the name, though of course it was for those who were acquainted with Sir Walter himself, the 'producers' of the name, to whom we consumers stand in a relation of semantic deference (for the terminology and its application, see Evans 1982, ch. 11). But for our purposes we can ignore this feature of the example.

I take it that Brandom is in effect recommending a Fregean identification of propositions with the senses of sentences (Thoughts), and I hope I have said enough at least to dispel the presumption that that model is inevitable. But a reader who felt that the location of false as well as true propositions in the world (at the level of reference) was problematic would not be the first person in the history of philosophy to be perturbed by that thought. For this feeling of anxiety is indeed the source of the classical problem of falsity (as that emerges, for example, in Plato's *Theaetetus* and *Sophist*), which may be expressed as follows: if false propositions exist in the world (at the level of reference) in just as good a sense as do true propositions, does that not mean that false propositions will be, at least in some sense, true? This problem will not unduly trouble Brandom, of course; and McDowell, likewise, thinks he can afford to be disparaging about it:

What makes it look as if false statements might not be possible is a conception according to which meaningfulness in general, including the meaningfulness of statements, is a matter of a relation—something along the lines of the name–bearer relation—to something actual. Such a difficulty in making room for falsehood does not (at least, not any longer) pose a worthwhile task for philosophy. (1998g, p. 58)

The problem (or pseudo-problem, if that is what it is) arises for the following reason: if we agree that the meaningfulness of declarative sentences (McDowell's 'statements') consists in their bearing a referential relation to something actual, it seems but a short step from there to our having to concede that the something actual on the worldly end of the relation must be something true; which renders falsity impossible.

I have argued (§§1–2) that we are forced by metaphysical and semantical considerations to locate a reference relation running from declarative sentences to worldly propositions. And that argument to the existence of propositions at the level of reference was utterly neutral on the status of those propositions in respect of their truth-value. So I maintain that the meaningfulness of declarative sentences—false as well as true—does indeed consist in their bearing a referential relation to something actual. Hence I am bound to hold that if this model does in any way appear to make the phenomenon of falsity problematic, we cannot simply dismiss the appearance but must proceed on the provisional basis that the problem is indeed a genuine one and so still presents a worthwhile task for philosophy. In fact I believe that the classical problem of falsity can be solved, but I do not pretend that the solution I favour will dispel all puzzlement about the nature of falsity, and to that extent I do not think that the classical problem of falsity is spurious. The correct solution to the problem, in my view, is simply the observation that the 'short step' from agreeing, on the one hand, that the proposition to which a declarative sentence refers is something actual to conceding, on the other, that it is therefore true, is in fact an illegitimate slide. False propositions at the level of reference are indeed actual, or real, in as good a sense as are true propositions at that level. False propositions as well as true ones have to be housed at the level of reference because false sentences as well as true ones are meaningful, and the level of reference exists to provide a home for meanings. (We need a level of sense as well, of course, for sentences and their semantically significant parts, but as I have argued the level of sense cannot meet the need for a reference-level repository for propositions.) Given that the level of reference is identical with the world, we have no option but to allow the reality, or actuality, of false propositions. But there is nothing in that line of reasoning which would warrant the further step to conflating false with true propositions.

Hence it is not the application of the referential model, as such, to sentences which gives rise to the apparent problem, but rather a fallacious (and dispensable) piece of reasoning extraneously built upon that application. So the problem can be neutralized, but I sympathize with anyone who feels that the solution does not dispel all puzzlement surrounding the nature of falsity in the context of an assumed referential model for the semantics of sentences. The residual worry is, I think, something along these lines. We have a metaphysical economy in which both true and false propositions inhabit the level of reference, and the solution to the classical problem of falsity assures us that these classes of proposition are indeed distinct, or at any rate that the application of the referential model to sentences gives us no good reason to query their distinctness. But what, it might naturally be asked, does their distinctness consist in? It hardly seems enough to be told that propositions in the one class are *true*, whereas those in the other class are *false*, and that the classes are mutually disjoint. What does this really tell us? It was presumably a worry along these lines that led Russell in 1910 to pronounce the existence of the Meinongian 'false objectives' he had formerly believed in—in effect, these were false propositions at the level of reference—to be 'almost incredible'.[42]

There are several things one might say in response to the general question: what is distinctive about true propositions? Russell himself tried one avenue when, in his critique of Meinong, he wrote that there is 'an ultimate ethical proposition' to the effect that 'it is good to believe true propositions, and bad to believe false ones'.[43] In more contemporary terms, one might say that it is a distinctive feature of truth to be normative for the conduct of inquiry. Additionally, one might suggest that what is distinctive about truth, and in particular what distinguishes it from falsity, is the fact that the predicate 'is true' is disquotable, whereas the predicate 'is false' is not. McDowell suggests that these two features of truth are intimately connected: 'Norms of inquiry are normative for the process of inquiry precisely because disquotability is the norm for its results'.[44] What he means can be gathered from a later text:

[W]hat makes it correct among speakers of English to make a claim with the words 'Snow is white' (to stay with a well-worn example) is that snow is (indeed) white. ... For a given sentence to be true—to be disquotable—is for it to be correctly usable to make a claim just because ..., where in the gap we insert, not quoted but used, the sentence that figures on the right-

---

[42] 1994, p. 152. Worldly propositions had been part of the metaphysical picture offered in *The Principles of Mathematics*: see e.g. 1903, §51.
[43] 1973, p. 76.   [44] 1994, p. 150.

hand side of the T-sentence provided for the sentence in question by a good
Tarskian theory for its language ... Truth in the sense of disquotability is
unproblematically normative for sentences uttered in order to make claims.
(2000*b*, p. 116)[45]

The idea is that inquiry can be counted as successful if and only if its
results (which are delivered in the form of declarative sentences) can
be disquoted or, put slightly differently, if and only if our assertions
of the sentences reached at the end of inquiry are interpretable as
assertions *that* (schematically) such and such is the case. For our
present purposes it suffices to point to the normativity of truth and
the disquotability of the truth-predicate as providing us with a
general answer to the question what is distinctive about truth. This
answer is not *yielded* by the semantical treatment of sentences I have
recommended, this being derived from other considerations: but it
does not *conflict* with that treatment either. I do not see this as a
difficulty: we should not expect an account of the semantics of
sentences to provide answers to all the puzzles we might have
about the nature of truth and falsity.

VI.4. TRUTH AND INTRINSICISM

One traditional answer to the question 'What is distinctive about
truth?' which we do *not* want is that provided by the so-called
correspondence theory of truth. We might try to motivate a correspondence theory by raising the following difficulty for the account I
have offered of the semantics of sentences and their parts: given that
the lowest level in my semantic hierarchy is still, so to speak, a level
of *meaning*, surely we need to posit a fourth, still lower level, at
which something utterly *non-linguistic* can be housed, if we are to
give a satisfactory account of the distinction between truth and
falsity. The objection might be expressed so: surely my level of
reference is, despite its label, still really a level of *sense*, so that a

[45] Cf. 1998*h*, pp. 38–9.

further level, one which is genuinely of *reference*, needs to be supplied. (Of course it need not be part of this objection to suggest that my level of sense is redundant. And it would not be sensible to press any such suggestion: for items at my level of reference—whether that be styled a level of reference or a covert level of sense—still need to be presented in some way. There are different *ways* of understanding *what* we understand.) The idea would be that, at this ultimate level, we would find entities—facts of a radically non-linguistic character—which would in some sense correspond to some propositions located at my level of reference: those propositions at the level of reference which enjoyed such a correspondence relation would count as true, the others, lacking such a relation, as false. The incoherence of this theory becomes manifest when we try to specify in language (we have no other way of doing it) what the entities purportedly on the ultimate-level end of the correspondence relation are like. Of course we have to make them proposition-like—otherwise there could be no question of correspondence with genuine propositions—and we are thus forced into the awkwardness of positing a level in the semantic hierarchy which houses entities that are purportedly both proposition-like and not in any sense linguistic.

We might try to circumvent this inconvenient upshot by abandoning the proposal to add a fourth level to the semantic hierarchy, and relocating the putative non-linguistic 'facts', whose correspondence with some propositions is supposed to render those propositions true, at the original level of reference. But in view of my remarks at the end of §1 above, together with what has just been said, this strategy fails. We have just seen that if a correspondence relation between some propositions and other entities is genuinely to be capable of grounding the truth of those propositions (and similarly, if the absence of any such relation is to ground the falsity of the remaining propositions), the entities in question would need to be propositionally structured. The usual candidates to play the role of truth-makers are states of affairs, that is, true (or obtaining) entities of the form *that a is F.* But, as we noted at the end of §1, these entities are not distinct, in form, from propositions at the level of reference:

to seek to prise such states of affairs apart from propositions at my level of reference is nothing more than an exercise in creating spurious distinctions. The wonderful isomorphism which ensues between existent such states of affairs and true propositions is no more than an artefact of their identity.

At my level of reference, some propositions are true and some are false; and there is no underpinning of this distinction either at the level of reference itself or at some purportedly lower level in the semantic hierarchy. There is no lower semantical level—and so *a fortiori* no lower ontological level—at which propositionally structured entities are not yet in the frame: there is no lower level housing mere objects, or mere concepts, or both; and any entities of the right form to be truth-makers turn out, on inspection, to be nothing other than the very propositions themselves which our purported truth-makers are designed to verify. It follows that though, for semantic and ontological purposes, we need a notion of reference as what grounds understanding, we do not, for those purposes, need a notion reference as what grounds the distribution of truth-values.

That takes me to a position on truth which Wright has labelled 'intrinsicist'.[46] Intrinsicism is the view that truth is an intrinsic—that is, non-relational—property of propositions. Wright concedes that intrinsicism may well be right about necessary truths, but contends that it cannot handle contingent truths:

> For the truth-value of any contingent proposition must co-vary with hypothetical changes in the characteristics of things it concerns—so that a hypothetical change, for instance, in the location of my coffee cup may entail an alteration in the truth-value of the proposition that there is no coffee cup on my desk, even though that proposition and the particular coffee cup in question are quite distinct existences. (1999, p. 208)

The example is rather cleverly chosen, for Wright's coffee cup and the proposition that there is no coffee cup on his desk are indeed 'logically distinct existences'. At least, they are logically distinct existences in the only intelligible sense that can be given to that

---

[46] See his 1999.

expression in this context, namely that the *sentence* 'That coffee cup exists' (here demonstrating the cup in question) neither entails nor is entailed by the *sentence* 'The proposition that there is no coffee cup on Wright's desk exists'—for of course there can be no question of spatio-temporal objects like cups enjoying logical relations, just as such: logical relations obtain between *sentences*[47]—and clearly the former sentence might be true while the latter was not true (if the embedded proposition did not exist, because, say, Wright did not exist, in which case the sentence as a whole would itself express no proposition), and the latter sentence might be true while the former sentence was not true (because, in the absence of any relevant cup, it would express no proposition).[48]

But as soon as we have registered that point, it becomes apparent that Wright's general contention is unstable. For that coffee cup (here I demonstrate a particular cup in my cognitive vicinity) is not a distinct existence from, let us say, the proposition that that cup is on some desk or other: whether that proposition be true or false, the sentence 'That coffee cup exists' both entails and is entailed by the sentence 'The proposition that that coffee cup is on some desk or other exists'. For if the former sentence is true, the relevant proposition does indeed exist (whether it is true or false), and so the latter sentence, which asserts the existence of the proposition, is true; and if the latter sentence is true, so is the former. What this suggests is that the intrinsicist would do well to persist, and not be put off by Wright's apparent counter-example. Obviously what is required is a distinction between *basic* and *non-basic* propositions, that is, between basic propositions, on the one hand, which are not true, when they are true, in virtue of the truth of other propositions, and non-basic propositions, on the other, such as general and molecular propositions, which, when true, are mediately or immediately true in virtue of the truth of basic propositions. The claim will then be that the intrinsicist account applies to *basic* propositions (contin-

---

[47] See my 1997*a*, §6.
[48] See on both these cases McDowell's 'Truth-Value Gaps', 1998*c*, pp. 199–213.

gent as well as necessary): these are, when true, not true in virtue of anything at all. The truth of non-basic propositions will indeed be a relational matter, but the relevant relations will be (ultimately) to basic propositions, not to anything non-propositional in the world. Any candidate for something in the world which could—to follow the correspondence theorist's rhetoric—*make* a basic proposition true will turn out to be something which, when specified adequately, is identical with the proposition in question.

VI.5. *DER MENSCH SPRICHT NICHT ALLEIN*

If McDowell had admitted concepts and propositions to the realm of reference, he would surely have expressed himself more favourably towards an idea which he mentions only to reject, that of 'objects as speaking to us in the world's own language'.[49] For the location of propositions at the level of reference surely provides a sense in which the world itself speaks: it speaks the propositions—true and false — which inhabit the level of reference. Now although McDowell officially repudiates this idea, he is actually not hostile to all forms of the image according to which objects speak to us. For he writes, in a passage of Ovidian delicacy:

A seen object as it were invites one to take it to be as it visibly is. It speaks to one; if it speaks to one's understanding, that is just what its speaking to one comes to. 'See me as I am,' it (so to speak) says to one; 'namely, as characterized by *these* properties'—and it displays them. (1998*d*, p. 468)

And, as Rorty points out, McDowell's appeal to the image of the non-human world as 'a sort of conversational partner' fits with his persistent tendency to personalize the relationship which we have in experience with the world, as when he talks about the world's 'doing

---

[49] 1998*d*, p. 470. Cf. Willaschek 2000, p. 36. The image derives from Rorty, who makes frequent and pejorative use of it: see e.g. 1979, pp. 298–9; 1982, pp. xxvi, 140, 171, 185, 191–210 *passim*; 1989, pp. 3–22 *passim*; 1998, p. 40. Cf. also Putnam's use of the image at 1995, p. 29.

you favours, showing you a kindness, vouchsafing facts'.[50] The image of experience as openness to the world (Chapter I, §4) already carries this connotation, given that the idea of *openness* has its literal home in the domain of rational, interpersonal relations.[51]

McDowell plainly faces a threat of inconsistency on this point: on the one hand he rejects the image of the world as speaking to us in its own language, but on the other he wants to accommodate the thought that objects speak 'to one's understanding'. He hopes to parry the incipient threat by insisting that:

Objects speak to us, in the metaphor that fits the position I am urging, only because we have learned a human language ... only in actualizations of conceptual capacities that are ours. (1998*d*, p. 470)

Here one wants to object that, although it might be correct to say that objects speak *to us*—in the sense that we understand their language—only because we have learned a human language, it would not be correct to claim that, in the metaphor, objects speak *simpliciter*—that is, that they display their properties linguistically, display their properties in ways that are essentially capturable in language—only because *we* have learned a human language. As an empirical claim this latter is simply false; the claim in that form can only be sustained in a transcendental sense. I shall return to this point shortly. For now the point to observe in connection with the first quoted passage is that it is hard to understand how it can be rendered consistent with what we have seen to be McDowell's official position, which does indeed suit the rejection of the image of objects as speaking to us in the world's own language. For McDowell's official doctrine that concepts—and hence propositions—are to be located at the level of sense rather than of reference, with its concomitant commitment to transcendental idealism in its unsatisfactory Kantian form, surely sits ill with *any* willingness to admit the image of objects as speaking to us, however hedged with provisos. There can be no coherent sense in which

---

objects at the level of reference, taken (as I have suggested McDowell is obliged to take them) as Kantian things-in-themselves, speak to us, even metaphorically, in the world's or in any language. There can be no coherent sense in which we are answerable, in judgement, to a realm comprising such objects. The threat of inconsistency I have mentioned can indeed be averted by McDowell, by jettisoning one of the claims that poses the threat: but unfortunately, given his other commitments, he is obliged to jettison the wrong one.

It is only when we restore concepts and propositions to the level of reference that we entitle ourselves to appeal to the image of objects as speaking to us; and once we have made that restoration, it will make perfect sense to picture objects as speaking—not only to us but to anyone who is capable of listening—in the world's own language. Indeed, something like that characterization of what is going on will be not merely legitimate but compulsory. For to say that there are propositions at the level of reference is tantamount to attributing quasi-linguistic structures to the world itself, identified with the level of reference; and to say that objects at the level of reference are essentially structured in such propositions—and this I take to be an implication of housing concepts at the level of reference, and of bringing objects and concepts together in appropriate combinations—is to say, with only minimal metaphorical licence, that objects speak to us by means of such structures. But those quasi-linguistic structures by means of which objects speak to us will then naturally not be organized into an empirical language—as it were an extra empirical language in addition to the already existing empirical languages with which we are familiar, and which are products of human devising; rather, they will be organized into a language which is an abstraction from—and constitutes the transcendental basis of—all actual (and possible) empirical languages.

We require this understanding of the theoretical position to be in place if we are to find any room at all for McDowell's claim that objects speak to us 'only because we have learned a human language'. McDowell himself is, I have suggested, not entitled to that claim, given his commitment to transcendental idealism in its unsatisfactory Kantian form. But there is a sense in which we can vindicate the claim if we follow my recommendation of locating concepts and propositions at the level of reference: we can vindicate the claim in a transcendental sense, as (to put it another way) trying to say something which can strictly only be shown. For there is no empirical sense in which an object's ability to speak to us—its ability to assert to all who are listening that it is characterized by *these* properties—depends on the *actual* development of one or more historical languages: that ability depends rather on the *possibility* of such a development. Of course the position I am recommending is in a sense, no less than McDowell's (Chapter V, §2), idealistic: but it is a form not of Hegelian absolute idealism, nor of Kantian transcendental idealism, but of a relatively unpretentious linguistic idealism. The world is construed as propositionally structured, and worldly propositions themselves have, as Rorty puts it (meaning to cast an aspersion on the position), a 'sentence-like appearance':[52] hence my characterization of the structure of the world as 'quasi-linguistic'. But, as I am stressing, the propositions (true and false) which compose the world are constituted as such by their essential expressibility in sentences not only of actual languages, but of possible languages too.

I want to guard against two potential misunderstandings of the idea, as it features here, of the world's own language. In the first place, it might be thought that the idea imported an assimilation— surely inconveniently, if so—of experience to testimony. But the transcendentalism of the linguistic idealism I am proposing ought to block any such conflation (which I have independently resisted: Chapter III, §3) of the case of experience with that of testimony. For the world's 'testimony' is delivered not in an empirical language, as testimony strictly so called is, but in its own language, which, as I have emphasized, is not one empirical language among others, but the transcendental basis of all empirical languages. Or we might alternatively bring out the difference by saying that, whereas testimony strictly so called is delivered in just one empirical language, the

52 2000, p. 126. Cf. 1989, p. 5; 1991, p. 137; 1998, pp. 35–6.

world's 'testimony' is delivered in them all (possible languages as well as actual). For we can indeed think of the world as speaking 'languages without end', as affirmed by Novalis in the quotation with which I opened this study:[53] we do so by thinking of the transcendental basis of all empirical languages, in which the world delivers its 'testimony', as collecting all actual and possible empirical languages. On this picture, although the world speaks no *one* empirical language, it might be said to speak them *all*, where this is understood in the transcendental way I am recommending. For the propositions which compose the world—the true and false propositions at the level of reference—can be thought of as determining equivalence classes of declarative sentences: a given proposition determines the class of all empirical sentences, actual and possible, which express (refer to) it.[54]

The second potential misunderstanding I wish to avert is a confusion between the position I am putting forward and the traditional conception of the world as, in Milton's phrase, 'the book of knowledge fair'.[55] According to this conception there are, in the words of Sir Thomas Browne,

two bookes from whence I collect my Divinity; besides that written one of God, another of his servant Nature, that universall and publik Manuscript, that lies expans'd unto the eyes of all; those that never saw him in the one, have discovered him in the other: This was the Scripture and Theology of the Heathens; ... surely the Heathens knew better how to joyne and reade these mysticall letters, than wee Christians, who cast a more carelesse eye on these common Hieroglyphicks, and disdain to suck Divinity from the flowers of nature. (*Religio Medici* I, §16; 1964, p. 15)

[53] The quotation is taken from the first part of *Das Allgemeine Brouillon* (1999, p. 500).

[54] One might have hoped that something stronger than a relation of determination would be available, that we might be able to *identify* worldly propositions with equivalence classes of sentences. But I have argued elsewhere (2001*b*) that this hope is forlorn, and that the relation of determination is the best that is to be had. Note that the existence of a determination relation running in this direction does not clash with the traditional doctrine that sense determines reference: that doctrine applies to *individual* senses and referents, whereas the determination relation with which we are here concerned connects a given referent with *all* (actual and possible) senses which present that referent.

[55] On the history of this conception, see Blumenberg 1981.

The difference between the metaphor of the world's own language, as I understand that, and the traditional conception of the book of nature, is that while the world's own language is, as I am emphasizing, not an empirical language but the transcendental basis of empirical languages, the book of nature, by contrast, was in effect held to be written in an empirical language (perhaps, as Galileo famously suggested, in the 'language' of mathematics), which it is then up to us to interpret, just as (in Browne's analogy, which has had widespread currency in the tradition) the hieroglyphics of the ancients were clearly elements of an empirical language, and one which it took effort to decipher. My 'book of nature', so to speak, is made up not of *symbols*, as in the traditional conception, but of the *meanings* of symbols. The world is propositionally structured; but it does not have any particular syntax.

It follows from the transcendentalism of the position I am recommending, combined with the fact that, as I suggested in Chapter IV, infants and animals can benefit transcendentally from our linguistic powers of designation and classification, that objects can speak not merely to us, but also to them. Indeed this is something McDowell at one point concedes, when he allows in his essay 'The Content of Perceptual Experience' that, alongside a 'sub-personal' story we can tell concerning informational transactions between different parts of an organism, and according to which the frog's eye can be said to tell the frog's brain things (cf. Chapter IV, §8), we can apply the metaphor of telling in such a way that an entire organism—in the example McDowell uses, the frog itself—is on the receiving end of an episode of telling. In this application of the metaphor,

what tells the frog things is the environment, making features of itself apparent to the frog ... This is a different metaphor of telling, not in competition with the 'sub-personal' one. It is essential not to be misled by the enormous capacity for illumination that the 'sub-personal' account has... into thinking that the 'sub-personal' account exhausts the content-involving truth in this area of biology. The second metaphor encapsulates a whole extra field of truths. What is more, the involvement of content here, and only here, is literal; underneath the metaphor of the environment telling the frog things, we have the literal truth that the frog becomes informed of things. (1998*b*, p. 349)

I noted in Chapter IV that McDowell's ascription in this essay of literal 'involvement with [sc. propositional] content' to frogs is inconsistent with his claim, elsewhere, that animals do not strictly enjoy mental states with propositional content. We find a corresponding inconsistency in connection with the topic of the present context, for there is an obvious clash between the claim, lodged by McDowell in the passage just quoted, that the environment (metaphorically) tells the frog things, and that the frog thereby (literally) becomes informed of things (that is, that the environment tells the frog, and it becomes informed of, *propositionally structured* things, things of the schematic form *that such and such is the case*), on the one hand, and his insistence, noted earlier in this section, that the conversation we enjoy with the non-human world arises 'only because we have learned a human language' and 'only in actualizations of conceptual capacities that are ours', on the other.

In Chapter IV I suggested that the way to remove the former of these inconsistencies, on McDowell's behalf, was to relativize the ascription of literalness to infant and animal content: relative to their 'sub-personal' states the ascription of content to whole organisms' mental states counts as literal; relative to our mentality it does not. But I made clear that the resulting position, though consistent, was unacceptable: for there is no tolerable intermediate position between allowing infants and animals to perceive objects (as they evidently do) and according strict propositional content to their mental states. That is, the right response to the inconsistency was to adhere to the more liberal policy propounded in his essay 'The Content of Perceptual Experience', without watering that policy down by trying to render it consonant with McDowell's other, divergent pronouncements on the subject. In the present context we should follow a parallel strategy and insist that, in the sense in which objects can speak to us, they can speak to infants and animals too, in spite of the fact that such languageless creatures have not (or have not yet) learned a human language. This upshot is secured by the fact that these languageless subjects can compensate for their lack of a faculty of spontaneity by exploiting, transcendentally, our powers of designation and classification, together with the fact that the role of our conceptual capacities in constituting the world's ability to speak to all who are listening is itself merely transcendental.

VI.6. EPILOGUE: THE UNITY OF THE PROPOSITION

The question exactly how concepts and objects form combinations to yield propositions at the level of reference is the question what constitutes the unity of the proposition. This is an issue which I have broached elsewhere,[56] and which demands extended treatment in its own right. It is also an issue which interests, or ought to interest, McDowell, given his view that the conceptual capacities exercised in judgement, and passively drawn on in experience, have a semantical or logical togetherness that is, broadly speaking, propositional in nature,[57] a claim which naturally throws up the question what the nature of that togetherness is. But without embarking on an extended treatment of the issue of propositional unity here, the point we need to note in concluding this study emerges as follows.

I have diagnosed McDowell's hostility towards locating concepts or universals at the level of reference as stemming from a fear that, if we put them there, we run the risk of sliding into an ultra-realism about meaning, according to which the concepts or universals housed at the level of reference manage to be constituted in absolute independence of our rule-following practices (in the sense of this phrase I suggested earlier: Chapter II, §5). For the purposes of this

---

[56] See my 1995*b*.
[57] 1998*d*, pp. 438–9; 2000*a*, p. 10. Cf. Brandom 1994, pp. 79–80.

diagnosis I have grouped concepts and universals together, as if they were the same thing, and when I first made use of this collocation of ideas I promised to return and comment on it. Are concepts and universals the same thing? Frege, of course, did not identify them, for he conceived concepts as being functions, and as such unsaturated or incomplete, whereas universals—taken as the referents of abstract nouns like 'wisdom'—were for him objects, and so saturated or complete.[58] The doctrine of the unsaturatedness of the concept was devised by Frege to solve the problem which I am calling that of the unity of the proposition (although, paradoxically, Frege did not locate propositions at the level of reference, as we have seen, but at the level of sense): his idea was that if we think of objects and concepts as being fundamentally different types of entity, and in particular if we conceive of concepts as essentially carrying gaps to be filled by objects, but of objects as carrying no such intrinsic slots for concepts, then no further difficulty concerning how these entities can stick together to form the right sort of unity remains.

But there are two problems with the doctrine of the essential unsaturatedness of concepts, an unfamiliar and a familiar one. The unfamiliar problem is an obvious upshot of considerations to which I have already drawn attention (but I have not seen it mentioned in the literature): I hinted at it in the last paragraph when I dubbed Frege's failure to locate propositions at the level of reference as, in the present context, paradoxical. The difficulty is this: if there are no propositionally structured entities at the level of reference for object and concept to combine to form, then it does not matter how skilfully we fit them up with pins and sockets for one another, they will not combine to form any kind of unity. On Frege's picture there simply *is* no appropriate unity—nothing propositional at the level of reference—for them to unite to form. The other, more familiar

---

[58] What about properties? Brandom states that Frege construed properties as unsaturated (as, in effect, concepts): 1994, p. 697 n. 67. This certainly corresponds to one use which Frege makes of the word 'property' (*Eigenschaft*): see e.g. 'Über Begriff und Gegenstand' (1892*a*), at p. 201. But as the rest of that article makes clear, properties or universals introduced by nominalizations like 'the property of being wise' counted, for Frege, as objects.

problem is the notorious paradox of the concept *horse*, the paradox of the concept which is not a concept because it is an object.[59] The difficulty is simply that the doctrine cannot be consistently stated: for in order to tell us that concepts help solve the problem of unity by being fundamentally non-objectual, Frege has to turn them into objects. As the reader will have observed, in presenting the doctrine in the previous paragraph I perforce reified the very things—concepts—which are not supposed to be objects. I used the word 'entities' to apply to both objects and concepts, in order to allow the doctrine at least the appearance of being stated without paradox. But the appearance is evidently illusory: for in calling concepts 'entities'—in talking about *them* at all—one inevitably makes objects of them. So there must be something wrong with Frege's solution to the problem of unity: either we must abandon the idea that solving the problem of unity requires us to find an unsaturated component of the proposition, in Frege's sense, or if we persist in attempting to solve the problem of unity armed with the chemical metaphor of unsaturatedness we must reconceive its nature.

But these are issues for another occasion. The point we need here is just this: however the problem of unity is to be solved, the solution will involve the uniting of objects (whatever these are) with universal entities—whether saturated or unsaturated—at the level of reference. (And of course we will have to site propositions at the level of reference to function as appropriate unities.) Even if Frege turns out to have been right that the account of the unity of the proposition must make essential appeal to unsaturated entities—concepts as he understood them—at the level of reference, such concepts will be universal rather than singular in nature: the paradox of the concept *horse* is the paradox of a *universal* non-object, and any purported solution to that paradox would have to respect that universality. Hence, whether concepts are conceived as saturated or unsaturated, to locate them at the level of reference, along with propositions, as part of a solution to the problem of the unity of the proposition will be, in effect, to avert the threat of Kantian transcendental idealism, which as we have seen in the course of this study so plagues McDowell's metaphysics; for the concepts located at the level of reference will be universal in nature, and will necessarily be united in the right way (whatever way that is) with the objects which, in the propositions in question, are said (truly or falsely) to fall under them.

A world which is identified with a level of reference populated by unified propositions, so conceived, is a world where things do not come separately, no matter how deep we dig ontologically, from the universal properties which they may be thought (truly or falsely) to instantiate. Moreover it should be clear that this picture commits us to a stronger form of realism about universals than the position often called Aristotelian realism—the doctrine that only instantiated universals exist. My linguistic idealism commits me to a more Platonic version of realism, for universal concepts exist at the level of reference wherever concept-expressions—possible such expressions as well as actual ones—are or could be available to refer to them. I submit that it is only in the context of this metaphysical and semantical picture that a genuinely minimal empiricism—a minimalist empiricism along the lines I have specified—will be able to make out its credentials.

References

Allison, H. (1997), 'We Can Only Act under the Idea of Freedom', *Proceedings and Addresses of the American Philosophical Association*, 71: 39–50.

Alweiss, L. (2000), 'On Perceptual Experience', *Journal of the British Society for Phenomenology*, 31: 264–76.

Aquinas, T. (1942), *Quaestiones Disputatae, iii. De Veritate* (Rome: Marietti).

Aristotle (1956), *De Anima*, ed. W. D. Ross (Oxford: Clarendon Press).

—— (1957), *Metaphysica*, ed. W. Jaeger (Oxford: Clarendon Press).

—— (1989), *Categoriae et Liber de Interpretatione*, ed. L. Minio-Paluello (Oxford: Clarendon Press).

Ayer, A. J. (1956), *The Problem of Knowledge* (Harmondsworth: Penguin).

—— (1969), *The Foundations of Empirical Knowledge* (London: Macmillan).

—— (1976), *Language, Truth and Logic*, 2nd edn. (Harmondsworth: Penguin).

Bäck. A. (2000), 'The Structure of Scotus' Formal Distinction', in I. Angelelli and P. Pérez-Ilzarbe (eds.), *Medieval and Renaissance Logic in Spain* (Hildesheim: Georg Olms), 411–38.

Bird, G. (1996), 'McDowell's Kant: *Mind and World*', *Philosophy*, 71: 219–43.

Blackburn, S. (2001), 'Normativity à la mode', *Journal of Ethics*, 5: 139–53.

Blumenberg, H. (1981), *Die Lesbarkeit der Welt* (Frankfurt/Main: Suhrkamp).

Boehner, P. (1958), *Collected Articles on Ockham*, ed. E. Buytaert (St Bonaventura, NY: The Franciscan Institute).

Brandom, R. (1979), 'Freedom and Constraint by Norms', *American Philosophical Quarterly*, 16: 187–96.

—— (1983), 'Asserting', *Nous*, 17: 637–50.

—— (1994), *Making it Explicit* (Cambridge, Mass.: Harvard University Press).

Brandom, R. (1995*a*), 'Perception and Rational Constraint: McDowell's *Mind and World*', *Philosophical Issues*, 7, Perception: 241–59.

—— (1995*b*), 'Knowledge and the Social Articulation of the Space of Reasons', *Philosophy and Phenomenological Research*, 55: 895–908.

Brandom, R. (1997*a*), 'Précis of *Making it Explicit*' and 'Replies', *Philosophy and Phenomenological Research*, 57: 153–6, 189–204.

—— (1997*b*), 'Study Guide', in Sellars (1997: 119–81).

—— (1998), 'Perception and Rational Constraint', *Philosophy and Phenomenological Research*, 58: 369–74.

—— (1999), 'Some Pragmatist Themes in Hegel's Idealism: Negotiation and Administration in Hegel's Account of the Structure and Content of Conceptual Norms', *European Journal of Philosophy*, 7: 164–89.

—— (2002), 'Non-inferential Knowledge, Perceptual Experience, and Secondary Qualities', in N. Smith (ed.), *Reading McDowell* (London: Routledge), 92–105.

Brewer, B. (1999), *Perception and Reason* (Oxford: Clarendon Press).

Browne, T. (1964), *Religio Medici and Other Works*, ed. L. C. Martin (Oxford: Clarendon Press).

Brueckner, A. (1993), 'Singular Thought and Cartesian Philosophy', *Analysis*, 53: 110–15.

Byrne, A. (1995), 'Spin Control: Comment on John McDowell's *Mind and World*', *Philosophical Issues*, 7, Perception: 261–73.

Campbell, J. (1982), 'Knowledge and Understanding', *Philosophical Quarterly*, 32: 17–34.

Cavell, S. (1969), *Must We Mean What We Say?* (Cambridge: Cambridge University Press).

Christensen, C. (2000), 'Wie man Gedanken und Anschauungen zusammenführt', *Deutsche Zeitschrift für Philosophie*, 6: 891–914.

Cleve, J. van (2004), 'Externalism and Disjunctivism', in R. Schantz (ed.), *The Externalist Challenge* (Berlin: Walter de Gruyter), 481–92.

Collins, A. (1998), 'Beastly Experience', *Philosophy and Phenomenological Research*, 58: 375–80.

Davidson, D. (1980), 'Reality without Reference', in M. Platts (ed.), *Reference, Truth and Reality* (London: Routledge and Kegan Paul), 131–40.

—— (1982), *Essays on Actions and Events* (Oxford: Clarendon Press).

—— (1984), *Inquiries into Truth and Interpretation* (Oxford: Clarendon Press).

—— (1990), 'The Structure and Content of Truth', *Journal of Philosophy*, 87: 279–328.

Davidson, D. (2001), *Subjective, Intersubjective, Objective* (Oxford: Clarendon Press).

—— (2005), *Truth, Language, and History* (Oxford: Clarendon Press).

Davies, P. (2000), 'From Constructive Philosophy to Philosophical Quietism', *Journal of the British Society for Phenomenology*, 31: 314–29.

Denejkine, A. (2000), 'Sind wir vor der Welt verantwortlich? John McDowell über Erfahrung und Realismus', *Deutsche Zeitschrift für Philosophie*, 6: 939–52.

Dennett, D. (1987), *The Intentional Stance* (Cambridge, Mass.: MIT Press).

Descartes, R. (1964–76), *Œuvres de Descartes*, ed. C. Adam and P. Tannery (Paris: Vrin).

—— (1985), *The Philosophical Writings of Descartes*, i, ed. J. Cottingham et al. (Cambridge: Cambridge University Press).

Dodd, J. (1995), 'McDowell and Identity Theories of Truth', *Analysis*, 55: 160–5.

Dretske, F. (2000), *Perception, Knowledge and Belief* (Cambridge: Cambridge University Press).

Dummett, M. (1981*a*), *Frege: Philosophy of Language*, 2nd edn. (London: Duckworth).

—— (1981*b*), *The Interpretation of Frege's Philosophy* (London: Duckworth).

Evans, G. (1982), *The Varieties of Reference* (Oxford: Clarendon Press).

—— (1985), *Collected Papers* (Oxford: Clarendon Press).

—— and McDowell, J. (eds.) (1976), *Truth and Meaning* (Oxford: Clarendon Press).

Frege, G. (1884), *Grundlagen der Arithmetik* (Breslau: Koebner); repr. 1987, ed. J. Schulte (Stuttgart: Reclam).

—— (1891), *Funktion und Begriff*, Vortrag Jena (=Patzig 1980: 18–39).

—— (1892*a*), 'Über Begriff und Gegenstand', *Vierteljahresschrift für wissenschaftliche Philosophie* 16: 192–205 (=Patzig 1980: 66–80).

—— (1892*b*), 'Über Sinn und Bedeutung', *Zeitschrift für Philosophie und Philosophische Kritik*, 100: 25–50 (=Patzig 1980: 40–65).

—— (1918–19), 'Der Gedanke: eine logische Untersuchung', *Beiträge zur Philosophie des deutschen Idealismus*, 2: 58–77 (=Patzig 1976: 30–53).

—— (1923–6), 'Gedankengefüge', *Beiträge zur Philosophie des deutschen Idealismus*, 3: 36–51 (=Patzig 1976: 72–91).

Frege, G. (1962), *Grundgesetze der Arithmetik* (Hildesheim: Georg Olms), a reprint of the 1893 and 1903 Jena texts.

—— (1976), *Wissenschaftlicher Briefwechsel*, ed. G. Gabriel et al. (Hamburg: Felix Meiner).

—— (1983), *Nachgelassene Schriften*, ed. H. Hermes et al. (Hamburg: Felix Meiner).

Fricker, E. (1982–3), 'Semantic Structure and Speakers' Understanding', *Proceedings of the Aristotelian Society*, 83: 49–66.

Gaskin, R. (1995*a*), 'Experience and Criteria', *Archiv für Begriffsgeschichte*, 38: 261–75.

—— (1995*b*), 'Bradley's Regress, the Copula and the Unity of the Proposition', *Philosophical Quarterly*, 45: 161–80.

—— (1996), ' "Kein Etwas, aber auch nicht ein Nichts!": Kann die Grammatik tatsächlich täuschen?', *Grazer Philosophische Studien*, 51: 85–104.

—— (1997*a*), 'Fregean Sense and Russellian Propositions', *Philosophical Studies*, 86: 131–54.

—— (1997*b*), 'Überlegungen zur Identitätstheorie der Prädikation', *Wissenschaft und Weisheit*, 60: 87–103.

—— (1997*c*), 'Russell and Richard Brinkley on the Unity of the Proposition', *History and Philosophy of Logic*, 18: 139–50.

—— (2001*a*): 'Ockham's Mental Language, Connotation, and the Inherence Regress', in D. Perler (ed.), *Ancient and Medieval Theories of Intentionality* (Leiden: Brill), 227–63.

—— (2001*b*), 'Proposition and World', in R. Gaskin (ed.), *Grammar in Early Twentieth-Century Philosophy* (London: Routledge), 1–27.

—— (2001*c*), 'Nonsense and Necessity in Wittgenstein's Mature Philosophy', in R. Gaskin (ed.), *Grammar in Early Twentieth-Century Philosophy* (London: Routledge), 199–217.

—— (2004), '*Complexe Significabilia* and the Formal Distinction', in A. Maierù and L. Valente (eds.), *Medieval Theories on Assertive and Non-Assertive Language* (Rome: Leo S. Olschki), 495–516.

Gaynesford, M. de. (2004), *John McDowell* (Cambridge: Polity).

Geuss, R. (1999), *Morality, Culture, and History* (Cambridge: Cambridge University Press).

Gibson, R. (1995), 'McDowell's Direct Realism and Platonic Naturalism', *Philosophical Issues*, 7, Perception: 275–81.

Glendinning, S. and Gaynesford, M. de. (1998), 'John McDowell on Experience: Open to the Sceptic?', *Metaphilosophy*, 29: 20–34.

Green, T. H. (1908), *Works of Thomas Hill Green*, i. (London: Longmans, Green and Co.).

Greenberg, S. and Willaschek, M. (2000), 'Is McDowell confronted with an Antinomy of Freedom and Nature?', in M. Willaschek (ed.), *John McDowell: Reason and Nature* (Münster: Münsteraner Vorlesungen zur Philosophie 3: LIT), 51–4.

Grice, H. P. (1967), 'The Causal Theory of Perception', in G. J. Warnock (ed.), *The Philosophy of Perception* (Oxford: Clarendon Press), 85–112.

Gubeljic, M., Link, S., Müller, P., and Osburg, G. (2000), 'Nature and Second Nature in McDowell's *Mind and World*', in M. Willaschek (ed.), *John McDowell: Reason and Nature* (Münster: Münsteraner Vorlesungen zur Philosophie 3: LIT), 41–9.

Habermas, J. (1999), *Wahrheit und Rechtfertigung* (Frankfurt/Main: Suhrkamp).

Hazlitt, W. (1967), *Lectures on English Philosophy*, in *The Complete Works of William Hazlitt*, ii, ed. P. P. Howe (New York: AMS Press), 121–284.

Heck, R. (1995), 'The Sense of Communication', *Mind*, 104: 79–106.

—— (2000), 'Non-conceptual Content and the "Space of Reasons" ', *Philosophical Review*, 109: 483–523.

Hegel, G. W. F. (1988), *Phänomenologie des Geistes* (Hamburg: Felix Meiner).

Heim, I. and Kratzer, A. (1998), *Semantics in Generative Grammar* (Oxford: Blackwell).

Heßbrüggen-Walter, S. (2000), 'Spontaneity and Causality: McDowell on the Passivity of Perception', in M. Willaschek (ed.), *John McDowell: Reason and Nature* (Münster: Münsteraner Vorlesungen zur Philosophie 3: LIT), 21–5.

Honneth, A. and Seel, M. (eds.) (1998), Introduction to *John McDowell, Wert und Wirklichkeit: Aufsätze zur Moralphilosophie* (Frankfurt/Main: Suhrkamp), 7–29.

Hume, D. (1975), *Enquiries concerning Human Understanding and concerning the Principles of Morals*, ed. P. H. Nidditch (Oxford: Clarendon Press).

—— (1978), *A Treatise of Human Nature*, ed. P. H. Nidditch (Oxford: Clarendon Press).

James, W. (1975), *Pragmatism and The Meaning of Truth* (Cambridge, Mass.: Harvard University Press).

Kant, I. (1929) *Critique of Pure Reason*, trans. N. Kemp-Smith (London: Macmillan).

—— (1998), *Kritik der reinen Vernunft* (Hamburg: Felix Meiner).

Kaplan, D. (1989), 'Demonstratives', in J. Almog et al. (eds.), *Themes from Kaplan* (Oxford: Oxford University Press), 481–563.

Kern, A. (2000), 'Einsicht ohne Täuschung: McDowells hermeneutische Konzeption von Erkenntnis', *Deutsche Zeitschrift für Philosophie*, 48: 915–37.

Kripke, S. (1982), *Wittgenstein on Rules and Private Language* (Oxford: Blackwell).

Kurbacher, F. A. and Heßbrüggen-Walter, S. (2000), 'Self-Criticism as a Way of Life', in M. Willaschek (ed.), *John McDowell: Reason and Nature* (Münster: Münsteraner Vorlesungen zur Philosophie 3: LIT), 59–67.

Larmore, C. (2002), 'Attending to Reasons', in N. Smith (ed.), *Reading McDowell* (London: Routledge), 193–208.

Lockwood, M. (1989), *Mind, Brain and the Quantum* (Oxford: Blackwell).

Lyne, I. (2000), 'Openness to Reality in McDowell and Heidegger: Normativity and Ontology', *Journal of the British Society for Phenomenology*, 31: 300–13.

Macarthur, D. (2003), 'McDowell, Scepticism, and the "Veil of Perception" ', *Australasian Journal of Philosophy* 81: 175–90.

McDowell, J. (1973), *Plato: Theaetetus* (Oxford: Clarendon Press).

—— (1982), 'Falsehood and Not-Being in Plato's *Sophist*', in M. Schofield and M. Nussbaum (eds.), *Language and Logos* (Cambridge: Cambridge University Press), 115–34.

—— (1986), 'Critical Notice of Bernard Williams, *Ethics and the Limits of Philosophy*', *Mind*, 95: 377–86.

—— (1990), 'Peacocke and Evans on Demonstrative Content', *Mind*, 99: 255–66.

—— (1994), *Mind and World* (Cambridge, Mass.: Harvard University Press).

—— (1995*a*), 'Précis of *Mind and World*' and 'Reply to Gibson, Byrne, and Brandom', *Philosophical Issues*, 7, Perception: 231–9, 287–300.

McDowell, J. (1995*b*), 'Eudaimonism and Realism in Aristotle's Ethics', in R. Heinaman (ed.), *Aristotle and Moral Realism* (Boulder, Colo.: Westview Press), 201–18.

—— (1996*a*), *Mind and World*, paperback edn. (Cambridge, Mass.: Harvard University Press).

—— (1996*b*), 'Incontinence and Practical Wisdom in Aristotle', in S. Lovibond and S. G. Williams (eds.), *Identity, Truth and Value: Essays for David Wiggins* (Oxford: Blackwell), 95–112.

—— (1997), 'Brandom on Representation and Inference', *Philosophy and Phenomenological Research*, 57: 157–62.

—— (1998*a*), 'Précis of *Mind and World* and 'Reply to Commentators', *Philosophy and Phenomenological Research*, 58: 365–8, 403–31.

—— (1998*b*), *Mind, Value, and Reality* (Cambridge, Mass.: Harvard University Press).

—— (1998*c*) *Meaning, Knowledge, and Reality* (Cambridge, Mass.: Harvard University Press).

—— (1998*d*), 'Having the World in View: Sellars, Kant, and Intentionality', *Journal of Philosophy*, 95: 431–91.

—— (1998*e*), 'Comment on Hans-Peter Krüger's Paper', *Philosophical Explorations*, 2: 120–5.

—— (1998*f*), 'Referring to Oneself', in L. Hahn (ed.), *The Philosophy of P. F. Strawson* (Chicago and La Salle, Ill.: Open Court), 129–50.

—— (1998*g*), 'Response to Crispin Wright', in C. Wright et al. (eds.), *Knowing Our Own Minds* (Oxford: Clarendon Press), 47–62.

—— (1998*h*), 'The Constitutive Ideal of Rationality: Davidson and Sellars', *Crítica*, 30: 29–48.

—— (1999*a*), 'Scheme-Content Dualism and Empiricism', in L. Hahn (ed.), *The Philosophy of Donald Davidson* (Chicago and La Salle, Ill.: Open Court), 87–104.

—— (1999*b*), 'Comment on Robert Brandom's "Some Pragmatist Themes in Hegel's Idealism" ', *European Journal of Philosophy*, 7: 190–3.

—— (2000*a*), 'Lecture' and 'Responses', in M. Willaschek (ed.), *John McDowell: Reason and Nature* (Münster: Münsteraner Vorlesungen zur Philosophie 3: LIT), 3–18, 91–114.

—— (2000*b*), 'Towards Rehabilitating Objectivity', in R. Brandom (ed.), *Rorty and his Critics* (Oxford: Blackwell), 109–23.

McDowell, J. (2000c), 'Comments', *Journal of the British Society for Phenomenology*, 31: 330–43.

—— (2001), 'Comment on Richard Schantz, "The Given Regained" ', *Philosophy and Phenomenological Research*, 62: 181–4.

—— (2002a), 'Responses', in N. Smith (ed.), *Reading McDowell* (London: Routledge), 269–305.

—— (2002b), 'Gadamer and Davidson on Understanding and Relativism', in J. Malpas et al. (ed.), *Gadamer's Century* (Cambridge, Mass.: MIT Press), 173–93.

—— (2002c), 'Knowledge and the Internal Revisited', *Philosophy and Phenomenological Research*, 64: 97–105.

—— (2003), 'Hyperbatologikos Empeirismos', *Deukalion*, 21: 65–90.

—— (2004), 'Reality and Colours: Comment on Stroud', *Philosophy and Phenomenological Research*, 68: 395–400.

Neale, S. (1995), 'The Philosophical Significance of Gödel's Slingshot', *Mind*, 104: 761–825.

Novalis (Friedrich von Hardenberg) (1999), *Das Allgemeine Brouillon*, in *Novalis: Werke, Tagebücher und Briefe*, ii, ed. H.-J. Mähl (Darmstadt: Wissenschaftliche Buchgesellschaft), 473–720.

Park, R. (1971), *Hazlitt and the Spirit of the Age* (Oxford: Clarendon Press).

Patzig, G. (1976), *Gottlob Frege: Logische Untersuchungen* (Göttingen: Vandenhoeck and Ruprecht).

—— (1980) *Gottlob Frege: Funktion, Begriff, Bedeutung* (Göttingen: Vandenhoeck and Ruprecht).

Peacocke, C. (1998), 'Nonconceptual Content Defended', *Philosophy and Phenomenological Research*, 58: 381–8.

—— (2001), 'Does Perception have a Non-conceptual Content?', *Journal of Philosophy*, 98: 239–64.

Pettit, P. and McDowell, J. (1986), Introduction to *Subject, Thought, and Context* (Oxford: Clarendon Press), 1–15.

Plato (1962), *Platonis Opera*, iv, ed. J. Burnet (Oxford: Clarendon Press).

—— (1995), *Platonis Opera*, i, ed. E. Duke et al. (Oxford: Clarendon Press).

Porphyry (1887), *Porphyrii Isagoge et in Aristotelis Categorias Commentarium*, ed. A. Busse (Berlin: Georg Reimer).

Priest, G. (2002), *Beyond the Limits of Thought*, 2nd edn. (Oxford: Clarendon Press).

Pritchard, D. (2003), 'McDowell on Reasons, Externalism and Scepticism', *European Journal of Philosophy*, 11: 273–94.

Putnam, H. (1978), *Meaning and the Moral Sciences* (London: Routledge and Kegan Paul).

—— (1981), *Reason, Truth and History* (Cambridge: Cambridge University Press).

—— (1992), *Renewing Philosophy* (Cambridge, Mass.: Harvard University Press).

—— (1994), *Words and Life* (Cambridge, Mass.: Harvard University Press).

—— (1995), *Pragmatism* (Oxford: Blackwell).

—— (1999), *The Threefold Cord: Mind, Body, and World* (New York: Columbia University Press).

—— (2002), 'McDowell's Mind and McDowell's World', in N. Smith (ed.), *Reading McDowell* (London: Routledge), 174–90.

Quante, M. (2000), 'Zurück zur verzauberten Natur—ohne konstruktive Philosophie? McDowells Naturbegriff in "Mind and World" ', *Deutsche Zeitschrift für Philosophie*, 48: 953–65.

Quine, W. V. (1953), *From a Logical Point of View* (Cambridge, Mass.: Harvard University Press).

—— (1960), *Word and Object* (Cambridge, Mass.: MIT Press).

Reichenbach, H. (1952), 'Are Phenomenal Reports Absolutely Certain?', *Philosophical Review*, 61: 147–59.

Rorty, R. (1979), *Philosophy and the Mirror of Nature* (Princeton: Princeton University Press).

—— (1982), *Consequences of Pragmatism* (Brighton: Harvester Wheatsheaf).

—— (1989), *Contingency, Irony, and Solidarity* (Cambridge: Cambridge University Press).

—— (1991), *Objectivity, Relativism, and Truth: Philosophical Papers*, i (Cambridge: Cambridge University Press).

Rorty, R. (1998), *Truth and Progress: Philosophical Papers*, iii (Cambridge: Cambridge University Press).

—— (2000), 'Response to John McDowell', in R. Brandom (ed.), *Rorty and his Critics* (Oxford: Blackwell), 123–8.

Russell, B. (1903), *The Principles of Mathematics* (Cambridge: Cambridge University Press).

Russell, B. (1912), *The Problems of Philosophy* (Oxford: Oxford University Press), paperback reprint 1967.

—— (1918), *Mysticism and Logic and Other Essays* (London: Longmans, Green and Co.), paperback reprint 1963 (London: Allen and Unwin).

—— (1956), *Logic and Knowledge*, ed. R. C. Marsh (London: Allen and Unwin).

—— (1973), *Essays in Analysis*, ed. D. Lackey (London: Allen and Unwin).

—— (1994), *Philosophical Essays* (London: Routledge).

Sainsbury, R. (1979–80), 'Understanding and Theories of Meaning', *Proceedings of the Aristotelian Society,* 80: 127–44.

Savigny, E. von (1994), *Wittgensteins 'Philosophische Untersuchungen'* (Frankfurt/Main: Klostermann).

Schantz, R. (1996), *Wahrheit, Referenz und Realismus* (Berlin: Walter de Gruyter).

—— (2001), 'The Given Regained: Reflections on the Sensuous Content of Experience', *Philosophy and Phenomenological Research,* 62: 167–80.

—— (2004), 'Empiricism Externalized', in R. Schantz (ed.), *The Externalist Challenge* (Berlin: Walter de Gruyter), 89–111.

Sedgwick, S. (2000), 'Hegel, McDowell, and Recent Defences of Kant', *Journal of the British Society for Phenomenology,* 31: 229–47.

Sellars, W. (1956), 'Empiricism and the Philosophy of Mind', in H. Feigl and M. Scriven (eds.), *Minnesota Studies in the Philosophy of Science,* 1 (University of Minnesota Press): 253–329; reissued in 1997 as a monograph (Cambridge, Mass: Harvard University Press), with an introduction by R. Rorty and a study Guide by R. Brandom.

Sextus Empiricus (1983), *Adversus Mathematicos* in Sextus Empiricus, ii. *Against the Logicians*, ed. R. Bury (Cambridge, Mass.: Harvard University Press).

Spade, P. V. (1990), 'Ockham, Adams and Connotation: a Critical Notice of Marilyn Adams, *William Ockham*', *Philosophical Review,* 99: 593–612.

Stern, R. (1999), 'Going Beyond the Kantian Philosophy: On McDowell's Hegelian Critique of Kant', *European Journal of Philosophy,* 7: 247–69.

Stich, S. (1979), 'Do Animals Have Beliefs?', *Australasian Journal of Philosophy,* 57: 15–28.

Strawson, P. F. (1966), *The Bounds of Sense* (London: Methuen).

Strawson, P. F. (1979), 'Perception and its Objects', in G. F. Macdonald (ed.), *Perception and Identity* (London: Macmillan), 41–60.

—— (1985), 'Causation and Explanation', in B. Vermazen and M. Hintikka (eds.), *Essays on Davidson: Action and Events* (Oxford: Clarendon Press), 115–35.

Strobach, N. (2000), 'Platonism and Anti-Platonism', in M. Willaschek (ed.), *John McDowell: Reason and Nature* (Münster: Münsteraner Vorlesungen zur Philosophie 3: LIT), 55–8.

Suhm, C., Wagemann, P., and Wessels, F. (2000), 'Ontological Troubles with Facts and Objects in McDowell's *Mind and World*', in M. Willaschek (ed.), *John McDowell: Reason and Nature* (Münster: Münsteraner Vorlesungen zur Philosophie 3: LIT), 27–33.

Tarski, A. (1956), 'The Concept of Truth in Formalized Languages', in *Logic, Semantics, Metamathematics*, 2nd edn. trans. J. Woodger and ed. J. Corcoran (Indianapolis: Hackett), 152–278.

Thornton, T. (2004), *John McDowell* (Chesham: Acumen).

Tugendhat, E. (1976), 'Die Bedeutung des Ausdrucks "Bedeutung" bei Frege', in M. Schirn (ed.), *Studien zu Frege*, iii (Stuttgart: Frommann-Holzboog), 51–69.

Wallace, J. (1977), 'Only in the Context of a Sentence do Words Have any Meaning', in P. French et al. (eds.), *Contemporary Perspectives in the Philosophy of Language* (Minneapolis, Minnesota: University of Minnesota Press), 305–25.

Wiggins, D. (1984), 'The Sense and Reference of Predicates: a Running Repair to Frege's Doctrine and a Plea for the Copula', in C. Wright (ed.), *Frege: Tradition and Influence* (Oxford: Blackwell), 126–43.

—— (1995), 'Eudaimonism and Realism in Aristotle's Ethics: A Reply to John McDowell', in R. Heinaman (ed.), *Aristotle and Moral Realism* (Boulder, Colo.: Westview Press), 219–31.

—— (1997), 'Meaning and Truth Conditions: from Frege's Grand Design to Davidson's', in B. Hale and C. Wright (eds.), *A Companion to the Philosophy of Language* (Oxford: Blackwell), 3–28.

Willaschek, M. (2000), 'On "The Unboundedness of the Conceptual" ', in M. Willaschek (ed.), *John McDowell: Reason and Nature* (Münster: Münsteraner Vorlesungen zur Philosophie 3: LIT), 35–40.

—— (2003), *Der mentale Zugang zur Welt* (Frankfurt/Main: Klostermann).

Williams, B. (1973), *Problems of the Self* (Cambridge: Cambridge University Press).

—— (2002), *Truth and Truthfulness* (Princeton: Princeton University Press).

Williams, M. (1996), 'Exorcism and Enchantment', *Philosophical Quarterly*, 46: 99–109.

Wittgenstein, L. (1922), *Tractatus Logico-Philosophicus* (London: Routledge and Kegan Paul).

—— (1958) *Philosophical Investigations*, trans. G. E. M. Anscombe (Oxford: Blackwell).

—— (1966), *Lectures and Conversations on Aesthetics, Psychology and Religious Belief*, ed. C. Barrett (Oxford: Blackwell).

—— (1969), *The Blue and Brown Books* (Oxford: Blackwell).

—— (1977), *Philosophische Untersuchungen* (Frankfurt/Main: Suhrkamp).

—— (1978), *Remarks on the Foundations of Mathematics*, 3rd edn., trans. G. E. M. Anscombe, ed. Anscombe et al. (Oxford: Blackwell).

—— (1984), *Zettel* in *Werkausgabe*, viii (Frankfurt/Main: Suhrkamp), 259–443.

—— (1989), *Bemerkungen über die Grundlagen der Mathematik* (Frankfurt/Main: Suhrkamp).

Wolf, S. (1990), *Freedom Within Reason* (Oxford: Oxford University Press).

Wright, C. (1980), *Wittgenstein on the Foundations of Mathematics* (London: Duckworth).

—— (1998*a*), 'McDowell's Oscillation', *Philosophy and Phenomenological Research* 58: 395–402.

—— (1998*b*), 'Self-Knowledge: the Wittgensteinian Legacy, in C. Wright et al. (eds.), *Knowing Our Own Minds* (Oxford: Clarendon Press), 13–45.

—— (1999), 'Truth: A Traditional Debate Reviewed', in S. Blackburn and K. Simmons (eds.), *Truth* (Oxford: Oxford University Press), 203–38.

—— (2001), 'Why Frege Does Not Deserve His Grain of Salt', in B. Hale and C. Wright, *The Reason's Proper Study* (Oxford: Clarendon Press), 72–90.

Wright, C. (2002*a*), 'Human Nature?' and 'Postscript to Chapter 8', in N. Smith (ed.), *Reading McDowell* (London: Routledge), 140–73.

—— (2002*b*), '(Anti-)Sceptics Simple and Subtle: G. E. Moore and John McDowell', *Philosophy and Phenomenological Research*, 65: 330–48.

Index